PEOPLE
— *over* —
POLITICS

PEOPLE

— *over* —

POLITICS

STEVE BESHEAR

GOVERNOR OF KENTUCKY 2007–2015

with Dan Hassert

PEOPLE OVER POLITICS
© 2017, A Stronger Kentucky, Inc.
All Rights Reserved.

The words, remembrances, observations, and opinions contained in this book are those of the author and reflect his memories and best recollection of experiences from his life and years in public service.

Front cover photograph of Jane and Steve Beshear provided courtesy of David Cronen.
Official and author photographs of Governor Steve Beshear provided courtesy of Marvin Young/Kentucky Office of Creative Services.
Author photograph of Dan Hassert provided courtesy of Jim Osborn.

Special thanks to the Kentucky Office of Creative Services, as well as to the additional photographers and organizations given credit herein, for providing the photographs featured in this book.

ISBN: 978-1-941953-45-7
Library of Congress Control Number: 2017904293

Printed in the United States of America

A Stronger Kentucky, Inc. is a corporation organized exclusively for charitable, religious, literary, educational, and scientific purposes under section 501(c)(3) of the Internal Revenue Code of 1986, as amended. The organization supports efforts to promote the health and well-being of the citizens of the Commonwealth of Kentucky. Funds were donated to A Stronger Kentucky, Inc. to produce and publish this book, and proceeds from the sale of the book will be donated to charitable and educational causes.

To purchase a copy of this book or donate to A Stronger Kentucky, Inc., visit www.astrongerkentucky.com.

STEVEN L. BESHEAR
Governor of Kentucky
2007–2015

To Jane, my partner and best friend for almost 50 years. Of all the wonderful and exciting moments of my life, by far the best was the day I met and fell head over heels in love with her. And to our grandchildren, Nicholas, Will, and Lila, and all of Kentucky's grandchildren who would benefit from a return to civility and common sense in politics.

CONTENTS

Section VII: Memories

Section VIII: Conclusion

Section I

INTRODUCTION

THE LAZARUS
CANDIDATE

If it weren't for Teddy Roosevelt, I might never have been governor.

The famous American statesman and I were of different political parties and were born in different centuries, but during a crushing time in my early political career, his words gave me consolation and strength. And 20 years later, a coincidental use of those same words inspired me to come out of political exile and run again for the office I had previously failed to win. In the process, I became—as influential Kentucky journalist Al Smith was to write about me—"a hero of the second chance."

My political career had started out with a string of successes at an early age. Elected to the state House of Representatives in 1973 at age 29, I was named outstanding freshman legislator by the capitol press corps and I won re-election twice. In 1979, I ran for state attorney general at age 35 and won, and four years later, I was elected lieutenant governor, still not yet 40 years old.

Following the natural progression of others before me, in 1987, I set my sights on the governorship. But I didn't make it. Instead, I suffered a disappointing loss in the Democratic primary, finishing a distant third behind businessman Wallace Wilkinson and former Governor John Y. Brown Jr. In fact, I gained just 18 percent of the vote to Wilkinson's 35 percent and Brown's 26.

My political ambitions had come crashing down around me. Given the magnitude of the defeat and the array of up-and-coming Democratic officeholders, it appeared that my political career was over. Quite honestly, I was devastated.

It was then that I stumbled on the words of Roosevelt. They came from a now-famous passage called the "The Man in the Arena," which was part of a speech he gave in Paris, France, in April 1910. (Today that passage is familiar to many people—thanks to the Internet, its use by President Obama, and a 2015 television ad for Cadillac—but it was considerably less known back in 1987.)

The passage goes like this:

> It is not the critic who counts; not the man who points out how the strong man stumbles, or where the doer of deeds could have done them better. The credit belongs to the man who is actually in the arena, whose face is marred by dust and sweat and blood; who strives valiantly; who errs, who comes short again and again, because there is no effort without error and shortcoming; but who does actually strive to do the deeds; who knows great enthusiasms, the great devotions; who spends himself in a worthy cause; who at the best knows in the end the triumph of high achievement, and who at the worst, if he fails, at least fails while daring greatly, so that his place shall never be with those cold and timid souls who neither know victory nor defeat.

Roosevelt's words consoled me. I had failed, that was true. But it was also true that I had actually been "in the arena" and that I had failed "while daring greatly."

Nevertheless, I had a family to take care of and two boys to raise and send to college, so I picked myself up and started over with my law career. With rhetorical comfort from Roosevelt and strong support from a loving wife and family, I got back on my feet and became a successful lawyer and community banker.

Little did I know that I hadn't heard the last of Roosevelt. Almost two decades later, by coincidence, those words would be thrust in front of me again, this time by someone who wanted me to again strive valiantly and again risk stumbling.

The year was 2006. Democrats Brereton Jones and Paul Patton and Republican Ernie Fletcher had followed Wilkinson into the governor's office, and thanks to a new constitutional succession amendment passed by voters, Fletcher was running for a second term (as Patton had been allowed to do before him).

I was a member of a small group that was actively seeking the best Democrat to run against the GOP incumbent, but we were unsuccessful. None of the Democrats we were recruiting was willing to step up. It was then that my close friend Tracy Farmer, a horseman and entrepreneur, came to me and urged me to run. The Democrats needed to put up a credible candidate, he said, and besides—who knew what might happen?

I laughed off his suggestion. The thought of running for governor again had not crossed my mind, and the memory of my 1987 loss (and a subsequent loss in the 1996 US Senate race) still stung. But Tracy persisted, and at a meeting at his house that December, he handed me a card that contained the passage from "The Man in the Arena."

"You may end up losing," Tracy said, "but you won't know if you sit on the sidelines and watch—you'll have to get *into the arena.*"

I was taken aback. Tracy had not known of my connection to that passage, but here he was, using it to sway me.

It seemed like a sign.

So I had several discussions with my wife, Jane, my college

sweetheart. We had married in 1969 and she had been by my side through all the ups and downs of my political life. She was surprised ("You want to do *what?*") and frankly more than a little unenthusiastic at the prospect of re-entering public life, but she told me she would support whatever I decided. My sons, Jeff and Andy, now grown with their own soon-to-be-expanding families, also promised their support.

So with their blessing, I decided to risk it all "in a worthy cause" by entering "the arena" again.

In May 2007, I won a crowded seven-way Democratic primary, and that November, I defeated the incumbent Republican governor by winning almost 59 percent of the vote.

It had taken 20 years, but this time I experienced what the late Republican president had called "the triumph of high achievement."

As a couple of friends jokingly suggested, the "Lazarus candidate" had risen from the dead!

In retrospect, that 20-year wait made me a better governor. At 63, I was a different person than I was at 43. More mature, obviously. Having seen more of life and dealt with a broader range of people, I was less surprised by things. More importantly, I was more patient and had a thicker skin. I was content to let roll off my back criticism that might have gotten to me 20 years earlier. I was less worried about winning every little legislative and political battle and instead set and followed strategies designed to win the proverbial war. I was able to see the bigger picture more readily. And when other leaders reacted stridently to things, I was less likely to get distracted and more likely to remain focused on the goal of the moment.

Obviously, having experienced both losses and victories on the campaign trail, I was more eager to take advantage of the opportunity in front of me and more willing to take risks in order to succeed. And thanks to the words of Teddy

Roosevelt, the Governor's Office—and the chance to have an impact on my beloved commonwealth—beckoned. I was ready to get to work.

KENTUCKY:
SUDDENLY A LEADER

When the end of the world comes, I want to be in Kentucky,
because everything there happens 20 years after it happens
anywhere else.

—Popularly attributed to Mark Twain

Which state was the first to adopt the Common Core State Standards for learning? The second state to adopt the Next Generation Science Standards? Which state was the winner in both 2014 and 2015 of a prestigious national award for attracting the most large-scale economic investment per capita? Which state has been the recognized leader in making health coverage available to its people and is a top-10 state in high school graduation rates?

New York? California? Maryland? Massachusetts?

Actually, it's Kentucky. That's right, Kentucky.

Surprised? I don't blame you, because when you look at Kentucky's history, Twain's words have a ring of truth—whether or not Twain actually said them.

While sporadic progress had been made in some areas, in 2007, Kentuckians' overall health was abysmal, our economy seemed stuck in the 19th century, and most of our kids were graduating from high school ready for neither college nor a career. Our enduring image in Hollywood seemed to be one tired hillbilly stereotype after another.

Given this inauspicious past, what happened over the last few years to cause words like "first" and "leader" and "role model" and "progressive" and "innovative" to suddenly be used to describe the Bluegrass State, and for things unrelated to horses, bourbon, or college basketball?

Why did the president of the United States give Kentucky a shout-out in his 2014 State of the Union address? Why were governors of other states coming to me, Kentucky's governor, for advice? And why did residents of the commonwealth who admitted they didn't support me politically suddenly seek me out to tell me how proud they now were to be from Kentucky?

Why indeed?

I was Kentucky's governor from 2007 to 2015, and if there was one thing I heard during those eight years, it was that Kentucky had a fascinating story to tell.

This book is that story.

This is not a chronological account of my administration or a comprehensive look at everything that happened in Kentucky during those eight years. Rather, it's a look at the intersection of politics and governing, and the issues, challenges, and successes that came to the forefront along the way.

It's a story about how even in this political climate of derision and division—where partisan bickering and deliberate gridlock have drowned out collaboration and consensus building as the national mantra—you can grab hold of a state encumbered by fundamental weaknesses and turn it into one of the more progressive states in the country.

It's the story of a group of people who were determined to build a more competitive future.

This story is also a training tool for future leaders of this commonwealth and this nation. Politics doesn't have to be mean-spirited. Collaboration across party lines must be embraced, not denigrated. Progress happens when campaigning gives way to governing.

In short, there is an urgent need for our leaders to put people over politics, and I hope that this book will be useful in that endeavor.

This idea was at the core of commencement addresses I gave to college graduates while governor as well as speeches on leadership I've delivered around the country since I've left office. It was also the overriding message of the class on public health policy I taught at the Harvard T. H. Chan School of Public Health in spring 2017.

This book is loosely organized into topical sections, each containing several essays, but it's tied together by common threads woven throughout its pages.

The first theme is non-partisanship.

Too many elected officials have distorted priorities. With a 24/7 focus on campaigning, with the goal of increasing and retaining power for themselves and their party, too many of our leaders have forgotten the mission of governing, which is to strengthen the country or state they lead, and help the people who live there.

As a result, the system of governing in this country is broken. Thanks to Washington-style politics, trust in government is almost nonexistent, and voters feel disenfranchised, helpless, and hopeless. They increasingly are turning to unprepared outsiders just to try something different and to make a statement.

But during my eight years as governor, we in Kentucky rejected that narrative and resisted becoming another voice in the national shouting match.

We had a divided government in Kentucky, with Democrats controlling the House and Republicans the Senate. But that didn't keep us from working together to help our people survive the Great Recession and a record number of weather catastrophes. Nor did our differences keep us from making historic progress on fundamental weaknesses that have held Kentucky back for generations.

Divided government *can* work, but it *takes* work. Conscious effort.

You see that throughout this book.

The second theme is the power of relationships.

I got my first job as a 16-year-old because my mom and dad had developed a friendship with an important person. As governor, I took that lesson to a whole new level.

Knowing people in Washington on a first-name basis assisted me in getting health care for Kentuckians who needed it and helped me break through a bureaucratic logjam that was holding up generators we needed to save lives during a winter weather disaster. Likewise, my taking the time to build relationships with key Republicans on both the state and federal level helped us build two new bridges across the Ohio River, begin to diversify Appalachia's economy, and tackle prescription drug abuse across the state. And working to connect with business executives on a personal level helped separate Kentucky from the pack in the super-competitive race to create jobs, even from across the ocean.

Time and again, I acted with the knowledge that even when you're a governor, very little happens unless you partner with others.

And finally, a third major theme is the importance of leadership and courage.

I was advised to oppose the Affordable Care Act and shun President Obama because he was unpopular in Kentucky, and I was warned that associating myself with him and his most visible initiative would damage my credibility. I ignored that advice. Instead, I embraced the ACA because I recognized it as a powerful tool that would make health coverage available to hundreds of thousands of Kentucky families. By risking my own political support, we changed the course of not only those families' lives but also Kentucky's future.

Just recently, I received an unexpected e-mail stemming from a chance encounter that tells in a compelling manner the incredible difference the ACA made in one person's life. I've included that e-mail in the conclusion of this book because it crystallizes both the reward of public service and the reasons I embraced the president's initiative.

Similarly, I opposed a long-serving Senate president who was determined to cut funding to K–12 education and other agencies, seemingly to build support within the Tea Party, and I took on powerful health industry lobbies to push for a more aggressive approach to the scourge of prescription drug abuse. I won both of those fights because I was right, and because I had a lot of partners.

And finally, I alienated people on all sides of the same-sex marriage issue—and opened myself up to stinging criticism—by pushing for a US Supreme Court ruling that I knew was necessary for the commonwealth and this country to move forward in some united way. And when the Supreme Court ruled, I angered an equal number of people by immediately implementing that decision. Until now, I've declined to talk about my personal views on same-sex marriage because they were irrelevant. In this book, I explain in a personal and candid way why I opened myself up to criticism and what was in my heart.

On other issues, I wasn't so courageous, and I regret it.

The bottom line is that Kentucky needs brave leaders. We made considerable progress, but Kentucky still faces fundamental challenges. Our ability to improve the quality of life of our people, long term, and build a more competitive statewide economy will require electing officials who are willing to stand up and take risks by tackling difficult issues. We need elected officials who have courage, vision, and persistence—and who understand that sometimes they have to forego what's popular to do what's best.

That's one reason this book is so timely.

On one level, it's a lesson for Washington and the nation of what collaborative leadership can bring. But it's also a warning. Today, rank partisanship is jeopardizing much of the progress that Democrats and Republicans made together in the last eight years in Kentucky.

Kentucky must fight to recover the spirit of collaboration, and it must resist becoming a player in the Greek tragedy that is playing out on the national level. The 2016 presidential election—the before, during, and after—has exposed deep divisions in this country that threaten to tear it apart. Some politicians in Washington and Frankfort are mining those divisions and that anger for their own benefit.

Unfortunately, rank partisanship won't put food on a single table, create a single job, or enable a single person to go to the doctor. All it will do is slow the momentum of a state that—having grown tired of being mired in the past—had begun to leap forward in impressive fashion.

Good leaders build and unify. They don't divide and tear down. And true leaders genuinely care about the people they serve. In short, they put people over politics. Take it from me, a man who for eight years enjoyed his dream job—leading the state where he was born and grew up.

And for those eight years, we proved Mark Twain wrong.

Section II
GOVERNING

OFF TO A POOR START

The beginning of my first term as governor was a near disaster. With a shattered economy, an upside-down state budget, a lack of personal relationships with legislators, and no long-term focus, my administration got bogged down almost from the beginning and found it difficult to get traction.

One month in, SurveyUSA had measured my approval rating at a healthy 62 percent. Two months later, it had plummeted to 46 percent. A month after that, it had fallen even further to 38 percent.

Small wonder that morale in my office was low, and social media and editorial pages were depressing places to visit.

And it didn't bode well for the next three and a half years.

If they're honest, most people who become governor of a state will admit later that they had no real idea of the demands of the job until after they were in it. No matter how close you are to the Governor's Office, or how much you have observed someone else in the job, until you are there—until that 24/7 pressure descends upon your shoulders—you don't really know what you are getting into.

Having served in the state general assembly, as attorney general, and as lieutenant governor, I had been as close to the job as anyone can be. I also had lots of great ideas as to where I wanted to lead the state. So I entered office in December 2007 feeling prepared and optimistic.

I had no idea the hurdles that awaited me.

Now every new governor in every state faces challenges right off the bat. But in Kentucky, a new governor essentially has only five weeks in which to put together a staff, prepare a two-year budget, develop a legislative agenda, and build the relationships that help pass that budget and agenda. It's not nearly enough time. But those challenges are anticipated and they apply to every new governor. I had more pressing and specific problems.

My first hurdle had to do with money. All of those great ideas I proposed during my campaign? They came crashing down around my head as the worst global recession of our lifetimes hit us full in the face almost immediately after the inauguration. Things like universal preschool and kindergarten, teacher raises, and investments in higher education all required money, and because of the economy, we didn't have any. The recession turned everything upside down and set us adrift almost from the beginning.

A second hurdle had to do with staff. I had been out of active politics for most of the previous 20 years, with a failed bid for the US Senate in 1996 being my only experience since losing the governor's race in 1987. Virtually everyone I had worked with in the '70s and '80s had moved on. Most had successful careers and were unwilling to return to state government. In essence, I had to start anew, finding people to fill dozens of important positions.

Fortunately, I *was* able to reach back and grab a few people whose hair was as gray as mine, or who had lost their hair altogether, and although I was criticized by the media for bringing back the "geriatric crowd," in the long run, it proved to be one of the best decisions I made in my first year.

And a third hurdle concerned the general assembly. Because of my 20-year absence, I had few close relationships with legislators. And the body as a whole was an entirely different animal than I was used to—in the decades since I'd been in Frankfort, the legislative branch had become almost a full-time group. It was also much more independent of the executive branch, and it took great pride in that independence.

I inherited a split legislature, with the House controlled by the Democrats and the Senate by Republicans. Both chambers presented challenges. I thought I would have natural allies in the Democratic House, but sadly, I was mistaken. Under my predecessor, the House had reveled in its independence and the thrill of doing battle with a Republican governor, and the prospect of following the lead of a Democratic governor didn't seem all that exciting to them. In fact, a Democratic legislator began likening me to Rip Van Winkle because I'd been gone so long from Frankfort.

And of course, those problems were exacerbated by internal leadership struggles within the House. I wasn't the only one who felt that way. As numerous newspapers reported, shortly after the session ended, House Majority Whip Rob Wilkey wrote an e-mail blasting leadership for what he said was focusing too much on retaining their positions and not enough on the people's business.

"I also thought there was a conscious effort to embarrass this governor during this session," Wilkey wrote. "It worked. He could have done a better job of building a relationship with the House, but I also feel he was misled into believing that we would work with him. We didn't."

Meanwhile, I had an even bigger challenge in the Republican Senate, which for several years had been led by Senator David Williams. Senator Williams, who would later run against me in the 2011 governor's race, was a forceful personality who dominated his caucus. In fact, it seemed to me that many Republican senators were literally afraid to disagree with him.

The divide between the Republican Senate and Democratic House was deep. It also didn't help that Kentucky's legislature had begun suffering from the same disease then infecting Congress and many state legislatures around the country—the inability to put partisanship aside and work together for the common good.

With that background, there is little wonder that my first session of the general assembly was not the most successful.

My biggest challenge was balancing the budget in the face of the historic recession. Indeed, during our first few weeks in office, we had to cut some $434 million out of the current year's budget just to keep it balanced. But those reductions paled next to the challenge of writing the next two-year budget when revenues were expected to fall almost $900 million short of even the current year's spending.

Making these multi-million dollar cuts in important programs was a very painful process for me. At one point, my wife, First Lady Jane Beshear, looked at me and sympathetically asked, "Is this what we ran for this office for?" I knew exactly what she meant, but we had no choice.

However, an important philosophy emerged from that first budget-cutting experience, a thoughtful approach that we utilized time and time again in the budget cuts to come.

Many states faced with this dilemma simply cut across the board: determine what the deficit is, then cut every program the same percentage to balance the budget. While that was certainly the easiest way to do it, in my mind it wasn't the smart way to do it. Why? Because although every state-funded program was important to someone, some were more important than everything else. So we made tough choices. We protected core priorities like education, health care, job creation, and public safety—even though that meant harsher cuts elsewhere. In short, we used a scalpel instead of a blunt hatchet. While this was much riskier politically because of the constituencies we angered, in the long run, this willingness to prioritize placed Kentucky in a position to recover from the recession faster than most states when the economy turned around. But the budget blood pooled deep just the same.

In addition, two of my priorities—proposals to reform the public pension system and to strengthen state ethics laws—fell apart late in the session. We also failed to pass expanded gaming.

Gaming had been a great campaign issue that had separated me from other Democrats in the primary and from my GOP opponent, but getting it through the general assembly proved to be another thing altogether. It would have created significant new revenue, but I found out quickly that for every 100 people in the horse industry, there were 100 different opinions on any issue. To try to get them to reach consensus on what an expanded gaming program should look like proved impossible. My proposal was introduced late in the session and went nowhere.

On one level, it wasn't surprising. In a Bible Belt state like Kentucky, most legislators ran for cover on an issue like expanded gaming. So it didn't even get a vote.

Small wonder that "disappointing" was the word of the day in every story that talked about my first legislative session.

I was proud that we had worked with the general assembly to balance the budget without raising taxes, and we did it without cutting a few core priorities like per-pupil classroom funding and Medicaid (although we cut just about everything else). That was a huge accomplishment. We also had some limited but important successes related to Adventure Tourism, increasing penalties for people who sexually abused children, and increasing the use of booster seats. But our broader agenda with its specific initiatives went nowhere.

Obviously, things had to change, and I knew it.

After the legislative session ended, I called a strategy meeting of my top staff and my consultants, David Eichenbaum and Fred Yang, who with fund-raiser Scott Gale, had helped me win the election. In addition, the Democratic Governors Association offered the services of consultant Doug Sosnik. Sosnik, a longtime adviser on policy and strategy, is somewhat of a legend in Washington political circles, having worked with Bill Clinton, John Kerry, Chris Dodd, and many others.

That meeting helped turn my governorship around.

We realized we had to come to terms with having no money and find ways to make progress anyway. We started planning a year ahead instead of a month ahead and began getting out around the state and building my influence by building my personal brand. I also set about to methodically develop personal relationships with individual legislators.

In the next few months, several things happened.

With the help of my then-Communications Director Jay Blanton, and Katie Dailinger, an aide who later became director of policy and communications director, we set in place a more strategic, coordinated, and integrated plan to build statewide support for my priorities. With the help of my scheduler, Courtney French, and later her successor, Liz Roach, we created a breathless schedule that had me leaving Frankfort regularly to make policy announcements, ramp up aid programs, build ties with local officials, and deliver funding for their projects. In the second part of 2008, I went on three multi-stop campaigns of the state. I did the Beshear About Kentucky town hall "listening tour" with cabinet secretaries in July; several events in September to publicize an aggressive program to sign up eligible kids under the Kentucky Children's Health Insurance Program; and a series of visits in December to explain my plan to fill yet another half-a-billion-dollar projected hole in the state budget.

And I became more aggressive and strategic about setting the agenda instead of letting it be set for me. For example:

- Saying we could no longer wait for the legislature to act, in late May, I issued an executive order strengthening the ethics policies governing the executive branch. (One of the strongest advocates for this action was my close friend Bob Vance, who served not only as a cabinet secretary but also as one of my closest informal advisers for six and a half years. In fact, the Kentucky Executive Branch Ethics Commission later gave Bob its prestigious Livingston Taylor Ethics Award for the 2011–13 biennium.)

- In late June, I called legislators back into town for a special session, then helped build consensus on a comprehensive plan to put the ailing Kentucky Retirement Systems on the path toward financial stability.

- In August, I unveiled a new road-building strategy called "Practical Solutions" that would help us be more pragmatic and efficient about how we designed and built roads, given Kentucky's woefully inadequate Road Fund. (My first Transportation Cabinet Secretary Joe Prather championed this initiative. His aggressive leadership cleaned up a cabinet that had long been tainted by corruption and scandal.)

- Over the autumn months, I announced an array of initiatives to help families and the state survive the recession. These included a novel financing plan to preserve student loans, a new website to link residents with assistance programs, a program to help seniors get needed medicine, doubling of heat assistance for low-income families, and new task forces on early education and college affordability. (Many of these ideas originated with the innovative Jonathan Miller, who was then Finance Cabinet secretary.)

- And in November, I worked with Energy and Environment Secretary Len Peters to unveil a seven-point comprehensive plan for changing how Kentucky produced and consumed energy over the next few decades.

In short, I took control of our future. Instead of reacting to others, I found ways to make progress despite the financial mess we inherited.

I took my message straight to the people. With frequent visits, Kentucky's communities got to know me and my administration, and they began to understand my goals for the state. They saw me standing strong for them and recognized that I was determined to improve not only their immediate quality of life but also the long-term capacity of the commonwealth.

It didn't happen overnight, but slowly and steadily, we recovered from the disastrous first six months, changed the narrative of my administration, and established a tone and a focus that we never lost.

Incidentally, when I left office in December 2015, my approval rating stood at 57 percent, so something worked.

A LEGACY FINDS ME

Shortly after I became governor, several of my advisers began to talk about what our legacy would be.

Most of them felt that I needed to pick one priority and concentrate on it. "Governor [Martha Layne] Collins is remembered for bringing Toyota to the state," they said. "Wallace Wilkinson created the lottery. Paul Patton reformed our higher education system." All seemed to agree that I would be remembered for one effort, at most, and that I needed to choose what that would be sooner rather than later.

They also felt that envisioning a legacy would focus not only me but also the entire staff on making the biggest impact in the shortest time, and it would give a sense of urgency to our work. And on that level, the exercise seemed to make sense.

But in the end, I simply couldn't do it. I didn't want to do just one thing. I wanted to do it all.

Kentucky has a series of fundamental weaknesses that must change for us to become one of the leading states in this country, and many of those challenges involve broad areas like education, workforce development, job creation, and health. We had made progress since the 1990s in education, but we remained in the middle of the pack because other states were making progress as well. Our economy was just average, with many low-paying jobs. Our workforce wasn't as educated and skilled as it needed to be. And our health statistics were abysmal—Kentucky was at the bottom of the heap in virtually every category.

So finally, I told my advisers, "Look. First of all, I can't spend my time worrying about what my legacy might be. Others will determine later what, if anything, we will be remembered for. And second, for Kentucky to get where I want it to be, we have to improve ourselves in *several* categories, not just one, and I want to try my best to make it happen."

As it turned out, over eight years, we were able to make significant progress on those fundamental weaknesses. After leading Kentucky through the worst recession of our lifetimes, we built a thriving economy, taking our unemployment rate from almost 11 percent to 4.9 percent, setting export records five years in a row, attracting investment from around the world, and creating almost 90,000 new jobs. We also moved Kentucky into the top 10 states in high school graduation rates, took our college and career readiness rate from 30 to 68.5 percent, and raised our dropout age from 16 to 18.

But ironically, it was in the area of health that we made the most dramatic difference, when an unexpected opportunity thrust Kentucky into the national headlines and a national leadership role.

Our aggressive implementation of the Affordable Care Act allowed us to change the course of Kentucky's history by providing to every single Kentuckian—for the first time ever—access to affordable health coverage. For many, it was the first time in their lives they had had such coverage.

During the first few years of my administration, we had no idea that we would have the opportunity to affect the health care of Kentuckians in such a significant way. But along came the Affordable Care Act, and we had the guts to embrace it in a state where President Obama had a 30 percent popularity rating.

My legacy, it seems, had created itself.

THE LONG, HARD SLOG

Of all the negative impacts of modern-day sound-bite campaigns, one of the most dangerous is the notion that a governor or other elected official can ride into town and, in his or her short time in office, solve all the state's problems.

News flash: It's not that easy.

Kentucky faces weaknesses at its core that have held the state back for generations—weaknesses like poor health, lack of education attainment, a workforce that isn't as trained and agile as the marketplace demands, too many children getting a poor start in life and in school, and an economy that isn't as diversified as it needs to be.

On challenges like these, there is no quick fix. No magic formula. No super pill and no silver bullet.

Governors, legislators, and voters need to understand that solving those problems takes a long time—decades, not years. It takes a lot of hard work and big-picture vision. And it requires broad partnerships that involve lots of stakeholders across the spectrum.

Raising the quality of life of a people is a long, hard slog. It's complex work. And the commonwealth can't afford to lose focus.

You usually don't hear realities like that during an election campaign. Instead, you hear lots of promises—simple, sexy-sounding promises that suggest quick results. A lot of slogans, a lot of platitudes, a lot of simplification.

But the reality is that once you take office, you realize the complexity of the job. You realize that promises have unintended consequences that must be taken into consideration, and that few issues are as clear-cut as the public understands them to be.

You also begin to recognize that to truly make a difference in the state, to actually create a better world for your children and grandchildren and their children, you have to tackle the difficult issues.

You have to start trying to shove that boulder up the hill a few inches at a time, knowing that four years or even eight years won't be enough time to get there and that—if the boulder ever gets to the top—you'll be so long gone that you won't get any credit for it.

Governors come into office with fresh ideas, and that's a good thing. But they often let their elections go to their heads. They tend to want to tear up everything their predecessor did and start completely new on virtually everything. And that's a huge mistake.

Some governors, as the saying goes, are reluctant to raise "stepchildren"—the programs, policies, and priorities pushed by their predecessors, partly because they'll have to share the credit for any successes. But on some issues, that's *exactly* what the state needs to make sustainable progress on big weaknesses.

When I came into office, I had fresh ideas and priorities of my own, but I also recognized the good work of governors who had served before me. So I *did* raise some stepchildren. My aggressive effort to court international businesses was an offshoot of work by Governors Martha Layne Collins and John Y. Brown Jr. My focus on early childhood development built upon the ideas pushed by Governor Paul Patton and First Lady Judi Patton. A number of governors since the 1990s have supported increased and equitable funding of our public schools and universities, and we continued that commitment. I recognized the powerful work of Governor Ernie Fletcher in the area of substance abuse and not only continued but also expanded the Recovery Kentucky program. I also kept the commitment that Governor Fletcher had made to Louisville to build the KFC Yum! Center, investing time and money to put in place a significant piece of downtown redevelopment.

Just as important was the evolution of the priorities of my administration.

When I was sworn in as governor in late 2007, I arrived determined to restore the people's trust in state government, to bring common sense to an out-of-control state budget, and to end the acrimonious partisan warfare that was interfering with good decisions.

Then the global economic recession hit with all its fury, and like governors across the nation, my top priority became helping Kentucky families and businesses survive.

But I also realized that survival wasn't enough. I wanted Kentucky to emerge from the recession not shell-shocked and shattered but able and ambitious, poised to do great things. And so—even as we were needing to trim state spending in order to balance the budget—we took aim at Kentucky's fundamental weaknesses.

Rather than get distracted by issues that might win me the next news cycle or election or the Internet for that day, I concentrated on long-term goals related to education, job creation, our workforce, health care, and preparing our children for school.

These efforts weren't quick fixes but were part of a long-term, multi-faceted strategy that helped Kentucky begin to strengthen its core. As I prepared to leave office years later, I issued a press release to call attention to these long-range strategies; to praise the many leaders, agencies, and organizations in both the public and private sectors who partnered with my administration on Kentucky's needs; and to issue a warning.

The release listed some specific progress on a "baker's dozen" of broad issues, such as:

- dramatically improving access to health care by reducing the number of Kentuckians without health coverage from 20.4 percent to 9 percent (down to 7.5 percent as of late 2016);

- raising the dropout age from 16 to 18;

- begin building a plan to build 3,000 miles of middle-mile fiber infrastructure to expand access to high-speed broadband in the furthest corners of the commonwealth;

- drastically expanding access to substance-abuse prevention and treatment programs;

- making changes that would potentially put 5,125 more kids in preschool and ensure all children enter kindergarten ready to do the work expected of them; and

- strengthening our future workforce by investing almost $200 million in new buildings at our two-year colleges, building an advanced manufacturing training center, and beginning a variety of apprenticeship programs.

But although we made measurable progress, that progress was vulnerable, I said. In order for Kentucky's long-term strategy to work, I wrote, "We need to hit the accelerator—not the brakes."

Unfortunately, Kentucky's new governor has been stomping on the brakes. He cut spending for higher education and attempted to cut spending for K–12 education. He vetoed an increase of some 8,000 more kids in preschool. He dismantled the state's award-winning health benefits exchange, and he is pulling back on Medicaid expansion, changes that will make it harder for the poor to get health care.

I'm reminded of North Carolina's recent experience. Since the 1960s, that state had a series of governors, both Democrat and Republican, who were willing to build on the efforts of their predecessors and were committed to public education and job creation. As a result, North Carolina vaulted ahead of most southern states. But, in the last few years, its political system has been taken over by right-wing politicians whose priorities are focused on things like "bathroom laws," and as a result, North Carolina is no longer viewed by many business, sports leagues, and others as the place to be. (However, the 2016 election of a moderate Democrat as governor is a hopeful sign.)

In a press conference in the waning days of my administration, I used an analogy to talk about the necessity of leaders committing themselves long term to progress.

"Think about it this way," I said. "If you want to turn a barren field into a forest, you plant seedlings. As those seedlings grow into saplings, you tend to them, protect them, nourish them, and fortify them. You don't run out in the fields every four or eight years and cut down your saplings and start over. Because if you do that, you'll never have a forest."

After decades of political leadership in Kentucky willing to nurture the saplings, our young forest is now in danger.

Philosophical differences are to be expected as new governors come in and legislatures change membership. So are shifts in priorities and focus. But undoing good work that is already beginning to pay off in a measurable way—just because of whose name is on it or which political party championed it— is destructive. It wastes time and resources, and it unravels progress made toward solving long-term problems. So much more momentum could be created if that energy was focused on positive efforts.

THE BUDGET STORM:
"COLD, HARSH REALITY"

The celebratory mood didn't last long.

The day after I was inaugurated during a beautiful ceremony in December 2007, budget director Mary Lassiter took me aside and smacked me with the reality of taking office at the leading edge of a global economic recession. "Governor," she said, "I hope you enjoyed yesterday. Because today we have to start figuring out how to cut $434 million out of the current year's budget to keep it balanced."

And just like that, my plans to move Kentucky forward by creating universal preschool, expanding kindergarten, raising teacher pay, and investing in higher education were put on hold.

I had a more urgent challenge to confront.

The $434-million gap had to be solved in six months—by June 30, 2008—the end of the biennium. That was bad enough. What was even worse was that experts told me that revenue in the coming two-year budget cycle would be about *$900 million less* than existing expenditures. By law, I had to write a balanced two-year budget proposal based on those revenue projections, and I had only a month to do it.

Kentucky, like every other state, was being crushed in a financial vise that was being cranked tight by levers beyond our control.

As I explain elsewhere in this book, the recession was historic in nature, officially labeled by the International Monetary Fund as the worst downturn since World War II. In fact, the country was so precariously close to slipping into a deep depression that two presidents and Congress passed monstrous stimulus packages that not only bailed out the nation's key industries but also protected core government services like education.

These were truly extraordinary times that required extraordinary responses.

Consequently, in a speech on January 29 to the joint session of the general assembly, I unveiled a budget—the first of my administration—that I called "austere to the point of pain."

"Last year while running for governor, I envisioned this first budget address to be a night where I unveiled a plan brimming with bold and creative new programs," I said in my televised speech. "However, that evening will have to wait. Because tonight, we deal with cold, harsh reality."

Now ... fast-forward eight years.

Taking to heart the edict to leave things better than you found them, I finished my second term in December 2015 and left behind a financial picture that was far rosier than any I had confronted. Rather than inheriting a mid-year shortfall and an upside-down revenue projection, my successor was gifted with a surplus and projected revenue growth.

In fact, a couple of days after I left office, the state Consensus Forecasting Group (the same experts whose projections provide the basis for every governor's budget proposal) predicted that Kentucky would end the 2015–16 biennium with a $223-million surplus. They also projected that revenues for the coming two-year budget cycle (fiscal years 2017 and 2018) would grow 3.2 percent and 2.4 percent, respectively.

Furthermore, in July 2015—just months before I departed—I made an $82.5-million deposit into the state's Budget Reserve

Trust Fund, bringing the so-called Rainy Day Fund's balance to $209.4 million, the highest in almost a decade.

How did we turn around the state's financial condition?

Well, the recipe was simple, even if the actual work wasn't.

First, we addressed the revenue side by working 24/7 to create jobs by attracting new businesses and helping existing businesses expand. This obviously created more tax revenue—not by raising taxes but by growing Kentucky's economy.

And second, we addressed the expenditure side by bringing "common sense" to state spending.

This second step—reining in the state budget—was neither easy nor done haphazardly. We had three basic strategies:

Our first move was outright cuts. All told, we reduced or rebalanced the budget 15 times in eight years, cutting $1.6 billion in spending while trimming the executive branch workforce to its lowest total in decades. I even instituted voluntary 10 percent pay cuts for myself and senior staff and mandatory furloughs for most state workers.

Some of this "right-sizing" was needed, but some of it hurt. Agencies that did important work like making sure our workplaces were safe, ensuring the water we drank was clean, and teaching postsecondary skills, had their budgets cut by 20 percent to 40 percent over my eight years. But to their credit, these agencies adjusted and still delivered the services Kentuckians needed and deserved.

Our second move was to make government more efficient in how it managed physical assets and spent money on an ongoing basis.

Through what we called the Smart Government Initiative, we sold surplus land and buildings, consolidated offices, merged information technology contracts, sold two little-used airplanes on eBay, and ended the practice of take-home cars in the Governor's Office. We also renegotiated and rebid service contracts, refinanced bonds, asked landlords to voluntarily reduce their rent, centralized postal and printing functions, and bought more goods in bulk across state agencies.

Then we moved on to look at updating procurement and revenue collection processes, installing GPS into fleet cars to track travel, installing energy-saving software in our buildings, and so on.

Some of the SGI's financial benefits were easy to measure as one-time shots of money, such as $230,000 for the planes and $7.45 million in surplus property. But we also embedded future savings by changing how we did business; for example, by saving almost $30 million a year with a technology consolidation of all infrastructure across all agencies.

In short, we did what people around Kentucky did to survive the recession: We sat down at the proverbial kitchen table, and we made tough decisions to identify how and where we could do without.

Our third strategy was to work to reduce the skyrocketing costs of ongoing and growing liabilities like public pension payments, health care for public workers, and corrections costs— what the Kentucky Chamber of Commerce called Kentucky's "leaky bucket."

Now, did we permanently resolve all these challenges? Of course not. These are systemic, long-term issues, and they will take consistent, aggressive, but measured attention by many administrations to get under control. In other words, it took a long time to get into those messes, and it'll take a long time to get out of them. But during my eight years, I worked with the legislature to put sustainable plans in place that—if future Kentucky leaders follow them—will address those challenges, long term.

Plus it's important to remember that Kentucky isn't the only state with these so-called leaky buckets, and that many of these costs—such as those for health care—will require national solutions.

As to how my budget strategies played out, I could go into detail and bore readers to no end with numbers and more numbers. And I'm sure that the two people who served as my budget director, Mary Lassiter and Jane Driskell, would love it if I did. Instead, I will quickly mention a few principles that guided our efforts.

The first was the sanctity of public money. Taxes are a sacred investment, and government can inspire confidence by taking good care of that investment. In bringing common sense to Kentucky's budget, we not only restored the public's confidence in us as stewards of their money but also preserved the ability of government to fulfill its role.

That leads to the second principle: Tax revenues are a tool to do good things. Short term, government lends help to those in dire need. It rescues, and it protects. Long term, government oversees the basic societal infrastructure that enables Kentuckians to pursue a more secure and rewarding future for themselves and for their children. That infrastructure includes things like health care, education, job training, public safety, and economic viability. If tax revenues aren't improving Kentucky long term, then they aren't being used wisely.

And that leads to the third principle: long-term payback. Making these huge cuts in important programs was painful, but it forced us to focus on what was most important. Instead of taking the easy way out and cutting every program by the same amount, like many states did, we made tough choices. We protected priorities like education, health care, job creation, and public safety—even though that meant harsher cuts elsewhere. Some states laid off state troopers and teachers and kicked Medicaid recipients out of the program, but we didn't. By preserving our core, we were in a better position to grow once the economy started recovering. But that took a long time.

In fact, the budget outlook was so bad for so long that we gave Mary—who later also led my executive cabinet—a nickname.

We call her "Cloud," because she was always raining bad news. Depressing numbers seemed to hover around her, like a gloomy storm system.

In reality, however, the nickname belied Mary's personality. She was always cheerful, was full of ideas and solutions, and had both a top-notch intellect and an incomparable work ethic. Having served under a half dozen governors, she led an experienced budget staff whose steady work helped guide us through those difficult times. And she was respected on both sides of the partisan aisle.

In the end, we *did* put Kentucky on better financial footing. Much better. Our aggressive and thoughtful strategies enabled us to make important investments in our education system and workforce in the 2015–16 budget, and it positioned us to create a stronger Kentucky long term.

Now, we didn't permanently solve Kentucky's budget pressures, because you never have enough money to do everything you want to do. Challenges are *always* present when you craft a budget, and every governor is forced to make tough decisions. But we did protect Kentucky's needs while also investing in the strengthening of our core.

Shepherding Kentucky through the recession turned out to be one of our hardest jobs during my eight years, but with the help of a great team, we did it with our integrity and our priorities intact. We left the state in better shape than we found it and left the incoming administration with a positive budget picture to boot.

Given that fact, perhaps I should have changed Mary's nickname.

THE RELUCTANT
FIRST LADY

I may be biased, but I'm still sure I'm right: There has never been a First Lady of the commonwealth who has tackled as many important issues as aggressively and with as much success as Jane Beshear.

That's ironic, because she never wanted to be First Lady in the first place.

See, early in life, I had some success in politics: elected to three two-year terms in the state House of Representatives, then four years as attorney general, and four years as lieutenant governor. Then in 1987, disaster struck, and I lost the governor's race. My political career was over, and as deeply disappointed as I was, I had to get on with life.

I went back into the law practice and became engaged in community banking. Jane entered the real estate business. We set about raising our two sons, Jeff and Andy, who at that time were 13 and 9. We went to soccer games, and I coached baseball. Jane was able to get back into the love of her life: horses. She not only enjoyed foxhunting but also became an accomplished event rider, winning blue ribbons all across the South. The boys had started riding as soon as they could walk, and when they followed her into foxhunting, soon I did too (realizing it was the only way I was going to get to see my family on the weekends). We also took up skiing and spent several holiday vacations as a family on the ski slopes.

Later, when we got the boys through college and through law and veterinary school and we became empty nesters, Jane and I began to travel with friends to faraway places like England, France, Italy, Austria, China, and Russia. We also went sailing several times in the Caribbean.

In short, we had become very comfortable financially and were blessed to enjoy a life that relatively few have experienced.

Then in 2006, a small group of us began talking to three or four leading Democrats about running against incumbent Governor Ernie Fletcher in the 2007 race. The thought of me running never crossed my mind that whole year. It wasn't even a possibility. But in November, after our potential recruits announced one by one that they weren't interested in the race, my friend Tracy Farmer and a few others urged me to run.

So one afternoon soon thereafter, I came home and sat down with Jane. "I am thinking of running for governor," I told her. Well, if looks could kill, I would have been dead right there! She could not believe her ears. We had built a wonderful life uncomplicated by politics, and she highly valued both her privacy and her time to spend with her horses and the first of our grandchildren. She was very reluctant to give that up.

Ultimately, however, she told me in an incredible display of love and unselfishness, "If this is what you want, then let's go do it."

So while the last thing Jane wanted was to be First Lady, once we won the election, she realized that for the next few years, she would be in a position where she could positively affect the lives of lots of people—in short, she had a unique opportunity to make a difference.

And brother, did she make the most of it!

Over the next eight years, she continued to be my closest and most trusted adviser, as well as my confidante and sounding board. She was able to cut through all the noise on key issues and help me focus on what was important.

But she also worked on her own to use the Office of the First Lady to lead the charge on a diverse list of more than a dozen significant issues. These included persistent and devastating problems like spouse abuse, breast cancer awareness, and substance and alcohol abuse. It also included changing state law to help more kids graduate from high school; help military spouses; build new biking, hiking, and riding trails; conserve energy; and create new incentives for the film industry.

I wasn't surprised. I told Kentuckians in my final "About Kentucky" weekly video message in November 2015, "It has been an easy role for her to fill. All her life, Jane has been generous with her time and compassionate with her heart. As a former teacher, as a mother and a grandmother, when she sees people hurting, she feels compelled to help them. She's genuine, and she's persistent. That's a good combination."

A 21-page report at the end of our second term gave some details of the Office of the First Lady's work under Jane's leadership and the capable direction of Jane's steady chief of staff, Susan Rieber.

Kentucky greatly expanded breast cancer awareness, screening, and treatment referral with the Horses & Hope program, geared toward workers in the horse industry. This effort included a new mobile screening van funded by a $1.5 million campaign.

Jane also worked with the Kentucky Coalition Against Domestic Violence to change state laws to better protect dating couples and to increase funding for domestic violence shelters and other programs. This included securing state money and raising almost $4 million in private donations since 2009 through the Shop and Share program.

In the area of education, Jane was a fierce advocate, and her persistence through the Graduate Kentucky initiative was the main reason that Kentucky finally updated a nearly 90-year-old law and raised its high school dropout age to 18. She also helped increase our focus on early childhood education and furthered literacy efforts through the Feed the Mind program.

Jane led the charge to upgrade the Kentucky Horse Park into a world-class facility, which then hosted the highly successful World Equestrian Games in 2010. She pushed Kentucky to expand its Adventure Tourism attractions. And thanks in great part to her, Kentucky built the first two phases and started the third phase of the Dawkins Line Rail Trail, a new 36-mile recreation and tourist attraction in far Eastern Kentucky.

She also co-chaired the Recovery Kentucky Task Force that expanded and enhanced the peer-based substance-abuse treatment program started by former governor Ernie Fletcher. Recognizing a powerful initiative when we saw it, we provided funding to complete Governor Fletcher's original plan to build 10 new residential treatment centers, and we also provided funding to plan and build four additional centers. Jane also created a foundation to raise money for the Recovery Kentucky program. These were significant steps forward in helping Kentucky families devastated by addiction.

Furthermore, Jane worked to create the Military Spouse Task Force to help our military families, for which she was later honored at the Pentagon by First Lady Michelle Obama and Defense Secretary Leon Panetta. Jane worked to increase Kentucky's chances to attract filmmakers and directors and to revitalize the Old Governor's Mansion in downtown Frankfort. She helped expand energy-efficiency efforts and worked to build the Capitol Education Center for Kentucky's schoolchildren. She also helped raise a $1-million endowment on the 100th anniversary of the Governor's Mansion to fund future renovation.

In short, Jane was a devoted advocate and tireless worker for all Kentuckians and especially for women and children. Time and again, people came to me while I was governor and said, "Jane is fantastic. She really cares about this state and its people, and she just keeps on going."

I knew that already, of course, but it was gratifying that so many other people recognized that as well.

As First Lady, Jane fell in love with the people of Kentucky, and they fell in love with her. That included many in the news media. In the early days of 2011 as I was beginning my re-election campaign, a journalist stopped me on my way into the office and jokingly said, "Governor, are you aware that Jane is more popular than you?" To which I responded, "Let me put it to you this way—if she announces for governor, I am out of the race."

She was a big reason not only for my election successes but also for our administration's successes and our popularity across Kentucky. And it will be a long time before Kentucky sees the likes of a First Lady like Jane Beshear again.

A LESSON FROM FDR

As the freezing rain began slashing down from the sky early on January 26, 2009, and the ice began to build up to perilous levels on trees, roads, power lines, and cell phone towers, I turned to Franklin Delano Roosevelt for guidance.

I'm not old enough to have heard FDR's "Fireside Chats" during the Great Depression of the 1930s. But in high school history class, I had read about them and heard recordings, and my parents told me about huddling around their radio listening to the president. "During those terrible times, we knew he cared about us," they told me, "and he gave us hope that things would be better."

That lesson stuck with me as I grew into adulthood and won elected office: A leader must show people that he cares about them, and during hard times, he must give them not only tangible help but also reassurance and hope.

Nothing demonstrated the truth of this principle more than that historic 2009 ice storm.

During my eight years as governor, Kentucky suffered a record 16 weather-related disasters that rose to the level of federally declared major disasters. They formed a biblical plague of calamities that included tornado outbreaks, horrendous windstorms, paralyzing snow and ice, flash flooding and sustained floods, landslides, mudslides, and rockslides. The first series of storms—with flash flooding and tornadoes—hit just two months after I took office, but nothing compared to the ice and snowstorms that hit in late January almost a year later.

By most measures, it became the worst natural disaster Kentucky has ever suffered.

As the freezing rain fell and fell over a couple of days—followed by a week or so of snow—the damage was widespread and severe.

- The weight of the ice snapped not only trees by the tens of thousands but also demolished power lines, telephone lines, and entire transmission towers.

- As a result, communities were cut off as landline service, cell phone service, Internet service, and even emergency communications died, and some 4,000 miles of roads were impassable.

- Nearly 800,000 families, businesses, hospitals, and nursing homes—representing almost 36 percent of the state's energy consumers—lost electrical power. And water supplies to more than 230,000 people were affected.

- When it was over, 36 people were dead, 110 of our 120 counties and about 100 cities had declared states of emergency, and communities spread over more than 32,000 square miles needed assistance.

Calling on every resource at our disposal—federal, state, local, public, and private—I set in motion a relief effort of a magnitude never seen before in the commonwealth. The response included a "major disaster" declaration from President Obama himself, the installation of more than 150 massive generators, and the establishment of about 200 shelters.

And even though we deployed thousands of dedicated and tireless state employees—road crews, public health workers, state troopers, forestry officials, Division of Water inspectors, fish-and-wildlife officers, emergency management officials, and others to work alongside local responders—I knew that it wouldn't be enough.

Our local emergency personnel and relief organizations were overwhelmed. Things were bad, and without electricity, clean water, and communications, they would get worse.

So I took the unprecedented step of ordering the mobilization of the entire Kentucky Army National Guard, plus selected Air National Guard units. There were some initial concerns expressed about the cost of such an action. "We'll worry about the cost later," I said. "There are lives on the line. Call them all up."

So in what turned out to be the largest call-up in Kentucky history, about 4,500 soldiers and airmen and women—all who were available and eligible—came to the rescue of their fellow Kentuckians. They delivered food and water. They cleared roads. They provided medical treatment and transportation. Their expertise and wireless communication equipment helped bridge the gap among local authorities who could not communicate with each other. And they literally walked door to door in hard-hit areas to find people in need of help. Without a doubt, these visits alleviated suffering. Without a doubt, they saved lives.

I mean that literally. Two members of the Kentucky National Guard going door to door in Hardinsburg, for example, came across an elderly couple who appeared dizzy and confused. Suspecting a problem, the soldiers investigated and found the home was filled with carbon monoxide from an unvented heater—a level that was twice the lethal dose. They acted swiftly and the couple survived.

Other soldiers helped local officials rescue four teens from the roof of a vehicle stuck in the frigid waters of a creek in Daviess County on a 10-degree day. More lives saved.

As soon as we could get a Blackhawk helicopter off the ground, Jane and I started going around to towns and other remote areas of the state, sitting down with beleaguered community leaders who were exhausted from getting shelters set up and trying to secure generators to power water systems and hospitals. We passed out sandwiches, hugged families, gave pep talks to soldiers and road crews and relief workers, and generally made our presence known. People needed to know that the highest levels of state government were aware of their hardships and were working diligently to bring help.

Heroes were everywhere.

Before the Guard arrived, for example, firefighters walked five miles through snow and ice to check on people in the cut-off town of Dawson Springs. In Ohio County, the chairwoman of the school board turned a middle school into a shelter. And at Murray State University, students and staff slept on the floor at the campus radio station so it could broadcast the latest information about relief efforts around the clock, providing the only functional public voice for several days. I met with the Murray students in person. The blurry-eyed students at WKMS-FM had been on the air for a couple of days when I arrived. They gave me a microphone to tell people of the region that help was on the way, that the National Guard would soon be there, and that everything would be okay.

We repeated that experience in dozens of communities over the next couple of days.

The message must have resonated. In the months that followed, I heard time and time again from people in many different communities some version of: "Governor, we knew we were going to be okay when we heard your voice on the radio and saw the National Guard walking up the street."

FDR, it turns out, was right. Sometimes leadership is about just being there so people can see that you care about them, and about giving hope that things will be better.

"GET OFF OUR BACKS"

It was a fiery comment that I delivered to Kentucky's General Assembly before a statewide TV audience early in a hard-fought re-election campaign, and it drew rousing applause—even from my opponent.

But while it was undoubtedly a great political move, on reflection, it was not my finest hour as a leader.

The occasion was my 2011 State of the Commonwealth speech, just a few months before the May primary.

The topic was coal and the federal government's attempt to regulate how it's burned for energy.

And there I was, my left forefinger extended and jabbing into the air, exhorting the Washington crowd to "get off our backs!"

I practically yelled it into the microphone. And then I repeated it, energized by the sudden roar of legislators leaping to their feet and applauding.

Just four words.

But they quickly took on legendary status for opposite reasons among both those who felt I greatly understood the needs of this state and those who thought I was just another cynical political hack.

Truth be told, those four words represented a lot of things:

- a strong commitment to a centuries-old coal industry that helped build this state, as well as a manufacturing industry whose health depends upon the low electricity rates that coal has provided;

- fierce support for beleaguered miners and their families who were finding it increasingly difficult to keep food on the table in the aftermath of a global recession, especially as the number of coal jobs continued to shrink;

- a statement of defiance to a president whose push for cleaner air didn't seem to include a sensitivity to the economic havoc he was causing our people; and

- a political move that improved my support in a critical area of the state.

Even today, I don't back away from any of those messages.

I *did* and *do* support our coal-mining families. Kentucky *was* in a desperate race to retain each and every job in the coal and manufacturing industries. While I fought hard for President Obama and his initiatives when I felt they would help Kentucky, such as with the Affordable Care Act, I *was* willing to oppose him when I thought he was wrong—in fact, Kentucky sued the EPA over the arbitrary nature of proposed emissions regulations. And finally, yes, I *did* want to be re-elected, because you can't govern if you're not in office.

So why then do I regret the "get off our backs" exhortation?

Because it was too simplistic a message. Because it reduced a complex issue into a four-word, black-and-white sound bite. Because it settled on a singular explanation for coal's decline at the expense of all others. And because it helped further the deceptive message to the Eastern and Western Kentucky coalfields that the best way to build a vibrant future was to simply cling to the past.

As governor, I had an opportunity and an obligation to begin changing my state's narrative on coal, and at that moment, I didn't do it to the best of my ability.

There's precedent for my simplistic message on coal, of course. It's difficult to govern effectively in an era of short attention spans and media sound bites and in an age where the need to build public support and the pressure to get re-elected have created a 24/7 focus on perceived slights and retribution. The public doesn't have the time or inclination to listen to and think about complex and involved lectures on topics such as tax policy, pollution controls, economic trends, and health care delivery systems. And elected officials quickly realize that opponents and their handlers are watching every move, waiting to distort words and use social media to fan them into wildfires that incinerate any hope of progress.

So, yes, I, like many officials in Kentucky, was very sensitive when it came to talking about coal.

Coal is part of Kentucky's heritage. Families and many communities understandably feel strongly about the importance of mining, and a politician's position on the issue is viewed by many as a statement of whether he or she truly cares about them. Consequently, no elected official wants to be misunderstood about where he or she stands.

But the bottom line is that rather than dedicate that part of my speech to an in-depth discussion of the coal issue, I opted for a sound bite.

An effective one to be sure. But also one that worked against me and the region, long term, because it minimized much of what we were trying to do with our long-term comprehensive energy plan and with the later SOAR (Shaping Our Appalachian Region) plan for diversifying that region's economy.

The fact is, numbers speak to the current health of the coal industry in Kentucky.

According to preliminary numbers reported by the state in January 2017, Kentucky produced nearly 42.6 million tons of coal in 2016. That's down almost 31 percent since I left office and down 72 percent from 1996, 20 years ago. It's the lowest total in Kentucky since 1939. In fact, that production number dropped Kentucky to No. 4 in the nation. As recently as 1988, Kentucky was No. 1. The decrease in production in Eastern Kentucky was even steeper—down over 40 percent since I left office and down almost 86 percent since 1996.

The number of mining jobs continues to decline as well. The average employment at Kentucky coal mines in 2016 was 6,550—down 31 percent since I left office and down over 65 percent since 1996. Mining employment in Kentucky at the end of 2016 was at a 118-year low—the lowest since at least 1898. Again, the drop was even steeper in Eastern Kentucky, where average coal employment in 2016 was 3,833—down 35 percent since I left office and down almost 75 percent since 1996.

Kentucky's numbers mirror those across the country, where coal companies as large as Peabody Energy and Arch Coal, among others, have been forced to declare bankruptcy.

There are many reasons for coal's downturn, and certainly one of the factors is the federal Environmental Protection Agency's push for cleaner air, but it is not the only factor. If you follow the industry's own coverage of policy and markets in places like Environmental & Energy Publishing, their analysts say market conditions, like the increased availability of cheaper natural gas and other energy sources, have also been major factors in the bankruptcies of coal producers and the rapid reduction in the use of coal.

But my point isn't to write a comprehensive, in-depth analysis of the forces affecting coal production. It's to point out that merely "standing up" to proposed federal regulations with shouted get-off-our-backs moments is not going to change coal's future, no matter who says it and how often and loud they say it.

I fought hard to protect coal miners' jobs and to find help for our displaced miners and their families, and I'm proud of that fact. If I were governor again, I would continue to make those some of my highest priorities.

But I also would have worked more aggressively earlier in my administration to push initiatives like SOAR, which takes a holistic, long-term, and more sustainable approach to rebuilding the economy of Eastern Kentucky.

And I wouldn't have echoed the narrative that coal's problems lie entirely at the feet of President Obama, as Republican politicians and even some Democrats continue to do. In truth, the EPA and its regulations were headed in that direction under prior Republican, as well as Democratic, administrations.

In order for Kentucky, and Eastern Kentucky in particular, to enjoy a vibrant future, we need to do three things:

One, convince the utility companies that it makes economic sense to continue to have a diversified portfolio of both coal-fired and natural gas power plants and to continue investing in clean-coal technologies.

Two, diversify Appalachia's economy, which is the point of SOAR, as explained elsewhere in this book.

And three, diversify our energy production on a statewide basis.

I was engaged in this effort early in my administration, when I hired a nationally renowned chemical engineer, Len Peters, to head the Kentucky Energy and Environment Cabinet. We took one look at the energy landscape and knew we had to take action.

Back in 2008, gasoline prices were hovering around $4 a gallon and the demand for energy in Kentucky was expected to grow more than 40 percent by 2025. The shale boom leading to cheap natural gas and more abundant petroleum was still around the corner. And the push for stringent new greenhouse gas regulations was gaining momentum.

We knew we had to maintain energy production while protecting the environment, without hurting our economy. The three *E*'s were intertwined.

So Secretary Peters and I released a comprehensive seven-point strategy for energy independence called "Intelligent Energy Choices for Kentucky's Future." The executive summary began, "Kentucky's challenge for the 21st century is to develop clean, reliable, affordable energy sources that help us improve our energy security, reduce our carbon dioxide emissions, and provide economic prosperity."

Even then, we recognized the threats facing coal, and so we took steps to reduce our consumption and pollution, develop alternatives that would both supplement coal and create jobs, and advocate for clean-coal technologies.

Well, we had some promising results.

During my eight years, we succeeded in using innovative programs to reduce the growth in our non-transportation energy use for state government alone by more than 4 percent by 2015. That represented a savings of more than $2.3 billion in cumulative cost avoidance, as of September 2015.

We also reduced sulfur dioxide emissions by 41 percent and nitrogen dioxide emissions by 45 percent.

And in the area of renewable energy, we explored Kentucky's potential in interesting ways. Wind, geothermal, and hydroelectric power were never able to gain much traction in Kentucky. However, we used grants and incentives to help fund an array of solar and biomass projects, such as a four-year switchgrass biofuels experiment on 20 farms in northeast Kentucky; the Glasgow Landfill Gas (methane) Recovery System; and the state's largest-ever solar facility in Mercer County, operated by Louisville Gas & Electric Company and Kentucky Utilities Company.

In fact, some of the most fascinating stories to come out of Kentucky in the last few years originated in the fields, laboratories, and buildings housing these demonstration projects. I believe their findings and the lessons learned will have a lot of bearing on our ability to solve the energy challenge and create a vibrant future for Kentucky's economy.

But that's going to require that Kentucky's current and future leaders recognize that there is an energy challenge, commit themselves to addressing it, and have the courage to do so in a progressive way. Looking at this issue only through a political lens will cripple the conversation. It's time to end the blame game. In the end, it doesn't matter who or what caused the change in the coal economy. What matters is that instead of spending our time expressing anger about the past, we focus all our energy on how to make our future brighter for future generations.

Fortunately, the SOAR effort has helped to change the dialogue about coal's future in a positive way. Until recently, every time the coal economy took a dip, folks would simply hunker down and wait for it to come back, refusing to entertain the idea that we needed to diversify the economy. Not anymore. Most folks living in our coalfields are now willing to have a rational discussion about where the energy economy is headed and admit that it is time to broaden our economic horizons.

The bottom line is that coal helped build this state and this nation, and it will always have a place in our energy portfolio and our regional economies. But the size of that place is smaller because of irreversible forces. So, as leaders, we need to help our people accept that reality and act accordingly, just like our agricultural community did with tobacco.

A DEGREE IN
BRIDGE BUILDING

Shortly after 8 p.m. on a brisk winter's night, a cargo ship the length of a football field was traveling 11.5 mph and tried to pass under a bridge that had "insufficient vertical clearance," in the stilted and technical language of federal safety investigators who later swarmed the scene.

The noise must have been deafening.

When it was over, a 322-foot span of the Eggners Ferry Bridge had been ripped completely off its piers and was draped over the bow of the MV *Delta Mariner* like a 616,000-pound web of scrap metal. A large section of the span's pavement was inconceivably still intact and its steel beams dragged in the Tennessee River.

Miraculously, no one on the ship or the bridge was hurt in that accident, which occurred January 26, 2012, on the edge of Western Kentucky's Land Between the Lakes region.

But just like that, Kentucky had another multi-million-dollar bridge emergency on its hands. And just like that, another name was added to the list of bridge projects my administration tackled during its eight years.

As state Transportation Secretary Mike Hancock was fond of saying, "We didn't set out to do it, but we earned a degree in bridge building."

The bridge projects were certainly educational.

- The Eggners Ferry accident taught us a new word: "allision"—when a ship runs up against a stationary object or other ship.

- The Sherman-Minton emergency shutdown in Louisville reminded us of the importance of inspections.

- The Downtown Crossing in Louisville—half of the Ohio River Bridges Project and the largest single infrastructure project in Kentucky history—was a triumph of persistence and planning.

- The Milton-Madison Bridge replacement in Trimble County was an innovative engineering feat.

- And all the way to the end of my administration, the stalled Brent Spence Bridge replacement in Covington remained an exercise in frustration.

Led by my two Transportation secretaries, Hancock and before him Joe Prather, we were involved during my eight years with almost a dozen major bridge projects representing billions of dollars, including new bridges, bridge replacements, and emergency fixes. I want to discuss each briefly because of the collective lessons they leave for leaders *and* voters, including the need to invest in our infrastructure on an ongoing basis, even in this anti-tax climate; the importance of collaboration among leaders across state and party lines; and the advantages of thinking outside the box in this era of limited funding.

The national funding mechanism for building bridges and roads is broken, a victim of the anti-tax fervor that has kept the federal motor fuels tax frozen since 1993. Meanwhile, on a state level, the gas tax revenues that prop up the Road Fund fluctuate wildly with changing prices at the pump, especially when those prices drop. Because Kentucky's gas tax had a "ceiling" for increases but not a "floor" for decreases, our Road Fund took several mid-year hits before I finally convinced a bipartisan group of legislators in 2015 to stabilize the fund. Critics tried to characterize the legislation as a tax increase, but those legislators understood that it was more a matter of preserving the tax. And they understood that the health of our infrastructure was at stake.

Unfortunately, Congress isn't willing to take such a stand. While this country's infrastructure falls down around it, "taxes" and "tolls" are considered epithets because too many people think of them as burdens instead of the investments they truly are.

It's true that bridges (and roads) represent some of the most expensive investments a state makes. But a modern transportation system is critical to a vibrant economy, and my administration recognized that. All told, despite inheriting a recession that greatly affected our ability to fund transportation projects, we issued $8.2 billion in road and bridge construction contracts during my eight years as governor, which might be some kind of state record.

We did that because we knew that these projects not only created thousands of immediate jobs but also laid the foundation for future economic development. In other words, taxpayers received a huge economic return on their money. And we were able to stretch our dollars because we worked with designers and contractors to set aggressive construction schedules and pursue practical designs that represented the simplest and most cost-effective way to build roads and bridges.

Our bridge projects—besides being interesting stories—demonstrated some of our challenges and strategies.

In no particular order:

Eggners Ferry Bridge (Tennessee River)

The January 2012 allision between the *Delta Mariner* and the bridge is an excellent example of the old saying, "Timing is everything." The aging two-lane steel bridge, which was built in the 1930s and handled about 2,800 vehicles a day, was slated to be replaced and demolished, beginning in 2014. It carried the US 68 and KY 80 traffic across Kentucky Lake.

The accident happened when the cargo ship, a huge vessel that was carrying space rocket components to Cape Canaveral, tried to pass through what is known as the recreational channel, which has a lower clearance, instead of the shipping channel, which the vessel normally used. The impact simply lifted a whole span off the piers, and folded it across the bow of the ship.

It took a few weeks to clear the bridge debris from the *Delta Mariner* and inspect the remaining bridge. Fortunately, the piers weren't damaged. Fortunately also, we found the bridge's original plans and drawings, which were more than 80 years old.

Folks in Western Kentucky's lake region went into panic mode, because much of the area's economy is based on summer tourism, and the initial assessment by our Transportation Cabinet was that it would be at least September before the bridge would be reopened.

Being from west Kentucky myself, I knew how important the tourism trade was, so I urged Secretary Hancock to come up with a better answer. And he did.

On March 8, we awarded an emergency repair contract worth $7 million to Hall Contracting of Kentucky, with penalties if it wasn't finished by Memorial Day weekend. Using innovative techniques, they made it, and the bridge reopened on May 25, with appreciative Western Kentuckians emitting an audible sigh of relief.

The Sherman-Minton Bridge

Some 70,000 cars a day were taking Interstate 64 over the Ohio River in 2011, so when a crack was found in a load-bearing part of the bridge, and Indiana Governor Mitch Daniels and I agreed to close the bridge on September 9 of that year, it was a big deal.

Subsequent inspections found more troubling cracks, and so a bigger repair plan was needed.

We got together with federal highway officials and Indiana, which inspects and maintains the bridge, to share the repair costs. Hall Contracting won the $13.9 million contract, which involved attaching 2.4 million pounds of steel plating along both sides of the 1,600-foot structure.

Thanks to the lure of a $100,000-a-day incentive, the bridge reopened 10 minutes before midnight on February 17, 2012, almost two weeks ahead of schedule.

Ohio River Bridges Project

By far the largest project involved building two new spans (and rehabbing a third) between Louisville and Indiana as part of the $2.3-billion Ohio River Bridges Project.

Louisville and southern Indiana leaders had been talking about the need for a new bridge for nearly 40 years, but questions of cost and location lingered. So I got together with Governor Daniels and we decided to do whatever it took to push the project forward, including cutting costs and adopting tolls as a revenue mechanism. (The cooperative relationship between Kentucky and Indiana continued throughout the bridges project, even after Mike Pence replaced Daniels as Indiana's governor.)

Indiana took the lead on building a new upstream bridge (the East End Crossing extending I-265 into Indiana) while Kentucky supervised the Downtown Crossing project, which included a new bridge, putting a new deck on the existing Kennedy

(I-65) bridge, and reconfiguring the highway intersections called Spaghetti Junction.

On the eve of my last day in office, the mostly completed Downtown Crossing, named after Kentucky native son Abraham Lincoln, opened to traffic four months ahead of schedule. Walsh Construction Inc. had pulled off a stunning construction feat.

How excited was the region to see this bridge? The day before, police estimated that 40,000 to 50,000 people came out for a Walk the (new) Bridge event.

The entire project—both downtown and upstream—was essentially finished by the end of 2016. That's less than four years at $2.3 billion, compared to the original estimates of 16 years and $4.1 billion.

Milton-Madison Bridge

The innovative "sliding truss" approach to replacing the bridge between Milton, Kentucky, and Madison, Indiana, saved months and millions of dollars, lessened the traffic headache for commuters, and won numerous engineering awards.

About 11,000 vehicles traveled US 421 across the bridge each day, the only river crossing on a 72-mile stretch between Louisville and Vevay, Indiana. But it was small, deteriorating, and old, built in 1929.

We broke ground on November 30, 2010.

As described by Walsh Construction, the $103-million project involved building a whole new truss on temporary piers next to the existing bridge while it remained open to traffic. When traffic was switched to the new truss, the existing piers were strengthened and the old truss was demolished. The new 30-million-pound truss was then slid 55 feet into place on the strengthened piers, using steel cables and eight computer-controlled hydraulic jacks over a two-day period.

At 2,428 feet long, it was the longest bridge in North America—and perhaps in the world—to be slid laterally into place. On April 17, 2014, just one week after the "slide," the bridge reopened to traffic.

US 60 Bridge

The new $95 million bridge carrying US 60 over the Tennessee River at the border of McCracken and Livingston counties became a "rush" job (in the positive sense of that word), and a good thing it did.

The old two-lane Ledbetter Bridge had opened as a toll bridge in 1931. It served well, but was too narrow for modern truck traffic and was rapidly deteriorating.

We built the main piers for a new bridge a quarter mile upstream in 2008 and 2009 and broke ground to finish the project in September 2010. Then, in early 2012, concern about safety on the old bridge brought severe weight restrictions that relegated traffic to passenger vehicles and unloaded standard pickup trucks. So we worked out a deal to incentivize the contractors—Kay & Kay Contracting and Haydon Bridge Company—to expedite the project.

Thanks to their hard work, we ceremonially opened the new four-lane bridge on July 31, 2013, nearly 11 months ahead of schedule.

It's a good thing we did. Because of torrential rains the following spring, the bank began slipping under the old bridge. As a contractor began moving equipment to the site to carry out an emergency demolition contract, land-based piers and approach spans on the McCracken County side collapsed overnight June 22. We finished demolishing the entire bridge in September.

Lake Bridges

Construction of new four-lane bridges over Lake Barkley and Kentucky Lake in the commonwealth's Land Between the Lakes recreational region was among my highest priorities to improve transportation and economic development in Western Kentucky. The existing bridges—the Henry Lawrence Memorial Bridge and the Eggners Ferry Bridge—were horribly obsolete, having been built back in 1932 to cross the Tennessee and Cumberland Rivers long before they were impounded to form those lakes.

But the move to replace them was slow going and years in the making. In July 2009, I had the pleasure of unveiling the design that was ultimately selected for both bridges—the design called a basket handle, tied arch.

But it wasn't until February 2014 that we awarded the $131 million contract for the Kentucky Lake bridge, having already spent $25 million to build a smaller bridge over a lagoon leading up to the lake.

Construction was fast. A week before I left office in December 2015, Johnson Brothers Corp. lifted the main steel arch span into place with cranes. There's some pretty dramatic YouTube video of that event. And by April 2016, traffic had moved to the new (but not yet completely finished) bridge. Why? So the existing bridge over Kentucky Lake, the Eggners Ferry Bridge that we were forced to fix four years earlier, could be blown up. Funny how that works.

In February 2015, we awarded the $128-million contract for the second lakes bridge, the Lake Barkley Bridge, with an expected completion date of October 2017.

The bridges were important parts of our plan to build a four-lane US 68/KY 80 corridor from Mayfield to Bowling Green throughout our Western Waterlands region, which is not only a cultural and recreational treasure but also an economic engine.

Big Four Bridge

Talk about a recycling project.

For seven and a half decades, the Big Four (railroad) Bridge carried cargo and passengers across the Ohio River between Louisville and Jeffersonville, Indiana. But when the trains stopped and its approach spans were removed in 1969, the bridge became a slowly rusting hulk—known more for dropping debris in the river and catching fire than for any useful function.

Plans first developed by the Waterfront Development Corporation in the 1990s called for it to become a crossing for pedestrians and bike riders, but those went nowhere.

Then, in 2011, Indiana Governor Daniels and I—along with the City of Jeffersonville—committed $22 million to turn the bridge into a new pathway connecting Louisville's Waterfront Park to downtown Jeffersonville. The Kentucky side opened in 2013, and the Indiana side the next year, and the bridge is getting heavy use.

A pedestrian-and-bike route was originally intended to be part of the Ohio River Bridges Project. But building the pathway on the Big Four Bridge instead both got the pathway finished years earlier and shaved tens of millions of dollars off the cost of the bigger bridges project.

Ironton-Russell Bridge

This wasn't a Kentucky-directed project, but on May 3, 2012, I had the privilege of joining Ohio Governor John Kasich to ceremonially break ground on another long-awaited bridge replacement project, this one linking Russell, Kentucky, with Ironton on the Ohio side.

Big trucks had been banned from the existing 1922 bridge for some time. Originally an $81-million project, when finished, the cable-stayed bridge will have an incredible 900-foot main span. Ohio officials predicted it would be finished in 2017.

I include it here because the day gave me another opportunity to continue conversations with Governor Kasich about a number of topics, including the Brent Spence Bridge.

Brent Spence

This last project is one that we couldn't move forward in a significant way.

The double-decker Brent Spence Bridge carries both I-71 and I-75 as well as local traffic across the Ohio River between Covington and Cincinnati, so it's hugely important to both the region and the nation. But it's not up to the job. Federal officials have classified it as functionally obsolete because of its narrow lanes, absence of emergency shoulders, and limited visibility on the lower deck. For those reasons and because it carries almost twice the traffic it was originally designed to hold, the bridge is plagued by both traffic backups and frequent accidents.

For decades, the region has talked about the need to fix the Brent Spence. The latest design would rehab it and build a new one next to it. However, the project was held back by lack of leadership and consensus on funding.

For a while, things looked good. Ohio Governor Kasich and I began using the same bistate, bipartisan model that Indiana Governor Daniels and I had used on the bridges in Louisville. We signed a general agreement on cost sharing and directed our staffs to find ways to lower the $2.6 billion price tag. Both of us understood that tolls as well as some public-private partnerships would be needed to build the bridge, given the lack of federal support and problems with the federal Highway Trust Fund.

Unfortunately, Northern Kentucky legislators—bowing to Tea Party anti-"tax" sentiment—persuaded their colleagues to pass legislation that explicitly forbids tolls on any interstate bridge between Ohio and Kentucky. Privately, many of these

Northern Kentucky legislators told me that they knew that tolls would be necessary if the bridge was to be built, but nevertheless, they sold their region "down the river," so to speak, placing their own re-election desires ahead of the needs of their people.

For all intents and purposes, the Brent Spence project had come to a halt, just a year before construction was to begin.

A TRAGIC DEATH

Jane and I were flying back from a Democratic Governors Association meeting on August 12, 2012, when a cell phone call delivered news that struck like a lightning bolt out of a cloudless summer sky.

Mike Haydon, my chief of staff, had suffered a medical emergency and was dead. He was only 62.

Mike's wife, Lisa, had lost the love of her life. Their children— Blair, Kate, and Ben—had lost a caring and engaged father. The state had lost a dedicated official. And I had lost a friend and trusted adviser.

To honor his more than 30 years of public service as both an elected official and a high-level adviser, we decided that Mike's body would lie in state in the Capitol Rotunda. And three days later, we held a public memorial for him. There was sadness but also laughter. The truth is, Mike was not only a consummate public servant but also a genuine character.

So I told the crowd that I had decided to skip the somber, serious stuff and honor Mike the man.

"If he could speak to us," I said, "he'd tell us to sing a song, something like that Joe Diffie song, 'Prop Me Up Beside the Jukebox.' Mike would rather us laugh than cry, to celebrate his life and unique personality rather than simply mourn his death."

So I talked about how staff members had likened Mike to the Energizer Bunny, a Tasmanian Devil, a mini-hurricane, or one of those bumper cars that moved forward until it hit an obstacle, and then moved in a different direction until it hit another obstacle, and then in a different direction, and so on and so on in a relentless desire to find a way through the problem.

Constant motion. Continuous energy. A whirlwind of activity.

During one legislative session, his staff threatened to attach a GPS to his belt, so they could track him down. And Mike could talk for three minutes or three hours or three days on any subject, as long as he had a listener. The point is, Mike created hundreds of little spheres of influence over his public career. He was simply that engaged and engaging. He was also witty, upfront, and honest, not to mention blunt and creative with the rhetoric.

To me, he was invaluable. Pragmatic, honest, and candid, he told me what I *needed* to hear instead of what I *wanted* to hear. For a governor, that's the best trait a chief of staff can have. That, and loyalty.

The irony is that when I first became governor, I didn't know Mike that well, despite his long career in local and state government. He had been mayor of Springfield, Kentucky, and property valuation administrator in Washington County. He served under Governor Paul Patton as deputy secretary of the Governor's Executive Cabinet and secretary of the Revenue Cabinet. He also had been chief of staff for House Majority Floor Leader Rocky Adkins.

I was looking for a legislative liaison in the Governor's Office, and several people had recommended Mike. He was known as a savvy political operator, but I was concerned about whether his loyalties would lie with former employers or with me. So I brought Mike in for an interview and was upfront about my concerns.

"Governor," he assured me, "if I work for you, that's where my loyalty will lie and with no other person."

So I took a chance and put him on the staff, and it turned out to be one of the best decisions I made. Mike had both working knowledge of the legislative process and relationships with most Democrats and Republicans there. He also absolutely loved the game. He brought us many legislative successes, and I was so impressed that when Adam Edelen, my chief of staff at the time, left in 2010 to run for state auditor of public accounts, I appointed Mike as his replacement. (In addition to Edelen, I had two other excellent chiefs of staff, Jim Cauley and Larry Bond.)

One example will suffice to demonstrate Haydon's legislative prowess. In my first five years as governor, I had to call the general assembly back into special session five times to pass budgets for the executive branch or Transportation Cabinet, mainly because of roadblocks in the Republican-controlled Senate. This cost taxpayers more than $2 million for work that should have been accomplished during the regular session.

One of those special sessions came in 2011, when the Senate abruptly closed out the regular session without reaching agreement on fixing a $139-million hole in the Medicaid budget. I had proposed a relatively painless solution that "borrowed" money from the second year of the biennium and paid it back with savings we'd realize by moving to a managed-care delivery model in Medicaid. But the Senate wanted to fill the hole with drastic cuts to schools, higher education, and other core programs on top of cuts we'd been making all along.

Without legislative agreement, I'd be forced to slash reimbursement rates to Medicaid providers—which would have jeopardized the whole Medicaid program. So I called the legislature immediately back into session. But after two weeks of the special session (costing the taxpayers about $60,000 a day), the Senate was still balking at reaching any kind of compromise. After the House again passed my budget proposal, the Senate passed what House leaders and I thought was a totally unacceptable alternative, and sent it back to the House.

About that time, I was in Northern Kentucky to give a speech when my cell phone rang. It was Mike. "Governor," he said, "we have an idea of how we can get a budget passed to our liking."

Staff had reviewed the Senate budget and determined that by using line-item vetoes and striking various words and phrases, I could end up with a budget fix pretty close to the one I had initially proposed. I gave Mike permission to discuss this idea with House leadership, which he did, and I followed up with a formal discussion by phone that evening.

I told them to go ahead and pass the Senate's budget plan with its cuts to education and then adjourn, and they could trust me to take care of the rest with my veto pen.

In the next two to three days, by using line-item vetoes and striking certain words and phrases, I reshaped the entire executive branch budget into one that resembled the amended budget that we had proposed and the House had passed. In so doing, we had dissolved the gridlock the Senate had created, saved Medicaid providers from rate reductions, and protected our schoolchildren and others from politically motivated budget cuts.

And we did it thanks to Mike Haydon. To me, that story says a lot about Mike, his love of creative strategy, and his penchant for always looking for ways to make things happen.

To be clear, his death was devastating on both a personal and professional level, and the unexpectedness of it made some of us feel like we were living in some cruel *West Wing* or *House of Cards* episode driven by some director's need for a plot twist.

But we also knew that our lives and the administration were better for having had Mike alongside us. It was also clear that that legacy lived on long after his death. As chief of staff, Mike had gotten me more engaged in the legislative process, had improved my relationship with many of the 138 members, and had shown me how to be a better advocate for my legislative agenda. In the years ahead, that improved engagement paid off in numerous legislative successes, and thus long after his death, Mike still had a hand in helping us make things happen.

Surely, God broke the mold after making Mike Haydon!

P3s: A NEW TOOL

As politics becomes more and more partisan, legislators are less and less willing to raise revenues to provide essential services needed by our citizens. Even mentioning the word "tax" these days makes most politicians shudder.

The unfortunate result? There are fewer resources with which to move the state and nation forward. Instead, we hear the same refrain repeated over and over: "There is plenty of money to do everything we need; we just have to be more efficient and cut out all of the wasteful spending." I've said it myself from time to time, and although there is some truth to the statement, the reality is far different. One person's wasteful spending is another person's essential service, and even when you eliminate all the waste that people can agree to eliminate, the budget still comes up way short of what is needed to make smart investments in our future.

As a country or a commonwealth, we're not going to get over the anti-tax feeling anytime soon. But at least when it comes to infrastructure and other programs that require one-time monies, a new tool surfaced several years ago that, when used properly, can help implement needed improvements.

This tool is public-private partnerships, or P3s. That phrase means different things to different people, but in Kentucky, we used P3s in two ways that benefitted us immensely.

First, we utilized them to improve the delivery system for our Medicaid program, which at the time provided health coverage for one in five Kentuckians. Ever since the implementation of Medicaid, services had been delivered on a fee-for-service basis—meaning a provider would earn a fee every time the provider performed a covered service for a Medicaid recipient. It was a simple process: The provider rendered a service, sent in a bill, and the state paid it. Unfortunately, this system encouraged providers to perform as many procedures and services as possible, because they got paid for each one. Thus from a financial point of view, it actually *discouraged* the thoughtful use of preventive care.

Consequently, over many decades, Kentucky had seen little improvement in our collective health, and the Medicaid budget had continued to spiral upward at alarming rates. The old delivery model for Medicaid simply wasn't giving us results.

At the end of 2010, a budget crisis created by a Medicaid shortfall lent urgency to our reconsideration of that delivery model. The crisis was the result of a one-two punch. Not only did the recession hurt General Fund tax revenues (with which Kentucky paid its share of Medicaid costs) but it also swelled Medicaid rolls—in Kentucky's case by about 3,000 people a month—as people lost their jobs and health care, or their employer stopping supplying health care. Expected relief from Congress for the growth in Medicaid failed to materialize, at least to the extent Kentucky and many other states needed.

Faced with a Medicaid funding gap of hundreds of millions of dollars, I had several choices: I could cut benefits and services, including kicking eligible people out of the program. I could cut reimbursement rates to providers by about 30 percent. Or I could find a new delivery system that was more efficient and saved money. Well, I refused to cut benefits and enrollment, particularly at a time when more and more families were relying on Medicaid. And because cutting reimbursement rates would cause providers to flee the program, it would have the same effect of severely reducing services.

That left moving our Medicaid program into a managed-care delivery model, which we had already been exploring. Initial studies had indicated that it would save us significant money, and other states making the change had had good experience from a cost standpoint.

But it had taken those states two to three years to convert their systems, and we didn't have the luxury of time—this budget would be passed by April and go into effect July 1. Therefore, I decided to jump in with both feet and move most of our Medicaid program into managed care. Through a formal request for proposals, we invited the private sector in April 2011 to bid on the delivery of these Medicaid services, and we required that companies be able to do so in six months. Several companies at first thought we were joking with the tight deadline, but we assured them we weren't. We didn't have a choice.

Ultimately, come July, we signed contracts with four managed-care organizations (MCOs) in the private sector and shifted to a managed-care model (effective November 1) quicker than any other place in the country. It was certainly not without bumps in the road, and several providers were upset with those bumps. However, we stayed the course and worked through the problems. As a result, as of this writing, five MCOs deliver services to our Medicaid population. We pay them a monthly fee per member, and it's in the private partner's best interest to keep those members healthy. Those companies then manage that patient's care, which encourages not only efficiency but an emphasis on preventive services that keep more folks out of the emergency room and reduce in-patient days in the hospital.

After all, one of the keys to reducing long-term health-care costs is to manage health problems before they become chronic diseases and conditions or even worse.

This public-private partnership gets better every day and is an example of how government can team with the private sector to both deliver quality services and save money.

Now, another public-private partnership that will place Kentucky at the forefront of states is KentuckyWired, our statewide high-speed broadband initiative and one of the biggest infrastructure projects in the history of the commonwealth.

We have historically thought of essential services as things like electricity, sewers, paved roads and streets, telephone service, and clean water. But in today's world, essential services also include the ability to instantly communicate around the world and to quickly store, access, and share large amounts of information electronically. Whether you're thinking of job creation and economic development, education or health care, high-speed broadband is not only desirable but essential for success.

Individuals, of course, use the Internet for myriad things— from researching information for school papers to listening to college lectures, sharing photos, ordering Christmas presents, paying bills, and looking at the results of medical tests.

Businesses use it to share, store, and access large amounts of data and engage in commerce around the world.

Unfortunately, Kentucky ranked near the bottom or at the bottom in both Internet speeds and broadband availability. While most of Kentucky's urban areas have had access to high-speed broadband for years, many rural areas of the state still didn't. And private providers were not entering those rural markets because it was not profitable to do so.

Therefore, we needed to find another way to get those services to the rest of our people.

An opportunity to do so arose early in my second term when I received a call from Republican Congressman Hal Rogers, the powerful chair of the House Appropriations Committee. Congressman Rogers's district included most of Eastern

Kentucky, an area vastly underserved by the private sector when it came to high-speed broadband. He wanted to use state and federal money to create a system for Eastern Kentucky, and his idea prompted me to think of how we could include the whole state in such an effort.

Such a statewide project was far beyond the financial capability of state government, and so we brainstormed about a way to utilize the private sector.

To make a long story short, thanks to the leadership of Finance Cabinet Secretary Lori Flanery and the late Steve Rucker, commissioner of the Commonwealth Office of Technology, our state is now in a public-private partnership arrangement with Macquarie Capital, an Australian company, and its partners. The partnership will build what's called the "middle mile" of the system, the main trunks that serve as the link between the Internet backbone and the local service providers. The project, called KentuckyWired, will bring high-speed broadband into every community, and local providers (cable companies, telecoms, etc.) will provide the actual service—the "last mile"—into individual businesses and households.

The total cost of this project is estimated at $324 million, with only a fraction of that coming from public money. The state general assembly authorized the sale of $30 million in bonds in 2014 and federal grants provided some $23.5 million. The private sector through Macquarie is providing the rest.

In addition, the commonwealth was already paying about $18 million to private vendors for high-speed broadband service for its agencies and facilities, and we pledged to contract with KentuckyWired for that service once the project was finished. In essence, the state agreed to become KentuckyWired's first paying customer—you might say an anchor tenant.

Under the agreement, the commonwealth will own the middle-mile system and will lease it to Macquarie Capital for 30 years.

And since the state's needs will use only a portion of the fiber capacity (estimated at 25 to 50 percent), the excess capacity will be available for sale in the private sector on a wholesale basis to either providers (who would resell it) or straight-end users like a hospital complex. Macquarie will handle the commercial end of this and the commonwealth will receive the majority share of the revenues from the sale of the excess capacity, although that percentage was still being worked out at this writing. But it was anticipated that the income to the commonwealth would significantly exceed our yearly outlay for the bonds.

So another win-win situation for state government and the private sector. They make money, and we are able to provide a much-needed essential service to every community. As a result, job creation, increased entrepreneurship, educational opportunities, and tele-health will become available to every corner of Kentucky.

The project was delayed during the transition to my successor, but it now appears to be moving ahead as planned.

And we weren't the only ones who thought the deal was an innovative solution.

In November 2015, the KentuckyWired P3 deal received the top honor from the Council of Development Finance Agencies for its financing package and forward-thinking initiative. A month later, it also won the national "Deal of the Year" award from the *Bond Buyer*, a newspaper for the municipal bond industry, which said the deal "forged new territory in the P3 market with its unique, first-of-its-kind approach to broadband connectivity on a statewide basis."

So when you start feeling boxed in by budgetary constraints, sometimes the solution is to think *outside* the box.

THE GOVERNORS' CLUB

The US Senate is often referred to as "the world's most exclusive club," but for eight years, I belonged to a group that—with roughly half as many members—was even more exclusive.

I'm referring, of course, to the "club" known as sitting governors, which includes the elected "CEOs" of all 50 states and five US territories.

Much divided us. Geography, obviously. The demographics of our states. Partisan allegiances. And ages, backgrounds, and experience levels. And many of us had separate and distinct goals and policy priorities for our states.

But we also had a lot in common. As CEOs of states, we tackled similar challenges and felt similar pressures. The great recession came crashing down on all of our states, for sure. And we all struggled with things like health care, pensions, and finding money for education and infrastructure.

Those challenges often brought us together. It might be surprising to those outside state government just how often governors interact with each other, collaborate, seek advice from and counsel each other, and—on rare occasions—confront each other.

I met some of my gubernatorial colleagues during my first campaign and a good many more at conferences sponsored by organizations like the National Governors Association, the Democratic Governors Association, and the Southern Governors' Association.

Those relationships paid off in myriad ways during my eight years. Let me give you some examples.

A little more than two months before I took office as governor in 2007, more than 600 nurses at Appalachian Regional Healthcare went on strike. The hospital system operated nine hospitals in Eastern Kentucky and West Virginia, and so I was about to walk into a troubling situation that I knew very little about, but which was already having a huge and negative impact on health care in that region.

But shortly before I was sworn in, West Virginia Governor Joe Manchin, whom I had met during my campaign, called to discuss the strike. He was well versed in the dispute, gave me the succinct background, explained a plan for bringing the sides together, asked my opinion, and requested that I join with him in making the proposal. On December 6, five days before my inauguration, we jointly unveiled the proposal to speed up negotiations. By December 22, the two sides had reached agreement.

So even before I was officially governor, I saw firsthand how relationships could help.

As I describe elsewhere in this book, I met then-Arizona Governor Janet Napolitano during the 2007 campaign and our relationship grew during various meetings of governors associations.

Later, when Janet was appointed secretary of Homeland Security and a series of natural disasters hit Kentucky, that friendship paid off, as she went out of her way to make sure Kentucky families got the help we needed. And when red tape delayed some of that help, Secretary Napolitano was critical in fixing the problem.

I met Kathleen Sebelius when she was governor of Kansas and head of the Democratic Governors Association. Later, when she was appointed secretary of the federal Department of Health and Human Services, she really helped Kentucky leap forward to implement the Affordable Care Act. Whenever we ran into a hurdle, she took my phone calls and made sure her staff was responsive.

In return, I made sure Kentucky was helpful to other states who were looking to take the path we did on Medicaid expansion. During a luncheon at one of the governors associations, I addressed governors who were interested in expanding Medicaid, but who were opposed by their legislative chambers. I described my use of executive orders and the importance of establishing credibility by gathering facts. (In Kentucky's case, this included an independent economic impact study before my decision to expand, as well as a performance study after the first year.)

One of the governors who came up to me after the presentation was Alaska Governor Bill Walker, who had recently been elected as an independent. Walker had myriad questions, and I was happy to see later that year when he ignored his recalcitrant legislature and expanded Medicaid by executive order so Alaskans, as he said, "no longer have to choose between health care and bankruptcy."

I also worked with Republican governors on a host of critical issues. I talked to Indiana Governor Mitch Daniels almost weekly while we were working to build two new bridges across the Ohio River between our states. Officials in Louisville and Indiana had talked for decades about the need for new bridges, but serious obstacles had kept it from happening. Governor Daniels and I were able to work through those issues, create both funding and construction plans, and persuade our transportation officials to work together. We belonged to different political parties, but we both understood the importance of these spans to our region's economy. This was a massive project, but we got it done. To say the least, I developed enormous respect for Governor Daniels. (I enjoyed a similar working relationship with Republican Mike Pence when he became Indiana's governor.)

Likewise, Ohio Governor John Kasich and I had numerous conversations about trying to jump-start a similar project—expanding capacity on the obsolete and unsafe Brent Spence Bridge between our states. We developed a plan to use the same bistate, bipartisan model that Governor Daniels and I used, but ultimately toll-shy legislators killed the funding model that supported it.

But Governor Kasich and I found success working together on another issue—fighting the misuse and abuse of prescription painkillers, which was a huge problem for our states. In August 2011, we announced a plan to share prescription medication data in order to crack down on both drug seekers who work across state lines and the so-called pill mills that exploit the loopholes in our prescription monitoring systems. We also announced the formation of an interstate task force with Tennessee and West Virginia that would find ways for the states to cooperate. Both were significant parts of a comprehensive, long-term effort to reduce addiction.

Another governor with whom I interacted on the prescription drug issue was Florida Governor Rick Scott, but we weren't on the same page, especially at first. That was unfortunate, because Governor Scott's delay in addressing his state's contribution to the national scourge of prescription drug abuse added to the suffering of families and communities in Kentucky and around the nation.

In a nutshell, Florida's regulation of pain clinics and its oversight of doctors' dispensing habits were weak, and well-organized traffickers took advantage by buying huge quantities of drugs and transporting them to other states like Kentucky. Governor Scott himself often pointed out that, nationally, 98 of the top 100 doctors dispensing Oxycodone were in Florida.

At the time, Kentucky authorities estimated that 60 percent of the prescription drugs sold and consumed illegally in the commonwealth came from Florida pill mills, with each trafficker bringing back, on average, more than $10,000 worth of drugs.

In 2009, for example, Kentucky State Police arrested more than 500 people from Eastern Kentucky in a widely reported drug roundup tied to Florida called Operation Flamingo Road.

Within our respective borders, Kentucky and many other states headed off such trafficking by electronically tracking prescriptions for controlled substances and sharing that data across state lines. Our electronic monitoring program, called KASPER, helped doctors ensure a person did not get prescriptions from several different sources, while also helping police investigate the diversion of pills to illegal sales. The effectiveness of KASPER increased tremendously under provisions of our 2012 legislation targeting painkiller abuse.

But Florida didn't have an electronic monitoring system, so criminals were able to bypass KASPER and other states' monitoring systems by going to Florida and coming back with literally trunk-loads of prescription drugs.

Aware of their state's reputation, the Florida legislature had voted to create an electronic prescription drug monitoring system in 2009. But Governor Scott declined to implement it, citing privacy concerns and the potential for security breaches. Instead, he opposed the system and vowed to get it repealed, favoring an approach focused primarily on law enforcement.

I spoke to Governor Scott on this issue at governors association meetings, as did West Virginia Governor Earl Ray Tomblin. We both urged him to get on board with the rest of us. I then joined officials from around the country in sending strongly worded letters in February 2011 urging him to support our efforts. Another official who wrote a letter was US Representative Hal Rogers, the veteran Republican congressman from Kentucky who had long been a warrior in the fight against prescription painkiller abuse.

But we were unsuccessful. So when US Representative Mary Bono Mack of California invited me in April 2011 to testify before a congressional subcommittee about prescription drug diversion, and to do so alongside Governor Scott, I had an immediate answer: "Tell me the time and the place, and I'll be there."

I was eager to raise the pressure on Governor Scott to a national level, because literally thousands of Kentuckians were dying.

It worked.

A few minutes before we were to testify, Governor Scott walked into the holding room and gave me some welcome news, saying that he was implementing an electronic monitoring system. I was delighted. When I began testifying a couple of minutes later, I made sure the subcommittee knew what I had just heard.

"The Department of Justice must focus more attention and resources on Florida, especially South Florida, to stop the flow of prescription drugs," I said. "And Governor Scott just told me right before this hearing that he is now going ahead with plans to create a prescription drug monitoring program. But that program is just a start. And it is just one piece of a much larger strategy. This is a national problem that demands national solutions. The sooner we come together to recognize that, the greater our success will be."

Suddenly, Florida's monitoring program became a primary focus of the committee's discussion.

A couple of months later, Florida enacted a comprehensive bill designed to reduce the flow of illegal prescription drugs—not just in their state but also to other states, including Kentucky. The bill strengthened Florida's prescription drug monitoring database, increased penalties for overprescribing narcotics, and required new permitting processes for all pharmacies.

Governor Scott signed it into law.

It was a major blow to interstate trafficking of prescription painkillers and began the process of filling a tremendous gap in the nation's fight against addiction. And it came about partly because governors and other elected officials saw their states not as islands but as integrated pieces of a nation that must work together.

CHANNELING CHICKEN LITTLE

If you suddenly lost your job and your family's income came only from your spouse's part-time, low-paying job, and your savings had been eaten up by, say, a medical catastrophe, where would you spend what limited funds you had left each month?

Would you make an extra-large payment toward your credit card debt? Or would you feed your kids, pay the water and electric bills, and make a reasonable credit card payment (all the while understanding and regretting that the balance would grow that month)?

If you chose the latter strategy—focusing on the necessities your family needed to survive until times got better—then you're halfway toward understanding why Kentucky's unfunded liability for its public pension systems grew during the recent historic recession and its aftermath.

There's no doubt that among state and local governing agencies, one of the biggest national conversations of the last few years has circled around the financial health of various defined benefit pension systems for retired public workers. In Kentucky, that conversation has been intense.

We are told that collectively, the retirement systems that cover Kentucky's state workers, state police, judges, legislators, and teachers (in short, everybody except county and city workers) have an unfunded liability of some $31 billion. That means that if the pension systems were closed today, those funds would be $31 billion short of being able to pay all of the current and prospective pensioners what they would be owed over their lifetimes. Depending on which method you use to calculate that figure, Kentucky's unfunded liability percentage is either the largest or second largest in the nation.

How did it get so big?

Over time and for a number of reasons.

One of the biggest reasons was underfunding. Beginning in 2003, the Kentucky General Assembly began passing budgets that put less money into the pension systems than what actuaries recommended.

Having said that, knowing one reason that Kentucky got into its current hole isn't enough. You also need to know a little about how the stock market reacts during a recession, how benefits are calculated, why people choose to work in the public sector, the inadequacies of Kentucky's obsolete system of taxation, the impact of health-care costs, what actuaries actually *do*, and the moving target posed by ever-shifting national accounting standards.

Now this essay won't try to explain all of those variables and issues—nothing would get this book chucked into the fire sooner. But the point is that the public pension problem is a long-term, complex challenge that won't be solved overnight by simplistic solutions and sensational sound bites that have caused fear in Kentucky and are being used to justify an unnecessary retreat from investments in our future.

But that's exactly what's happening.

With huge numbers being tossed around and doomsday prediction scenarios being peddled as political currency, it's little wonder that Kentucky's public workers and retirees fear that their safety net—the pensions they worked hard to earn and that they're counting on in their golden years—won't be around when they need them.

But let me say to retirees and state workers as forcefully as I can: The sky isn't falling, and doomsday is not around the bend. Your pensions *are* safe. You earned those pensions, and state government can and will honor them.

Now, I'm not minimizing the problem. No matter who is estimating the value of Kentucky's unfunded liability and no matter how they estimate that valuation, the liability is a big number and cause for legitimate concern. But 99 percent of the people who hear these numbers have absolutely no idea how they are derived or what they mean. And they have no idea how vested interests on both sides of the issue are using them to game the system.

So let me clear up some misconceptions about Kentucky's public pension problem with some context. Let me also—because some people ignore or lack knowledge of history—talk about the foundation that the legislature and I worked to put in place over eight years that national experts agreed would address this problem.

While the legislative underfunding began several years before I came into office, my first few budget proposals to the legislature also were guilty of underfunding pensions. But there's a reason for that. The Great Recession forced our hand. Monstrous revenue shortfalls caused by the global economic meltdown created huge holes in the budget. We had choices about what to fund: basic services for our people or large payments on future liabilities in public pensions.

Both the Democratic House and the Republican Senate joined me in protecting core priorities like education, health care for the most vulnerable, job creation efforts, and public safety. By doing so, we both reduced the suffering of our people and preserved programs that we later used to improve graduation rates, reverse the tide on poor health, and create explosive growth in our economy. In other words, our choices both protected families' short-term survival and helped the commonwealth rebound from the recession. That economic growth and our commonsense approach to state spending put Kentucky's budget in better health than it's been in a long time. In fact, we left the incoming administration a projected $223-million surplus.

Yes, we knew our budget choices caused the unfunded liability in our public pension systems to grow, but education, job creation, health care, and public safety were higher and more immediate priorities.

So, to answer the question I posed at the beginning of this discussion: We kept our family alive rather than make extra payments to pay off a credit card. And I'd make the same choice if I had to do it again.

But we didn't sit around and ignore the problem.

Underfunding wasn't the only reason that Kentucky's unfunded liability began to grow. There was an array of factors. Poor performance in the stock market caused the value of assets to decrease and caused those assets to bring in a lower return than anticipated. Kentucky's pension benefits continued to be rich, compared to other states, and past legislatures sweetened those benefits without paying for them. Kentucky also experienced an extraordinary number of retirements early in my term. And finally, changes in accounting standards and actuarial assumptions caused a massive increase, at least on paper (more on that later).

So, even as we made the best use of Kentucky's meager budget, I worked with the general assembly—both Democrats and Republicans—to take aggressive steps to address this issue. In fact, we worked throughout my eight years as governor to improve the long-term financial health of the pension systems.

When I took office, I was told that the Kentucky Retirement System (which handles pensions for all but teachers, legislators, and judges) would run out of money as early as 2022. So we put in place changes and a funding plan that experts said would—if followed—bring the pension systems back on sound financial footing over time.

The work included two comprehensive reform bills in 2008 and 2013 and a host of smaller pieces of legislation. In 2008, I also created the Public Pension Working Group. In 2011, I asked the state auditor of public accounts to do an audit. In 2012, the general assembly created the Kentucky Pensions Task Force and we brought in national experts from the Pew Center on the States. In 2013, we created the Public Pension Oversight Board.

The changes ran the gamut.

- We reduced benefits for future employees.

- We closed loopholes (for example, people earning multiple pensions).

- We required employees to contribute more to their own accounts.

- We sought strategies to control health-care costs.

- We expanded investment expertise on the pension boards.

- We reduced the retirement factors for early retirees.

- We improved openness with a new website.

- We improved legislative oversight.

- We created a hybrid cash-balance plan for employees hired after 2013.

- Finally, we put the system on a schedule to ensure adequate future funding by making the full actuarially required contribution (ARC) beginning in fiscal year 2015. (Indeed, in the 2015–16 budget, we fully funded the ARC.)

We were back on track with a long-term plan the experts said would solve the problem.

However, then the board that manages many of our pension funds suddenly decided the full value of the ARC had increased.

Why?

Well, the board uses numbers that are compiled by actuaries trained to make assumptions and project those assumptions out over a period of years (usually about 30 years when it comes to pensions). And those assumptions are complex. They include things like mortality rates, life expectancy, future employment and payroll levels, tax rates, and stock market performance—all out to 30 years. In so doing, they have to predict things like recessions, depressions, and wars.

To come up with an unfunded liability number, these actuaries make literally dozens of assumptions about future events. They use historical data, trends, and formulas, but in the end, they're simply making educated guesses. And the one thing that you can be sure of is that over a 30-year period, they're going to be wrong most of the time.

Now the frustrating thing for elected officials who rely on their work is that those same actuaries from time to time *change* their assumptions, which changes projections up and down the line.

That's what happened in Kentucky. At the end of 2014, the actuaries for the pension board decided that the interest rate that they had been assuming over the next 30 years was too high. Oops! Just like that, with a tap on the keyboard, Kentucky's unfunded liability increased by almost *$2 billion*, and KRS managers said the ARC payment needed had just increased by $95 million a year—this almost a year after we passed a budget that fully funded what those same actuaries had told us was the full ARC.

It reminds me of the quote attributed to former US Senate Minority Leader Everett Dirksen: "A billion here, a billion there, and pretty soon you're talking real money."

Talk about changing the rules in the middle of the game! And in many respects, it is a game.

Again, the unfunded liability was too high and we needed to reduce it. But it's an inexact figure, and it's a target that continues to shift. It was in the pension board's interest for the actuaries they hired to lean in the direction that would make that figure as high as possible, since it would increase the pressure on the legislature to allocate more money.

The only real solution is to put in place a long-range comprehensive approach that better controls benefits and commits a sufficient stream of revenue to keep the pension system functioning and building up its reserves over the long haul. And that's exactly what we did, with the help of national experts. It was a significant accomplishment, and an array of leaders on both sides of the political aisle and in both the public and private sectors recognized that.

In the press release announcing the passage of the 2013 reform bill, Senate President Robert Stivers, a Republican, said that Senate Bill 2 and House Bill 440 (which created funding to pay the full ARC in the next two-year budget) were "a shining example of how government should tackle pressing problems facing the state. Public pension reform was accomplished through a bipartisan, bicameral, and collegial way."

The Kentucky State Chamber of Commerce, in a newsletter to its members, called the legislation "the most consequential piece of fiscal policy passed in Kentucky in decades."

But as everybody also acknowledged, it was a plan that needed time to work and should be given time to work without new administrations coming in and spreading fear. After all, it took about 20 years for our pension systems to get in this shape, and it will take about the same amount of time to get them back on firm financial footing.

"You won't see it this year, you won't see it next year, but you get five, six, seven, eight years out, you'll start to see that unfunded liability be diminished," President Stivers was quoted as saying in a story on Kentucky's unfunded liability that was published in the *Lexington Herald-Leader* in March 2015. "We have made a commitment to make sure those systems are sound."

And what was the verdict in summer 2016 when one of the architects of Kentucky's 2013 pension reform—a pension expert from the Pew Center on the States—returned to Kentucky for a three-year checkup? According to the Kentucky Chamber of Commerce, which hosted his visit, the Pew expert's evaluation after three years showed "a positive path forward" and concluded "the system is now on the right track."

Now this same strategy can be used for the unfunded liability in the Kentucky Teachers' Retirement System (KTRS), which is part of the $31-billion estimate but wasn't part of many of the early reform efforts. With the KTRS, we focused first on the medical costs, shoring up the funding and structure to secure medical benefits for our teachers. We also made changes to improve the KTRS investment performance. When other reform measures failed in the 2015 session, we created the Kentucky Teachers' Retirement System Funding Work Group to work on long-term solutions that experts said, again, would put the system back on sound financial footing.

That's what Kentucky needs to do—come up with a solid, measured approach that, over time, will stabilize KTRS, just like we did with the KRS.

However, in the 2016 budget session, the new administration didn't create any long-term solution for KTRS. Instead, it simply persuaded the general assembly to put $1.2 billion into the state pension systems—primarily the teachers' fund—and $125 million in a newly created fund that could be used to stabilize the pension system in future years.

But to do so, it stripped the budgets of many state agencies, including colleges and universities. Many agencies were cut 9 percent on top of the 40 percent they were cut during the lean recessionary years of my two terms. And services and programs that didn't get cut but were due for funding increases—like classroom teaching and many other areas of K–12 education—didn't get those increases. Core K–12 funding was frozen even as costs were going up.

The consequences were tremendous. For example, this budget cut safety inspections in coal mines, leaving our miners at risk, and it cut funding for things like behavioral health. We retreated on many other services and investments as well.

And that retreat stands to get even more dramatic in the future, because this new administration has made it clear that public pensions are its top priority. And it's apparently willing to starve other services and programs to put more money there. (Interestingly, some of the very people and organizations who felt that the right solution to the pension issue had been found in 2013 (see quotes above) are now supporting this retreat from vitally needed investments in our future.)

Clearly, pension obligations are a need that must be honored. But simply dumping money into the system without putting any long-term plan in place is not the answer. And allowing that obligation to become a vacuum cleaner that sucks up state revenues at the expense of other core, critical services is not only unnecessary but will jeopardize the ability of the state to meet its many other needs and to strengthen its competitive capacity long term. A budget, after all, is a balancing act.

It's time to make thoughtful structural changes in KTRS like we did with KRS, and then have the patience to let those changes work.

THE FOURTH ESTATE: A CHANGING INDUSTRY

I had a fairly positive relationship with most of Kentucky's media members and respected their commitment. Sure, like all elected officials, I had my share of complaints: coverage I thought was off base, stories that failed to give "my" side its fair voice, and reporters who were consistently ill prepared, lazy, or biased. But in hindsight, most of that isn't worth discussing. As with public officials and every other career, some reporters are better than others. And even the good ones sometimes have a bad day. It's just the nature of the business.

However, few professions have changed more rapidly or drastically over the last few years than the world of journalism. The onset of the Internet and the creation of the 24-hour news cycle on television have turned the world upside down from an information standpoint. Print media outlets, in particular, are scrambling to survive, and it's still an open question as to whether they will.

Here in Kentucky, the changing nature of the industry created several trends that continue to negatively affect those who cover the news and those of us who want our news covered.

One was the decreasing size and experience of the Frankfort-based media.

With shrinking news holes, budgets, and staffs, the number of full-time reporters assigned to cover state government in Frankfort every day is a fraction of what it once was. When I started in politics, a dozen to two dozen reporters were either permanently stationed in Frankfort or regularly showed up to write stories. But when I left the Governor's Office, maybe a half dozen reporters were assigned to the Capitol on any given day.

Northern Kentucky, for example—with nearly 400,000 people in the three counties of Boone, Campbell, and Kenton alone, and with well over half a million in the region—had no regular media presence in Frankfort, not since the closure of the *Kentucky Post* in 2007.

In addition, as reporters retired or left the business, they were often replaced with green reporters who lacked institutional knowledge and sources. That wasn't their fault. But it hamstrung them.

The public's smaller appetite for news stories didn't help either. More than one reporter at the state's top newspapers complained that after a full day of work during a legislative session, he or she would be told not to bother writing any of the three or four stories they'd reported because "there wasn't any space." And so the public never found out what went on that day.

Now, a cynic might think that a politician would welcome the reduced oversight. That means fewer people to hold him or her accountable. But I didn't like it for a number of reasons.

For one thing, it made it more difficult to get information out. To get around that, like many governors, I used social media, employing Twitter, Facebook, and Flickr. I also had a YouTube channel on which I released a weekly video message called "About Kentucky," a several-minute talk featuring a timely program, idea, or news event. Sometimes, Jane joined me.

I also took the rare step of routinely appearing on a wide variety of radio talk shows. In fact, my staff set up a monthly schedule that included a regular rotation of a half dozen or more shows a month. Now this was a big risk—some of the shows had combative and unpredictable hosts, and most had conservative or *extremely* conservative slants. Most included a call-in format during which I was confronted with any number of questions from listeners. But I liked these, because they gave me opportunities to explain in much greater detail the rationale for important decisions and to respond to criticism. We had some interesting conversations, to say the least. But I often received praise for being willing to go "into the belly of the beast."

The second reason I didn't like the reduced media coverage was that too many complex issues didn't get the comprehensive treatment they deserved. Although there were noted exceptions, too many stories on a daily basis—whether in newspapers, on TV, or online—tended to be rushed, short, and simplistic, written to fit the space or accommodate the public's short attention span. And what reporters and their editors chose to cover seemed increasingly designed to increase the number of clicks on their social media and websites, rather than what was important.

The clickbait-like headlines and focus got to be silly after a while, and I found myself subconsciously avoiding those reporters who just wanted to stir things up to generate attention. But I also realized that some of the reporters themselves, or at least the serious-minded ones, were just as frustrated with the trend toward sensational coverage for its own sake.

That trend did a disservice to all involved: readers, leaders, stakeholders, the reporters, and the topic itself. I realize that individual media outlets are businesses that must adapt to changing market demands, but sometimes I wish they'd worry less about telling people what they *want* to know and more about what they *need* to know. In other words, stop trying to entertain so much and do more educating and informing.

Here in Kentucky, we desperately need the public to better understand the challenges facing this state.

Kentucky will never embrace badly needed tax reform, for example, until voters understand the degree to which our current tax structure holds us back. It's obsolete, old-fashioned, inefficient, and counterproductive. Now, I can say that all I want, and so can other governors and legislators. But we need independent voices to say it as well, and we need the media to write about such issues with regularity and authority in ways that people understand.

In short, we need more in-depth coverage of what's important to create more meaningful and sophisticated dialogue.

And as a historical footnote, that focus on entertaining instead of informing is what gave Donald Trump almost unlimited free publicity and helped a guy with few serious ideas and lots of drama become his party's nominee for president and subsequently president of the United States. From the very beginning of the presidential campaign, the collective media chose to ignore candidates with issues, ideas, and experience, and report instead Trump's latest inflammatory remarks. That gave him credibility, inflated his voice, and devalued the things on which voters should have been basing their choices.

Another trend involves the increased blurring of the line between reporting and editorializing. Most reporters understand that on any given story, they first gather the facts, which they hope will lead them to a clear conclusion. However, an increasing number of reporters decide what conclusion they want to reach in a story and then attempt to find facts that will support that conclusion. Many times if offered facts that contradict where they want the story to go, those facts are simply ignored. We have a few of those in Kentucky, and they are disliked not only by officeholders but by their own colleagues as well.

Most reporters want to do serious-minded work with a lasting impact, and they want to let the story go where the facts lead them, but their job descriptions have changed. And that's the harm of another trend in the media.

Increasingly, reporters are called to be not only purveyors of information but public personalities in their own rights. The act of reporting and writing or filming a story now only occupies a small part of a reporter's day. He or she then has to go on Twitter and other social media platforms to give different versions of those stories, give commentary about them, and advertise them. Media members appear on television talk shows to voice their opinions, write stories about themselves so readers and viewers "can get to know them," and they're encouraged to become part of the story.

The bottom line is that working in the media today is not easy, particularly if you're determined to do the job right. Thank goodness, many are still willing to give it a go.

THE SAME-SEX
MARRIAGE FIGHT

One moment the political Left was singing my praises as the defiant governor who had ignored his state's dislike of President Obama and boldly embraced and implemented health-care reform, the president's most visible and controversial initiative.

A short time later, those same voters were figuratively burning me in effigy.

Meanwhile, the Far Right—a group with whom I had disagreed on almost every single issue, and who for years had vilified me and all I stood for—suddenly was holding me up as the heroic defender of their beliefs and ideals.

To describe March 4, 2014, as a disconcerting moment is a huge understatement.

That was the day I announced Kentucky's appeal of a federal judge's decision that threw out the Kentucky Constitution's ban on gay marriage. That was the day I isolated my personal feelings and embarked on a lonely path that, in the eyes of some, tarnished my legacy of progressive leadership. But it was also the day that set in motion events that would bring clarity to one of the most contentious issues of our time.

I saw that contention firsthand. In my entire eight years as governor, no single social issue was more politically or morally sensitive than that of same-sex marriage.

Not surprisingly, there was also no issue on which my views and actions were more mischaracterized, misinterpreted, and misunderstood.

Now, I share the blame for that confusion, for a couple of reasons.

One, I played my proverbial cards close to my chest. Even as the media questioned me almost daily about my personal views on the subject of gay marriage, I declined to answer. This issue wasn't about Steve Beshear, I told them. It was much bigger. My own views on same-sex marriage weren't important. What was important was getting a decision from the US Supreme Court that would bring clarity and finality to this issue. My decision not to talk about the issue on that personal level left others to assume they knew my motivation.

The second reason for the misunderstanding was that my views on the subject had greatly evolved over time, much like those of this nation as a whole.

I want to explain that evolution, and in so doing, explain why I decided to appeal the decision. People then may still not agree with what I did, but at least they will know why I did it.

The long path to that moment began in my childhood, during a much different era. How different? In a 2015 Gallup survey, 60 percent of Americans said the validity of same-sex marriages should be recognized. As recently as 1996, that number was only 27 percent. And if you went further back to the '50s and '60s, when I was growing up, that number was probably in the single digits, if not close to 0 percent.

It's difficult to fathom in today's social environment, but back when I was growing up in rural America, gay marriage was not even on the radar screen as an issue. No one openly discussed homosexuality, and the only time the subject came up was in the occasional joke. Since my father was a Baptist preacher, the thinking in our household more or less matched the thinking in the broader religious community—that homosexuality was considered a choice, an aberration, and a sin.

But to be honest, we didn't think about it much.

My attitude slowly began to change when I went to college and law school. There, I was exposed to a more diverse group of people and a broader spectrum of thinking. That evolution continued when Jane and I moved to New York briefly to practice law—but it still wasn't complete. Later when we were back in Kentucky and raising our two young boys, I remember being vaguely concerned about them having a gay teacher. But of course, when I stopped to actually think about it, I realized that the number of cases of gay teachers preying on boys was considerably less than the number of heterosexual teachers abusing children, and that a gay teacher was no more likely to be a predator than a heterosexual teacher was.

One of the biggest changes in thinking—for both me and the nation—had to do with homosexuality itself. Back then, the general conclusion was that people chose to be gay, a notion that some critics used to prop up a pejorative narrative that people were switching their sexuality like they would change outfits— to be trendy and grab attention. That was and is a false narrative. After years of research, most psychologists had begun to reject that notion, concluding that sexual orientation was a deeply ingrained trait with which most LGBT people are born. Some studies even suggest sexual orientation might have a genetic or biological link. That thinking impressed me, and it helped erode much of my previous attitudes about both homosexuality and same-sex marriage.

Nevertheless, when I first ran for governor in 2007, and I was facing questions on the campaign trail, I still wasn't sure where I stood. Like much of America and Kentucky, I had grown up believing that marriage was defined as the union of a man and a woman. I had not yet come to the point of believing that that union—as approved by the government—should include two men or two women. In fact, when I was asked whether I had voted for the ban on same-sex marriages in 2004, I conceded that I had.

But that was then. As the issue of same-sex marriage gathered steam, I began to discuss it with more candor with some of our gay friends (some of whom were not yet convinced themselves that legally sanctioned same-sex marriage was the right road to take). My thinking continued to evolve, and whereas my conviction was slow to form, it nevertheless formed in a solid way. I came to believe that government was wrong to dictate that only mixed-sex couples could marry. Rather, if two people love each other, be they male and female, male and male, or female and female, they ought to have the right to enter into such a relationship, and that relationship should be recognized for legal purposes.

That is what I believe today, and that is what I believed when the lawsuit was filed in federal court in Louisville in 2013 challenging both the 2004 change to Kentucky's Constitution that essentially banned same-sex marriages and the 1998 law that preceded it.

As attorney general for the commonwealth, Jack Conway defended the constitutional amendment but lost at the District Court Level, when US District Judge John Heyburn ruled that the ban violated the equal protection clause of the 14th Amendment.

That wasn't surprising. About a dozen such lawsuits on this issue were being litigated around the country at that time, and most of the district judges had ruled the same way: Same-sex bans, whether defined in law or state constitutions, were unconstitutional under the US Constitution. Heyburn's decision indicated that Kentucky would have to both allow same-sex marriages and to legally recognize those performed in other states.

After much soul-searching, Conway decided he would not file an appeal, because he philosophically agreed with the federal

District Court's decision striking down the ban. I privately agreed that the judge was right, but as governor, I didn't think Conway's decision to forego an appeal was the right decision for that moment in time. Why? Because one judge's opinion in one of Kentucky's federal districts wasn't enough to settle the issue in Kentuckians' minds.

As I said in my statement announcing the appeal, "Both of these issues, as well as similar issues being litigated in other parts of the country, will be and should be ultimately decided by the US Supreme Court in order to bring *finality* and *certainty* to this matter. The people of this country need to know what the rules will be going forward. Kentucky should be a part of this process."

To me, getting the issue in the hands of the US Supreme Court was the No. 1 goal. The issue of same-sex marriage had to be settled, once and for all, by the highest court in the land. Until that happened, we would be left with a hodgepodge of different decisions in various areas of the country, and that would be an unacceptable and confusing resolution. Kentucky, like the country as a whole, needed clarity and certainty. That was one reason I appealed.

A second reason was this: As the elected governor and leader of the state—the *entire* state with its *entire* population—I felt some responsibility to the almost 75 percent of Kentucky voters who voted for the constitutional amendment in 2004. Because the amendment had passed by an overwhelming majority, I knew that for those voters to ever accept the outcome of a legal battle overturning that ban, the battle had to be fought to the highest level and the last inch of disputed ground. The ban needed its full day in court. If we had stopped Kentucky's case at the district level, thereby legalizing gay marriage in Kentucky without a US Supreme Court decision, there would have been widespread angst and divisiveness among our people.

And yes, to be candid, politics was a third reason for my decision—although not for the reason most people thought. There's no doubt that the appeal "froze" the gay-rights issue as a legal issue while the court battle played out, effectively heading off an array of lawsuits and legislative proposals that were waiting to be unleashed.

It also froze it as a political issue. The year 2014 was an election year in which every one of Kentucky's House seats was up for grabs. For years, the South had been trending Republican, and indeed Kentucky was the last southern state that still had a Democratically controlled chamber. The GOP had been slowly gaining seats, and they had vowed—with a lot of national money to back up their boast—that 2014 was the year they would flip the House. If they could manage that, they were almost certain to win the governor's race in 2015 (which they wound up doing anyway), and Kentucky would go solidly red like the rest of the South, probably for a long time.

Now, to me, the great tragedy of such a cataclysmic event wasn't that Democrats would be out of power. It was what the Republicans would do if they gained unfettered control, as shown in states like North Carolina. In my six years as governor, we had made incredible strides in making affordable health care accessible to every single Kentuckian. We had expanded preschool access, adopted a set of standards for learning, and protected classroom funding from across-the-board cuts. We had protected state workers' pensions from being tossed onto the mercy of an unstable Wall Street. And we had protected safety-net programs for our families.

If Republicans gained control, much of that progress would likely disappear, and more than likely, Kentucky would join other southern states in their race back to the 19th century.

If I went along with Conway and let Heyburn's ruling stand without an appeal, the issue of same-sex marriage would be used as a club to beat down Democratic House candidates across the state—no matter how they stood on the issue. That was political reality. I felt like the future of the state hung in the balance. Again, it wasn't a matter of Democrat vs. Republican but of keeping the state from retreating.

And then there was Andy, my son. He had kicked off his campaign for the office of state attorney general in November 2013. To be sure, this was an issue fraught with the possibility of missteps for him. We talked about the issue, and his conclusion was always the same: "Dad, forget about my campaign. Do what you feel is the right thing to do."

Nevertheless, deciding to appeal the case was not an easy thing to do.

Many of my more liberal friends felt betrayed and couldn't understand why I had made that decision. Many people, especially those in the LGBT community, vilified me, and much of the criticism was vicious and personal. It didn't matter that in my first six months in office, I had restored protections for LGBT state workers by signing an executive order barring state officials from making hiring or firing decisions based on sexual preference or gender identity. Nor did it matter that I had appointed a number of openly gay individuals to the state bench, to head state agencies, and to my executive staff.

Meanwhile, many far-right conservatives were suddenly praising me. That made me equally uncomfortable.

I also knew that many people on my staff were profoundly disappointed. A little over a month before, I had been invited to Washington, DC, to hear the State of the Union in person, and the president of the United States himself had given Kentucky a long shout-out, calling me a "man possessed" when it came to giving families access to health care. Morale and pride had been sky-high. But with the decision to appeal, that morale plummeted in one day's time. Even though my staff understood my strategy on an intellectual level, on an emotional level, they were devastated to hear the barrage of criticism, and to see the administration and the state being ridiculed across the nation as backward and bigoted.

On matters of health care, education reform, and job creation, we had been seen as leaders and we had won national awards. But now we were the butt of jokes on late-night TV shows and in editorial cartoons.

The members of my staff who are gay were especially hurt. Some of them had worked long hours with ferocious energy for many years to make me look good, and I knew they now felt betrayed on a deep level. I also knew the scorn they were being forced to endure from their friends and others in the LGBT community. Their voicemails, e-mail in-boxes, and social media sites were crammed with complaints and rants. As hard as it was for them, I really appreciate how they stood by me and recognized the long-term nature of my strategy. I had numerous individual conversations with them and other staff members to discuss the issue, but at the end of the day, the issue remained a sensitive one with hurt feelings on all sides. And I couldn't do anything to mitigate that hurt without undercutting either the legal or political strategy.

It gnawed at me, day in and day out. Many nights, I didn't get much sleep. But I endured because I felt like I was doing what needed to be done for the future of the issue and the state, because my staff kept working hard on my behalf, and because of the rare e-mail of outside support that was passed on to me. One woman who worked for the state said this in an e-mail:

I don't pretend to know everything that's going on regarding the marriage decision, but please let your boss know that this particular lesbian continues to support him strongly and I am VERY sorry to hear that he was booed today. I think the Feds HAVE to make this decision. If Kentucky is left to its own devices, I'll be an old lady before the job gets done. While I always love to hear a person stand firmly on conviction, regardless of how controversial it may be, I also recognize that that is not always the best way to get things done. The good guys need to stay in office or positive change will never occur.

———

I continued to steadfastly refuse to discuss my personal opinions in a public way because I wanted both sides to feel that we would pull no punches and would vigorously pursue the appeal. But I did take two steps over the next year that should have telegraphed to the public how sincere I was when I explained my motivation for the appeal as the need for clarity and certainty, not morality.

The first step had to do with whom we hired to appeal the case. With Conway declining to handle the appeal, Kentucky needed to hire outside counsel. We advertised for a law firm to take the case and received seven proposals, of which five were evaluated.

Two of the firms had a national reputation for involvement in cases against gay marriage. One of them promised to put nine lawyers on the Kentucky case. But an internal evaluation by the state Finance and Administration Cabinet noted that the firms were "grounded in a singular ideological viewpoint." It then concluded, "The interests of the Commonwealth are better served by representation unencumbered by an articulated ideological position on the legal issues to be decided." So, to much criticism from groups like the Family Foundation, we rejected those firms and instead hired a long-established Kentucky firm that scored highest in the evaluation, the Ashland law firm of VanAntwerp, Monge, Jones, Edwards & McCann. (By the way, they did a great job representing the state.)

The second step that spoke to my motivation came when we "won" that appeal. In November 2014, the Sixth Circuit broke ranks with the rest of the federal appellate courts and upheld same-sex marriage bans in Ohio, Michigan, Kentucky, and Tennessee. But instead of being satisfied with the victory, we filed a brief in which we agreed with the plaintiffs that the Supreme Court should hear the same-sex marriage case. "Win" or "lose," my opinion had not changed. (And in January 2015, when the Supreme Court agreed to hear the case, I issued a statement that called it "the right decision," and I said that "Kentuckians, and indeed all Americans, deserve clarity and finality on this matter, and the assurance that the law will be consistent across state lines.")

Now I knew from the beginning that the issue of same-sex marriage would make it to the Sixth Circuit and likely to the Supreme Court, with or without Kentucky. But we were an important member of the case, since our Kentucky case was the only one to involve both issues: the licensure of same-sex marriages within the state, and the recognition of such licenses issued in other states.

Well, the rest is history.

On June 26, 2015, the Supreme Court—in the landmark Obergefell v. Hodges ruling—held that the fundamental right to marry is guaranteed to same-sex couples by the 14th Amendment to the US Constitution. The ruling required that states license marriages between two people of the same sex and recognize such marriages that were lawfully licensed and performed in other states.

Kentucky's ban was officially overturned.

Saying that we finally had the clarity we needed, I immediately announced that Kentucky would recognize as valid all same-sex marriages performed in other states and in Kentucky. I directed all cabinets of the executive branch to alter any policies necessary to implement the decision. I instructed the Kentucky Department of Libraries and Archives to provide revised marriage license forms to county clerks for immediate use. And I sent a letter to the clerks explaining these actions and reminding them that they had sworn an oath to uphold the Constitution.

"Neither your oath nor the Supreme Court dictates what you must believe," I wrote. "But as elected officials, they do prescribe how we must act."

We received a handful of letters in opposition to the new rules, but in the end, I'm proud to say that the vast majority of county clerks—117 of 120—followed the law, upheld the Constitution, and performed their duties. *That* should have been the news story, but we all know that's not the way the media operates.

The county clerk from Rowan County, Kim Davis, was one of the three. She was sued by the ACLU, lost, called a federal judge's bluff, and defied his order. He then sent her to jail, where she stayed until her deputies began issuing same-sex licenses. Across the country, her case attracted the attention of presidential candidates and late-night comedians alike (and it was hard to tell the difference). She was both held up as a martyr and mocked in social media, and she blamed me for not supporting her.

Another of the recalcitrant clerks, from Casey County, Casey Davis, asked to meet with me, and I agreed. He was also a Pentecostal preacher, and I sympathized with his plight and told him so. But the law is the law. As elected officials, we are not allowed to force our personal religious beliefs on our constituents, and we are not allowed to choose which laws to uphold—no more than a police officer can or a judge can. That's not how this country works, and it's not the definition of religious freedom. Knowing my father was a Baptist preacher and that I had grown up in a religious household, the clerk asked me for my advice. I answered with sympathy, sincerity, and candor: Search your soul and your conscience, I told him. If your deeply held religious beliefs prevent you from fulfilling the clear-cut responsibilities of the job, then for the sake of your spiritual serenity, you should consider resigning.

It wasn't what he wanted to hear. When he talked to reporters after our meeting, he said I ordered him to issue the licenses or lose his job. He called me a "warrior against Christianity" and went on a bike ride across the state to hold himself and fellow clerk Kim Davis up as victims of persecution. I didn't bother to answer his charge or correct his account of the meeting. He either understood the law and the concept of religious freedom, or he didn't.

Besides, I had long ago gotten used to criticism for the way I handled the issue. And I still hear it sometimes today, from both sides. Was my strategy correct? I don't know. But if I had to do it all over again, I would probably handle it the same way. The fact is, if we had not taken the fight all the way to the US Supreme Court, Kentucky would have had dozens of Kim Davises defying the change, and we would have had to fight the same battle again and again in endless courtrooms across the state.

The bottom line is that today, same-sex couples across Kentucky can finally both marry and have their out-of-state marriages recognized in this state. I am proud that Kentucky played such an important role in getting this matter settled across the country, and I believe it was settled in the right way.

Recently I ran into some of the plaintiffs in the case. They didn't spit on me, yell at me, or curse my name. Instead, they seemed excited to see me, they gave me a hug, and they asked me to pose for a picture.

Love wins.

Section III

HEALTH CARE

AN URGENT NEED

Several months after I left the Governor's Office, I took my grandchildren, Will and Lila, bowling. When we went to the counter to get our shoes, the young employee waiting on us recognized me.

"You know, everybody in my family now has health insurance because of you," he said.

The very next day, a young lady at Starbucks who handed me my coffee smiled at me and said, "Thanks for my health insurance."

Months later, I was campaigning with Hillary Clinton in Hopkinsville when a woman yelled my name, ran up, and hugged me, tears in her eyes. "Governor," she said, "you saved my life."

These weren't isolated occurrences.

In the years I was governor and in the time since, I rarely go out in public or open the mail without hearing from Kentuckians whose lives were transformed for the better because of newly gained access to health coverage.

These aren't just numbers on a stat sheet. They are real people whose compelling stories of frustration and desperation are changing because they can finally get the health care they needed. Real examples include:

- a stay-at-home mom who hadn't been to the doctor in 10 years;

- an independent TV producer who had been repeatedly denied insurance because he had a pre-existing heart condition;

- a farmer who finally was able to check out a growth on his face—and who, a short time later, underwent surgery to remove cancer;

- a grad student not yet out in the real world; and

- an elderly woman who, as the only person in her extended household without health coverage, stayed awake nights worrying about being able to stay healthy so she could continue caring for her retired husband, a grown child with mental handicaps, and her grandchildren—because they looked to her for so much.

People like these, hundreds of thousands like them, are the answer to the question of why, under my watch, Kentucky was so aggressive in embracing federal health-care reform.

My actions ran counter to conventional political wisdom.

After all, Kentucky's electorate gave President Obama just barely a third of its presidential vote in 2012. And our US senators—Mitch McConnell and Rand Paul—were two very high-profile Republicans who regularly appeared on Sunday morning news programs to eviscerate the president and lead the charge against so-called Obamacare.

Yet there was I was, standing up as a lone and loud national voice to embrace and defend the president's most controversial initiative.

There I was, using my gubernatorial powers to both expand Medicaid eligibility in Kentucky and create a state-based health benefit exchange called "kynect."

I challenged Senators McConnell and Paul to their faces at the Kentucky Farm Bureau's annual ham breakfast. I wrote an op-ed in the *New York Times* and went on a national media tour to tout Kentucky's health-care story. I had the audacity to travel to Washington and advise Democratic leaders to make support of the Affordable Care Act a foundation of their campaigns, instead of hiding their support.

And I did everything within my power to force the health-care industry in Kentucky to operate under this new paradigm. In fact, I was so active and so aggressive that President Obama himself, in an internationally televised State of the Union speech, called me "a man possessed when it comes to covering his commonwealth's families."

To friends, allies, and pundits alike, it seemed like I was committing political suicide. I was sued. Leading Democrats hid from the issue. Gleeful rivals threatened revenge at the polls. Legislators vowed to overturn my executive orders and hold back funding.

But still I persisted. Why? Because I didn't see the issue through a political lens. Instead, all I kept seeing were the faces of those Kentucky families in need.

I knew that improving vulnerable Kentuckians' access to health care—no matter how I did it—was morally the right thing to do. And it was the smart thing to do as well.

Over the eight years I was governor, I had partnered with leaders of both parties in both the public and private sectors to lead Kentucky out of a historic recession and to begin addressing in an aggressive way the fundamental weaknesses that have held us back for generations. And the most stubborn of these weaknesses was poor health.

We all knew that Kentucky's collective health had long been terrible. In almost every measure there was, we had always ranked near the bottom or at the bottom. I'm talking about being ranked 50th in preventable hospitalizations, 50th in cancer deaths, 49th in poor physical health days, 44th in premature deaths, 49th in cardiac heart disease, 43rd in high cholesterol, 46th in high blood pressure, and 44th in annual dental visits.

The suffering was deep. Kentuckians were sicker than most. We died too early. And our families went bankrupt paying to treat diseases and chronic conditions.

At the same time, for our state as a whole, our poor health had had devastating consequences: Decreased worker productivity. Depressed school attendance. A poor public image. Difficulty in recruiting businesses. Huge health-care costs. And a lower quality of life for our people.

There was a clear and direct line between poor health and almost every challenge Kentucky faced, including poverty, unemployment, lags in education attainment, substance abuse, and crime.

One of the biggest reasons for our poor health was lack of access to health coverage. When we started, an estimated 640,000 people in Kentucky were uninsured. That was almost *one in six* Kentuckians.

Lack of health coverage was jeopardizing their health and financial security. These people would get up every morning, go to work and roll the dice, hoping and praying that they didn't get sick or hurt. They chose between food and medicine. They ignored checkups that would catch serious conditions early. They put off doctor's appointments, hoping a lump or a pain turned out to be nothing. And they lived every day knowing that bankruptcy was just one bad diagnosis away.

Furthermore, their children were going long periods without checkups that focused on immunizations, preventive care, and vision and hearing tests. Things like diabetes, asthma, and infected gums were going undiagnosed and untreated.

This left them in pain and their futures in jeopardy.

No one in America, the richest country on earth, ought to have to live like that.

Now some politicians talked about these people as if they were aliens from some distant planet. But they weren't. They were our friends and neighbors. Our former classmates and hunting buddies. We sat in the church pews with them on Sunday morning and in the high school bleachers with them on Friday night.

Many of them had jobs, but their employer either didn't offer insurance or it was priced out of reach. And insurance on the private market was even more expensive. These were people like substitute teachers, seasonal construction laborers, nurse's aides, new graduates at high-tech startups, grocery clerks, and farmers on their tractors.

In fact, I told the story of one such farm family one year speaking at the Kentucky Farm Bureau's annual ham breakfast.

The father was a seventh-generation farmer raising primarily beef cattle down in Casey County. Before Kentucky started its insurance exchange, the family couldn't afford health coverage. The father said he, his wife, and their daughters skipped doctor's visits, ignored health concerns and—when he or his family absolutely had to have care—paid outrageous out-of-pocket costs.

That wasn't a strategy for good health. But through kynect, the family was able to obtain insurance and one of the first things the father did was go to a dermatologist to have a disturbing-looking spot on his face checked out. He hadn't been able to afford to do so before. Good thing he did. That spot was skin cancer. He had it removed. As he said in the understatement of the year, kynect "lowers costs *and* saves lives."

The farmer and his wife were so thrilled with what their new health coverage had done for them that they later let their story be told in the magazine *US News & World Report*.

Before we embraced health-care reform in Kentucky, families like them had been left out in the cold. Before reform, good health and hope were difficult to find.

By any measure, lack of access to health care was a big problem for both the state *and* our families.

And while we were very slowly improving in some health areas, like smoking rates and signing eligible children up for care,

I knew that incremental progress was no longer sufficient. In the 50 years since Medicaid was created, Kentucky had spent more than $100 billion in public funding on health care for the most vulnerable. But we remained the sickest state in the nation, with some of the highest uninsured rates.

It was time to do something different. The old way wasn't working. Big problems demand big solutions. Bold solutions. Game-changing solutions.

On a national level, the Affordable Care Act was such a solution. In a transformative way, it helped me improve the future of our state and the lives of our families. I was resolved to make it work, no matter whose name was attached to it and no matter what partisan critics thought of me.

REFORM WITH A CAPITAL *R*

Now, lots of people have heard the story about how Kentucky became a national model in health-care reform while I was governor.

But most folks don't know the context for our work. Kentucky's aggressive embrace of the Affordable Care Act didn't happen in a vacuum. One, as I explained earlier, Kentucky was in dire need of good health. The time was right. And two, the ACA wasn't the only thing we did. Rather, it was just one piece of a fundamental overhaul of health care that included changes to core elements like *how* people access care, how that health care is *delivered*, *who* can access that care, *what services* they receive, who *oversees* that care, and how much it *costs*.

This truly was reform with a capital *R*.

During my eight years, Kentucky employed a series of game-changing solutions.

- We moved gradually but steadily toward electronic medical records that would improve the efficiency of care.

- We switched our Medicaid delivery model from fee-for-service to managed care.

- We expanded Medicaid eligibility standards to cover more people.

- We created a state-run health benefit exchange called kynect that became a national model for efficiency and effectiveness.

- We provided wider access to substance abuse and behavioral health treatment, two problems that have long plagued Kentucky.

- We appointed a task force on emergency room use that sought to solve the problem of "super-utilizers," the people who went to the ER for care—even though it was the most expensive care—as many as 121 times a year.

- We took steps to make pediatric dentists available in every Kentucky county.

- We established a multi-pronged initiative called "kyhealthnow" that attacked long-standing and stubborn health problems like obesity, smoking, dental decay, and heart disease.

While poor health had long been a problem in Kentucky, the biggest challenge was access to that care. Too many Kentuckians couldn't afford to go to the doctor often enough to maintain good health and to address problems and concerns before they became costly, chronic, and sometimes fatal diseases and conditions.

The Affordable Care Act gave us an opportunity to address this big problem in an aggressive way.

So, what did we do and how did we do it? First, we didn't rush into it. We had two decisions to make:

1. Whether to create a state-based health benefit exchange, or let the federal government handle it, and

2. Whether to expand Medicaid eligibility to 138 percent of the federal poverty level

The first decision was easy. Virtually every stakeholder in Kentucky—from providers to business organizations to advocates for the poor—urged me to create, manage, and operate a state exchange. It would give us control, flexibility, and accountability.

Officials in the Kentucky Cabinet for Health and Family Services began working on a state-based exchange on March 24, 2010, the day after President Obama signed the ACA into law. On July 28, they met with me and I formally blessed their work, effectively making health care one of my top priorities for the next five and a half years. They applied for and received three federal grants totaling more than $66 million to plan and implement the exchange.

But on July 17, 2012, after two years of work on the exchange, the general assembly's Capital Projects and Bond Oversight Committee tried to block it. Voting strictly along partisan lines, the committee rejected a proposal to lease office space. Unfortunately, the discussion didn't focus on health care and helping Kentuckians. Committee members instead wondered whether I had the authority to act. They wanted more say. They wanted to know whether policies on the exchange would cover contraception and abortion. They feigned surprise at my decision. And they were afraid that helping Kentuckians find health insurance would tie them politically to President Obama.

Honestly, it didn't surprise me that once again elected leaders were putting political considerations above the needs of our people. Unfortunately, today that is more the norm in politics than the exception.

But we were not going to turn back now. Look, the Affordable Care Act was neither perfect nor the end-all solution to health-care reform. But it was a start. And it was the law.

And the law required Kentucky and other states to either create an exchange or accept the federal model. We could hide and let the feds take over, or we could step up.

I stepped up.

I had the authority to override the committee's decision, and I did. I directed the Finance and Administration Cabinet to lease the space. And I issued an executive order establishing and defining the Kentucky Health Benefit Exchange, creating an advisory board, and laying out a process for stakeholder involvement.

A year later, on August 16, 2013, I announced the opening of a call center in Lexington that would serve as the hub for information related to kynect.

And after months of hard work, at midnight on October 1, 2013, we crossed our fingers, said a prayer, and threw the switch— and it worked!

People came out of the woodwork by the thousands. By 7 p.m. of that first day, we had more than 70,000 pre-screenings, almost 4,700 applications, and 940,000 unique page views. With IT people standing by, we worked out a few bugs caused by the overwhelming response, and we never looked back.

In the months that followed, Kentucky was inundated with questions about how we made our exchange work while the federal exchange struggled to get up and running.

At the risk of getting down in the weeds, here's my explanation, in a list, because it's important to understand both how carefully we planned this initiative and just how many partners we had in Kentucky. From health-care providers to insurance companies to IT specialists to advocates for the poor to business leaders, we invited everyone to the table and we listened to their ideas. Consequently:

- We set up offices for kynect in an old warehouse-looking office building filled with surplus furniture. Its open-air, stripped-down atmosphere created the feel of a business start-up where creativity abounded, collaboration was expected, and determination to succeed prevailed—a sense of mission that was contagious.

- We created a website that allowed Kentuckians to browse and plug in numbers without actually opening an account, giving them a no-risk way to get an estimate of their premium.

- We kept the website simple, free of the bells and whistles that made other sites more sophisticated but harder to use.

- After we selected the vendors who would build the system, we brought them in and surrounded them with all the state agencies involved in the products and services to be covered by the system, including our Insurance Department as well as the Cabinet for Health and Family Services. So under the same roof were IT experts who knew how to build complex systems in the health-care universe, people who knew how to determine eligibility, and folks who understood Kentucky's insurance laws and regulations.

- We built a single system to determine eligibility for both the exchange's private insurance subsidies and Medicaid.

- We tested our system early and often, including a complete test of the whole system, top to bottom, three months out.

- I picked strong leaders: Audrey Tayse Haynes, the secretary of Health and Family Services, was a former deputy assistant to President Clinton and chief of staff to Tipper Gore. Carrie Banahan, executive director of the exchange, had extensive experience in Medicaid, health policy, and insurance regulation.

And the chairwoman of the kynect advisory board, Sharon
Clark, was Kentucky's insurance commissioner.

- I created an open-door policy that encouraged communication
  and joint decision making, so I wasn't surprised by events
  surrounding the exchanges like some other governors were.

- We built a huge network of people to publicize kynect and
  to identify and enroll the uninsured, including Kentucky's
  insurance agents. We also engaged all the sister agencies
  within the cabinet to educate their clients about kynect.

- To act as "kynectors," we hired local health departments and
  community-based agencies who were already on the front
  lines, especially in impoverished communities. Since many
  people didn't trust state government, we used the people they
  did trust.

- The kynect Mobile Tour traveled across the state, attending
  everything from the Bourbon Festival to the Woolly Worm
  Festival to Festival Latino, not to mention college football
  games, Ironman competitions, and minor league baseball games.

- Our PR firm, Louisville-based Doe-Anderson, developed
  an ad campaign with a catchy tune that featured cartoon
  figures with which any demographic group in Kentucky could
  identify: black, white, male, female, in a wheelchair, a single
  mom, a two-parent family, or a young professional.

- And finally, we carefully separated the politics of the Affordable
  Care Act from the health-care impact of kynect. It was a
  fine line. Nationally, I had become the face of Obamacare,
  calling out those who stubbornly kept trying to dismantle the

Affordable Care Act and who talked about it in a disingenuous way. But at home in Kentucky, my emphasis was not on politics but on people. "This isn't about me or President Obama. It's about your families," I told people. "Check it out."

Well, the people of Kentucky took me at my word. They did check it out, and in the first six-month enrollment period, more than 400,000 Kentuckians were enrolled in health coverage, many of them for the first time. That number continued to increase as kynect was hailed as a model for the nation for its smooth performance.

———

The second decision—whether to expand Medicaid—required a little more thought.

There was no doubt that it was sorely needed. At the time, some 640,000 Kentuckians were uninsured. It was estimated that about 308,000 of them actually had jobs, but their employers didn't provide health care coverage, it was too expensive for them to afford on their own, or they didn't qualify for Medicaid under current guidelines.

They were doing all they could to pay bills, put food on the table, and keep a roof overhead, but they had to go without health care. So they were stuck.

The expansion would increase the Medicaid eligibility guidelines to 138 percent of the federal poverty level—$15,856 for an individual, $21,404 for a family of two, and $32,499 for a family of four.

In so doing, it actually would eliminate the disincentive that kept some current Medicaid enrollees from working—under the expansion, impoverished families could work their way up to the middle class without the fear of losing insurance coverage.

Studies show that people without insurance were much more likely to skip regular checkups, to go without needed medicine, to delay examinations that catch early symptoms of serious problems, and to delay seeking treatments from specialists. When they do end up seeking treatment, often in an emergency room, their problems are more advanced and thus more difficult and expensive to treat.

So it all sounded good, but the *big* question loomed: Could we afford it? Because although the federal government covered 100 percent of the cost of the expansion until January 2017, in the years that followed, Kentucky would have to start paying a portion of that cost, maxing out at 10 percent in 2021. So before I made that decision in May 2013, I sought advice from the preeminent actuarial firm PricewaterhouseCoopers and the University of Louisville's Urban Studies Institute.

These independent groups concluded that expanding Medicaid would inject $15.6 billion into Kentucky's economy over eight years, create almost 17,000 jobs, protect Kentucky hospitals from the impact of cuts in indigent care funding, and turn costly federal mandates into an $802-million positive budget impact. That budget impact took into account a vast array of changes both positive and negative, including the tax revenue from new jobs as well the phased-in state match.

In short, PricewaterhouseCoopers and U of L told me, "Governor, you can't afford *not* to do this."

I'd always felt strongly that expanding Medicaid was the right thing to do morally. Now I knew that it was also the smart thing to do financially. Most called it a no-brainer. It wasn't a surprise that numerous health-care advocacy groups, as well as medical providers and local officials, supported the expansion. In fact, we had a list of about 100 organizations that expressed support, including groups like AARP Kentucky, Children Inc., the Kentucky Council of Churches, Louisville Metro Board of

Health, and Eastern Kentucky University.

In April 2013, I held a several-hour meeting with top staff members and a large team from the Cabinet for Health and Family Services to discuss the results of that study. At the end of the presentation and discussion, I was convinced. "We're going to do this," I told them. Top CHFS leaders later told me they cried all the way back to their offices, then gathered in Cabinet Secretary Haynes's office to celebrate. "We started screaming and jumping up and down," Audrey recounted.

It was also time to tell the world.

So on May 9, we held a press conference to explain our decision, and we held it in the majestic State Reception Room . on the second floor of the State Capitol. In the very first sentence, I set the tone:

"Today we change the course of Kentucky's history."

I carefully laid out both the moral and financial case for expansion, and I did it with the authority of someone who knew he was right. But I also knew that the unbiased and independent studies and the mountain of facts and evidence would not sway critics, and so I ended my remarks with an admonition whose most poignant line became an Internet meme:

> As for the naysayers, they express vague and broad anxieties about cost, fears which the facts refute ... and they fall back on partisan national politics.
>
> If Kentucky expands Medicaid, they ask, won't Kentucky be supporting "Obamacare"?
>
> To them I say: "Get over it."
>
> The Affordable Care Act was approved by Congress and sanctioned by the Supreme Court.
>
> It *is* the law of the land. ...
>
> If you want to embrace Washington-style politics and evoke Washington-style arguments and embroil Kentucky

in a Washington-based debate ... go to Washington, because we don't need you here.

This is Kentucky.

I'm Kentucky's governor, and I'm going to do what's best for Kentucky's people.

Those were strong words and a bold promise, and Kentuckians knew it. A few days later, *LEO Weekly*, an alternative news magazine in Louisville, put me on the cover of its weekly edition wearing a stethoscope emblazoned with one of the Obamacare logos and the headline "Get over it."

I had made my stand.

As for history making, the next few years proved me prophetic, but that's another essay.

GRABBING THE MICROPHONE

For more than three years, Kentucky's work on health-care reform had been purposely quiet.

On August 22, 2013, that changed in a big way. I let loose … and the nation took notice.

In a speech before a large group of farmers and farm advocates that served as a thinly veiled lecture to the two US senators sitting beside me, I laid out a passionate case for why Kentucky needed the Affordable Care Act. I expressed disgust with the critics whose partisan-based opposition and continued efforts to overturn the act were hurting our families. In so doing, I unintentionally lit the fuse to a publicity explosion that propelled me to become not only a national voice for health-care reform but also arguably the ACA's loudest defender, proudest torchbearer, and most ardent flag-waver other than President Obama himself.

Truth be told, I had no idea what I was setting in motion that day. I just knew that I had grown weary of leaders who cared more about political gain than about the people they were elected to represent.

The prospect of bringing desperately needed health coverage to desperate Kentuckians had filled us with eager anticipation. But all around us, the mood was negative.

On a national level, the Affordable Care Act was in jeopardy, being buried under a partisan avalanche of skepticism and scorn. And many Republicans throughout Kentucky were copying their national colleagues and trying to undercut the initiative even before it was implemented, although they had no ideas of their own. Meanwhile, ACA supporters were scared to embrace it.

With the benefit of good timing and a powerful message, I seized the microphone.

The event was the Kentucky Farm Bureau's Country Ham Breakfast and Charity Auction, an annual event that brings elected officials to the state fair to honor the farm industry and auction off a prize-winning ham to raise money for charity. In 2013, the speakers included Senators Mitch McConnell and Rand Paul, both of whom were actively working to repeal the Affordable Care Act.

I told my speechwriter that I wanted to challenge the senators and the partisan gridlock in Washington for leaving our farmers out in the cold by failing to approve the Farm Bill in a timely manner. But then I wanted to segue from the "safety net provided by crop insurance" to another safety net for farm families, the one provided by affordable and accessible health insurance.

"Make the rhetoric pretty tough," I told him, "and I'll ramp it back if I feel the need to."

Well, he did make the rhetoric tough, and I didn't ramp it back. Or at least not very far.

With the senators sitting right beside me, I told the crowd that it was "amazing how the people who are pouring time, money, and energy into defunding the Affordable Care Act … sure haven't put that same kind of energy into trying to improve the health of Kentuckians. And think of the decades they have failed to help on that front."

"Look," I said, "when I think of Kentucky and its people, I don't see the *R* or *D* or *I* behind our names. I see the farmer driving the tractor to the barn long after dark, the teacher staying up late to grade papers, the Kentucky National Guard soldier saying good-bye to her family, the preacher in the pulpit, the truck driver, and the small-business owner. These people need our help, not our excuses and our political posturing."

Some in the crowd cheered. Others sat on their hands, stone-faced and annoyed.

Senator McConnell followed me to the microphone and merely repeated his vow to pull out Obamacare "root and branch," and Senator Paul—who told reporters later he had been caught off guard—gave his version of that same message.

Well, the speech got attention, to say the least. A reporter from the DC news magazine *National Journal* was in town covering the US Senate race. But after hearing me speak, she alerted her editor that she was immediately writing a breaking-news story for the *Journal*'s website.

With the headline "Obamacare Showdown Over a Ham Breakfast in Kentucky," the story described my advocacy as "striking in its intensity and how personally he approached the issue," and called me "a man on a mission, to make history by making a success of the Affordable Care Act in a red, Obama-resistant state."

A top official from the US Department of Health and Human Services e-mailed the story and kudos to my communications director and called it "a very inspiring read."

In the days that followed, my message gained even more traction as other publications followed with reports of their own. The online news site PoliticusUSA, for example, called my speech "a flip of the narrative from the defensive, taken-off-guard Democratic apology tour." The Virginia-based multi-media site POLITICO noted "the rare southern embrace of Obamacare."

For a moment, my staff and I were stunned. Who would have thought that people wanted to hear from a small state like Kentucky, one that rarely had a voice on the national stage?

Nevertheless, we all recognized the vacuum regarding ACA support in the national arena and we rushed to fill it.

The very day after the ham breakfast speech, I began working with my speechwriter and communications director on an opinion piece that we sent to the *New York Times*. It sat in the newspaper's pipeline for a few weeks before appearing in the September 27 print edition under the headline "My State Needs Obamacare. Now."

The last paragraph took aim at naysayers who refused to recognize that the ACA was the law of the land, approved by Congress and sanctioned by the US Supreme Court: "Get over it … and get out of the way so I can help my people. Here in Kentucky, we cannot afford to waste another day *or* another life."

What happened next might have been unprecedented in the history of the commonwealth and the Governor's Office.

The *Times* op-ed and quotes from it reverberated throughout the Internet—shared and linked so many times that an ad agency measured its online presence at close to 2 billion people.

Within days, it seemed that every news organization in the country (and some outside it) wanted to talk to me personally. My communications and scheduling staff could barely keep up with the requests.

Over the next few months, I appeared in traditional print media like the *Washington Post*, *TIME* magazine, the *Wall Street Journal*, the *Economist* and the *Atlanta Journal Constitution*. I appeared on broadcast media and programs like *Meet the Press*, *Hardball*, *Morning Joe*, *The Ed Show*, the BBC, CNN, C-SPAN, NPR, and *CBS Evening News*. And I was interviewed by and my words featured on websites like Slate, The Daily Beast, Huffington Post, and Daily Kos.

I also traveled to Washington, DC, a half dozen times to give speeches to public issue groups and health-care policy organizations that wanted to learn exactly what Kentucky was doing and how we were succeeding.

The headlines almost made me blush:

"How to Win Every Obamacare Argument: A Guide from the Experts," "How Steve Beshear Became Kentucky's Democrat Whisperer," "Kentucky's Governor Brilliantly Makes the Case for Obamacare," and "Kentucky's Unlikely Health Care Heartthrob."

My message was compelling for a number of reasons. One, I was an unlikely champion given Kentucky's national red-state leanings. Two, I was obviously not afraid to call out the leaders who were motivated by politics instead of the health of their people. And three, I was able to break the ACA's value into easily appreciated human terms, instead of getting bogged down in a wonkish explanation of its various provisions. With concise, clear, and interesting language, I stripped away the fluff and zeroed in on the original intent of expanding access to care.

The ACA wasn't about President Obama or myself, I told people; it was about helping people. It was a powerful tool for making families and the economy stronger, and we in Kentucky were making it work.

Lawmakers and advocates told my Washington staff, "Why can't the White House talk about health care the way Steve Beshear talks about it?" Media opinion-shapers said the same thing.

For a state like Kentucky, such publicity was not only unheard of but also valuable.

A public relations firm estimated the value of our earned (a.k.a. "free") media coverage in just the four months between September 26, 2013, and January 31, 2014, at $32.9 million for print and online media and $1.3 million for broadcast.

And it was positive value. Typically, if Kentucky is in the national spotlight at all, it's either for something like the Kentucky Derby or college basketball, or something negative or embarrassing related to the unfair stereotypes of our people. But here we were furthering the image of Kentucky as a progressive leader in health care, much like we did with school reform in the late 1990s and with our being the first state to adopt Common Core standards in education.

I was in the news so much that my name was even floated (in limited circles, I'm sure) as a possibility for a cabinet post or even as a vice presidential pick.

In retrospect, the whole experience seems surreal. Who's to say that my name was even given serious consideration, but it was indicative of the respect that we in Kentucky were receiving for our leadership on this issue. The nation's most powerful people and organizations were listening and watching as a governor from Kentucky defined a problem and implemented a solution—better than anyone else.

I knew I was doing something right when Republican after Republican came up to me during this period and said, "Governor, I saw you on TV last night. I don't always agree with you or even like you, but you sure are making me proud to be a Kentuckian."

A GRATEFUL
PRESIDENT

In early October 2013, the phone rang at the Governor's Mansion.

The president of the United States was on the line.

"I just called to say thank you," President Obama said. "Thank you for proving to the world that the Affordable Care Act can work. We are so proud of you in Kentucky."

As everyone knew, the president's most visible initiative was in trouble. Across the nation, most leaders were criticizing it, few were embracing it, and the well-documented struggles of the federal health benefit exchange to get up and running had made it—to be blunt—the butt of jokes across the nation, despite the president's best intentions.

But in Kentucky, I had recognized the ACA as a huge opportunity to help my people and improve our historically bad health statistics, and I had run with it. I forged ahead, embracing both of the ACA's chief provisions—Medicaid expansion and a state-based exchange called kynect—and I did so openly. Rather than be embarrassed to link myself with so-called Obamacare, I stood up and became its loudest supporter.

More than any other governor across the nation, I became the face of what Obamacare could do for people. I lashed out at critics, I publicized every step in Kentucky's implementation, I praised the president's vision, and I went on a national tour to brag about the historical events that were happening day by day in the commonwealth.

It helped that kynect—as opposed to the federal exchange—was working so well.

Those words from the president of the United States made me proud to be a Kentuckian. I thanked him for his courage and vision and for providing Kentucky with such a powerful tool to attack one of our most stubborn weaknesses. And I told him that it was his persistence in getting the ACA through Congress that had been the turning point.

Before he hung up, he thanked me again, then paused and half-jokingly said, "By the way, Steve, do you have any tech people you can send me so we can get the federal exchange working like Kentucky's?"

I just laughed and responded, "Mr. President, it will work eventually, because you are not going to let up until it does."

In the weeks that followed, the president went on to single out Kentucky for praise in speeches around the country, in places like Boston and Maryland.

But he wasn't finished showcasing Kentucky.

A couple of months later, the phone rang again.

It was the White House, and they were inviting me to sit in the president's box for the State of the Union address on January 28, 2014. I was blown away by the honor and eagerly accepted.

That day, Jane and I flew to Washington, DC, and we were taken to the White House, where First Lady Michelle Obama hosted a reception for all of the invitees who were to sit with her at the address. Jane and I felt honored to mingle with guests that included ordinary Americans like us, as well as those with lofty titles and accomplishments. The guests included Mary Barra, first female CEO of General Motors; Jason Collins, the first NBA player to come out as gay; two survivors of the Boston Marathon bombing; the District of Columbia's Teacher-of-the-

Year winner; Vice Admiral Michelle Howard, the first female four-star admiral in the history of the US Navy; San Francisco Mayor Ed Lee; and US Army Ranger Sgt. 1st Class Cory Remsburg, who had earned a Purple Heart.

While we didn't get to see the president, who was putting the final touches on his speech, we did receive the personal attention of Mrs. Obama and members of her staff. The First Lady thanked Jane and me profusely for showing the world that the ACA could be implemented successfully. Her chief of staff, Tina Tchen, added to the praise: "In those dark days of last October and November [when the federal exchange was struggling], Kentucky was a shining light in an otherwise dark period." She also shared that on several occasions during that time, the president would come into a staff meeting, look around and say, "Kentucky. Kentucky. The ACA is working in Kentucky."

After the reception, we were loaded into limousines and driven to the Capitol, where we waited in a holding room for a few minutes before I was taken to the president's box. As you can imagine, seating is limited on such occasions, but through the good graces of Congressman John Yarmuth of Louisville, Jane was seated in the gallery across the way.

Attending a State of the Union speech is quite an experience. Before the speech, members of Congress whom I knew were waving and shouting "hello" as the chamber filled to capacity. Then the president arrived with much pomp and circumstance and, after several standing ovations, began to talk.

I had not seen an advance copy of the speech, so I had no idea what the president would say about Kentucky. But when he came to the topic of health care, I found out:

And if you want to know the real impact this law is having, just talk to Governor Steve Beshear of Kentucky, who's here tonight. Kentucky's not the most liberal part of the country (that's not where I got my highest vote totals), but he's like a man possessed when it comes to covering his commonwealth's families. 'They're our neighbors and our friends,' he said. 'They are people we shop and go to church with, farmers out on the tractor, grocery clerks … they are people who go to work every morning praying they don't get sick. No one deserves to live that way.' Steve's right. That's why, tonight, I ask every American who knows someone without health insurance to help them get covered by March 31. Help them get covered."

It's impossible to describe the thrill and emotion that went through me when the president spoke those words. It was obviously exciting for me personally, but even more so, it was an honor for the Commonwealth of Kentucky to be recognized in front of tens of millions of people from around the world for our successful efforts.

I was astounded that his speechwriters had actually tracked down one of my speeches and included a snippet from it in his remarks. Apparently they felt that my message—that the ACA was about helping "our neighbors and friends," not politics—would resonate.

Afterward, Jane and I met up in the hallways of the Capitol. We were taken to a personal meeting with the president, where I thanked him for honoring Kentucky in such a way, and he thanked me again for leading the way in health care for our nation. I walked away reminded again of the man's dignity and sincerity.

Jane and I were then taken back to the White House and then on to the airport, where we returned to Kentucky that very night.

The next morning I got another surprise when I walked into my office. My staff greeted me with rousing applause and handed out T-shirts emblazoned with "Steve's right!"

That was touching, but little did I know that the president had also, with those two words, handed the more irreverent members of my communications staff the perfect piece of ammunition. For months afterward, just out of my earshot, they'd leave meetings in my office with a new list of tasks and, with a few laughs and a note of pride, send each other off with these parting words: "Hey, we better get on that, right away. After all … [pause for a three-count before they all chimed in]: 'Steve's right!'"

Smart alecks.

IT'S NOT ABOUT OBAMA

Kentucky's successful embrace of the controversial Affordable Care Act brought me some interesting opportunities, from appearing on the BBC to sitting in President Obama's box during a State of the Union speech.

And there was the time that Nancy Pelosi asked for political advice …

Well, she and others. See, as everybody knows by now, when it came to implementing the ACA, Kentucky got out of the gate like one of the Derby-winning Thoroughbreds for which the state is known. We enrolled about a thousand people a day through kynect, our successful state-based health benefit exchange. I was running around the state (and the country, for that matter) touting the positive impact that kynect and expanded Medicaid would have on our people and our economy.

But whereas Kentucky's system was seen as a national model, the federal exchange had fallen flat, and the president and national Democratic leaders were feeling enormous political pressure.

One day late in 2013, a staff member for Representative Pelosi, the House minority leader, called out of the blue to invite me to Washington to speak to the Democratic House Caucus. It seemed that many of the House Democrats were extremely nervous about the ACA and its possible effect on re-election chances the next year.

So on December 5, a Thursday, I flew to DC and went to a caucus room in the Capitol, where about 90 Democrat members waited for me. Congressman John Yarmuth—the unabashed liberal from Louisville who, from the beginning, had been a vehement supporter of the ACA—gave me a glowing introduction to a rousing round of applause.

It was a bit overwhelming. But I spoke for about 10 minutes or so, giving a pep talk about the success of the ACA in Kentucky and about why we as Democrats should embrace it instead of running away from it.

"Take a deep breath," I said, "because the Affordable Care Act is going to work and is going to be recognized for the good it is doing for our families." Kentucky was proof of that, I said, and ultimately, the political furor would die down and voters would recognize that health care is both a fundamental right and need.

Right after I spoke, the gathering broke into a sort of informal mingling. I was standing there when someone tapped me on the shoulder. I turned around and was face to face with the legendary Congressman John Lewis, the longtime public servant and civil rights leader. Among other things, Lewis had helped organize the 1963 March on Washington with Martin Luther King Jr. and suffered a skull fracture in 1965 in the march for voting rights across the Edmund Pettus Bridge in Selma, Alabama.

I was tongue-tied, but listened in amazement as *he* thanked *me* for my work on health care. "No," I told him. "I'm the one who is honored here." I then told him that he was a hero of mine and that I greatly admired his lifelong work against discrimination.

Soon thereafter, Representative Pelosi took me out in the hall for an impromptu news conference with the Capitol press corps. I reiterated the remarks I had given to the caucus: Take a deep breath because the ACA will ultimately prove to be a political benefit to the Democratic Party. My words were reported in news outlets around the nation, proving once again that Kentucky had something to say and the nation wanted to hear it.

As I told the news and opinion website The Daily Beast during my trip to Washington: "It's probably the most important decision I will get to make as governor because of the long-term impact it will have. … You may not see a change next week or next month or even five years from now, but over the course of the next generation … you're going to see a sea change in the health status of Kentuckians."

I spent the entire year of 2014 talking about improving Kentuckians' health. That message, combined with the tangible gains in the state's economy, helped Democrats hold on to the state House in the 2014 fall elections, even as the rest of the nation moved hard to the right. In 2015, Democrats were less successful in the races for statewide constitutional offices, but that election had a radically different dynamic in that serious talk of the issues in Kentucky was dwarfed by the national political landscape. The same dynamic occurred in 2016, when the effect of Democrat nominee Hillary Clinton's unpopularity in Kentucky trickled down to state House races.

Back when I was governor, however, I actually had separate strategies for talking about the ACA when it came to the politics of health-care reform—one for inside the state and one for the national arena.

Inside Kentucky, I de-emphasized the political angle. I talked to Kentuckians about the commonwealth's historically poor health, and how it held us back. I talked about families who desperately needed help. And I urged people to block out all the partisan rhetoric and focus on their own situation.

"You don't have to like the president, and you don't have to like me," I told Kentuckians. "Because it's not about the president, and it's not about me. It's about you. It's about your family. It's about your kids. So you owe it to yourself and to your family to get on the kynect website and see what you might qualify for. It won't cost you a dime to look, and I guarantee you'll like what you find."

That message worked to build support for kynect and to encourage people to enroll.

In fact, even the name "kynect" was adopted partly to create a brand distinct from the political bickering that plagued Washington. It wasn't surprising that a Marist poll of Kentucky voters in September 2014 showed a 61 percent unfavorable rating for Obamacare and only a 17 percent unfavorable rating for kynect. And national reporters gleefully quoted average Kentuckians who said they thought the coverage offered through kynect was better than that offered under Obamacare (even though they were the same).

That's why I encouraged families to ignore the names and check out the product.

But outside the state, my message focused quite a bit on politics. Why?

Because I was weary of leaders fighting against the ACA simply because it was President Obama's initiative. They needed to quit thinking about themselves and start thinking about the people they were elected to represent—especially since many of those who bad-mouthed the ACA had had decades to improve health care in the United States and hadn't done a damn thing.

Likewise, I was weary of members of my own party who were afraid to support the ACA publicly for the very same reason—that it was the president's initiative, and in some areas, he was unpopular.

In Greek mythology, the Lethe was a river in the underworld that wiped blank the mind of anybody who drank from it or passed through its waters. I sometimes wonder whether the Potomac River that wraps around our nation's capital has the same effect—it seems that too many Kentucky lawmakers who fly into Washington forget the hurt and suffering back home once they cross the Potomac. That's why the phrase "inside the Beltway" has come to symbolize the distorted reality that seems to exist for so many lawmakers, leaders, lobbyists, and others whose work revolves around the federal government.

As a governor, I was much too close to my people's needs to ignore the opportunity that the ACA provided to dramatically transform the commonwealth. Other governors—including Republican governors like John Kasich of Ohio, Jan Brewer of Arizona, and Brian Sandoval of Nevada—felt the same way. That's why in the *New York Times* op-ed I talked about the "huge disconnect between the rank partisanship of national politics and governors whose job it is to help beleaguered families, strengthen work forces, attract companies, and build a balanced budget."

And that's why I used every chance I could to call out the people who led the charge to try to undercut, weaken, and defund the various provisions of the Affordable Care Act.

It remains to be seen what will happen to health care following the 2016 elections. The new administration and the Republican-controlled Congress have vowed to repeal the program, but as of this writing, everything is still up in the air. Likewise, in Kentucky, key elements of the ACA are in jeopardy given the opposition of Governor Matt Bevin and some state legislators.

Even President Obama and other avid supporters of the ACA admit that the original act should be re-examined and refined, as needed. But I will say it again: Think how much better off the country and Kentucky would be if, instead of just obstructing and opposing, folks spent as much time and energy actually working to *improve* the ACA.

THE RIGHT TEAM

For a governor, having the right team in place is half the battle, the biggest difference in whether an initiative succeeds or fails.

Such was the case with Kentucky's implementation of the Affordable Care Act, which made health coverage available to every single Kentuckian for the first time in history. Kentucky was one of the few states to both expand Medicaid and create a state-based health benefit exchange, in our case called kynect.

It was a huge undertaking and required a huge team, including top advisers in the Governor's Office, leaders and staff in the Cabinet for Health and Family Services, the Department of Insurance, my communications staff, hundreds of "kynectors" (who helped people sign up for insurance), community-based organizations and advocates, providers, insurance agents, and private contractors like Doe-Anderson Advertising, PricewaterhouseCoopers, Deloitte Consulting, and Xerox.

Every chance I got, I heaped praise on the various elements of the team.

The tone was set by my top health advisers, including Audrey Tayse Haynes, secretary of CHFS; Medicaid Commissioner Larry Kissner; Carrie Banahan, executive director of the Kentucky Health Benefit Exchange; and Emily Whelan Parento, Carrie's successor as director of my Office of Health Policy. Leading the charge for the Insurance Department was Commissioner Sharon Clark.

I wasn't the only person to recognize the strong performance of my team.

- For her work leading kynect, Carrie Banahan was named one of *Governing* magazine's national Public Officials of the Year in 2014.

- Also in 2014, Kerri Richardson, my communications director who helped craft and manage the public messaging of my entire health reform effort, was named the Communicator of the Year by the National Association of Government Communicators. Kerri was helped by a fantastic staff, including her deputy, Terry Sebastian, who replaced Kerri when she left to enter the private sector.

- Chris Clark, the engineer who was the technology program coordinator for kynect (and was a big reason our exchange worked from the beginning), received one of three State Technology Innovator Awards from the National Association of State Chief Information Officers in 2015.

- And finally, Louisville's Doe-Anderson Advertising, who developed the marketing campaign for kynect, won a 2015 North American Effie Award, one of the most prestigious awards in its business.

In other words, professional colleagues recognized that these talented and committed public servants tackled a large, complex project and knocked it out of the proverbial park, and to honor that performance awarded them the highest honors in their fields.

But if you talk to any of them, they'll say that the biggest honor was giving hope and good health to so many hundreds of thousands of Kentuckians.

KENTUCKY'S STORY,
BETWEEN SOME COVERS

In early October 2013, lawyer-turned-award-winning-author Steve Brill emailed my office a request. He was fresh off writing an incredibly detailed 40-page special report for *TIME* magazine on health-care costs, and he said everyone he had talked to while researching the article had told him he had to go to Kentucky.

"Come on down," we replied. "We'll show you around."

So Brill did come down, we showed him around, and apparently he was impressed.

Because he said so in his 2015 book.

Pick up a copy of *America's Bitter Pill*—a work that the *New York Times Book Review* called "an energetic, picaresque, narrative explanation of much of what has happened in the last seven years of health policy"—and you see numerous references to Kentucky as the state that did things right and for the right reasons.

Brill paints a flattering picture with numerous vignettes and anecdotes about why and how Kentucky's ACA implementation was a model for the nation. His book concludes that, after the commonwealth expanded Medicaid and put its state-based exchange into operation, "everybody in Kentucky probably had benefited from, or knew someone who had benefited from" the new law.

Among the 243 people Brill interviewed for the book were an array of Kentucky officials, including me, as well as Kentucky families and advocates. His visit to kynect's headquarters must have initially given him pause, however.

Leaders from the Kentucky Cabinet for Health and Family Services said Brill told them that he had visited exchange offices in other states, and they were "plush." In contrast, he told us that the 30,000 square feet that we leased on Mill Creek Park in Frankfort to house kynect's 210 employees looked more like a warehouse filled with surplus furniture.

We just laughed. The office space *did* resemble a warehouse. And the furniture *was* surplus. That's why, as Brill noted in his book, the people who worked there called it "The Shack."

But although the space was modest, the work being done there was anything but.

The open-air, stripped-down atmosphere created the feel of a high-tech start-up where creativity abounded, collaboration was expected, and determination to succeed prevailed. Just like a start-up, we knew we were doing something new and innovative, and the sense of mission was contagious.

America's Bitter Pill describes a team of committed people in Kentucky ranging from engineers to health-care workers who were determined to succeed and did.

I feel honored by Kentucky's inclusion in the book (and not because he calls me "glib and charismatic.") I like it because books seem weightier and last longer than newspaper articles and broadcast news programs, and because Brill's work praised Kentucky as a leader in a transformative effort that gave so many people a more rewarding life.

For the diverse team that made Kentucky's ACA implementation a success, *America's Bitter Pill* is the bookshelf equivalent of a congratulatory plaque to hang on the wall.

IT'S KILLING US

My Executive Order 2014-747 had some state workers fuming ... and I admit I wasn't unsympathetic.

The order, which essentially banned tobacco use on state property, was a bold step for a tobacco state, and while it was intended to lead to better health for people of the commonwealth, I knew it wouldn't be easy for some people to comply with. Smoking is a highly addictive habit, and as a former smoker, I know how difficult it is to shake. Even many smokers who want to quit and try to quit are unsuccessful.

Nevertheless, it was time for state government—as Kentucky's largest employer—to set an example and take a stand against poor health. And as governor, I was going to make it happen.

Under my predecessor, Governor Ernie Fletcher, Kentucky had prohibited smoking inside state buildings. On September 4, 2014, I expanded that prohibition to the grounds surrounding those buildings, and I expanded it to include all tobacco products, including chewing tobacco, snuff, and e-cigarettes.

It was a major statement. The new rules affected some 33,000 state workers, plus hundreds of thousands of visitors to almost 3,000 state-controlled buildings on more than 26.4 million square feet of property.

On the one hand, smokers would have to travel off campus if they needed to light up. On the other hand, people wouldn't have to walk through a cloud of smoke to enter a building, nor watch the person next to them in a meeting spit tobacco juice into a plastic bottle. And importantly, state government would be a leader in creating a work environment that promoted better health.

Kentucky became the fifth state to make such a move, and I would argue that—given our historically high smoking rates—we had the most to gain. During the press conference announcing the decision, I rattled off then-current details about the damage caused in Kentucky by smoking: almost 8,000 lives lost each year, $1.92 billion in tobacco-related health-care costs each year, and an additional $2.3 billion in lost productivity each year.

Our rate for adult smokers was the highest in the nation, and for youth, it was sixth highest. Reducing Kentucky's smoking rate by 10 percent by the year 2019 was one of the goals of my kyhealthnow initiative led first by Lieutenant Governor Jerry Abramson and later by Lieutenant Governor Crit Luallen, and expanding tobacco-free policies to more executive branch property was just one move we took toward that goal.

The whole fight against smoking was a sensitive issue for a number of reasons. Even though the number of tobacco farms in Kentucky has greatly decreased over the years, we're still No. 2 in production, and I know burley leaf still provides a living for many farm families. Furthermore, Louisville was home for years to the headquarters of the former Brown & Williamson, then one of the country's largest cigarette manufacturers. I was cognizant of how difficult it was for smokers to quit, and I didn't believe in vilifying them. I also know that many smokers often see any anti-tobacco regulation as an affront to their personal freedom.

Nevertheless, as I said in my 2015 State of the Commonwealth address, it's time to stop denying that cigarette smoke is toxic. It's time to accept modern medicine and science, and both help smokers who want to quit and also protect our children and workers from exposure to secondhand smoke.

Kentucky has long had the highest smoking rate in the nation, and it's one of the biggest reasons we lead the nation in cancer, heart disease, respiratory illnesses, and other chronic diseases. In fact, when it comes to preventable illnesses and deaths, every single study concludes that *nothing* is as devastating to Kentucky as smoking and tobacco use.

I worked with the general assembly and health advocates to take a number of steps to reduce smoking and tobacco use. We raised the tax on cigarettes to help price them out of the reach of teens, while also banning the sale of e-cigarettes to youth. We encouraged schools and universities to implement tobacco-free campuses, and we encouraged cities and counties to pass ordinances that banned smoking in public areas. When I left office, about a third of Kentuckians lived in such communities.

Unfortunately, we were unable to pass comprehensive statewide smoke-free legislation before I left office, although we worked for four years to do so. However, in 2015, the House did pass smoke-free legislation for the first time in its history, so there is hope that people who care about good health and who believe in the science of medicine will one day prevail.

In the meantime, on a more practical level (à la treatment instead of law enforcement) we were able to drastically improve access to smoking cessation programs and medications. Long before the Affordable Care Act required smoking cessation to be a covered service, we made Medicaid recipients eligible for nicotine replacement therapy and tobacco cessation medications. We also encouraged more public employees covered by the state health plan to seek cessation prescriptions.

As a result, the number of adult smokers continued to fall between 2013 and 2014 from 26.5 percent to 26.1 percent and the number of youth smokers fell from 17.9 percent to 16.9

percent, as kyhealthnow noted in its 2015 "Scorecard." Those were marked improvements from 2011, when 29 percent of adults and 24.1 percent of youth smoked, according to the Behavioral Risk Factor Surveillance System and the Youth Risk Behavior Surveillance System.

Now Kentucky's smoking rates compared to other states are still nothing to brag about, but we're headed in the right direction. Furthermore, the impact of most efforts to improve health typically doesn't show up in statistics for years. I hope that, if the emphasis on smoking cessation continues, the numbers will look even better down the road.

Clearly, however, there is a lot of work to be done to further decrease smoking rates, and leaders in every sector need to take ownership of this issue.

The rewards are great: Our ability to attract jobs and investment depends in part on building a healthier workforce, our system of health care depends on us lowering costs, and our families' path to a higher quality of life is founded on good health.

A TALE OF
TWO MAPS

When people wanted to know whether the Affordable Care Act was working in Kentucky, we showed them "The Map."

Technically, it was two maps, color-coded to display the percentage of residents in each of Kentucky's 120 counties without health insurance. One map showed the numbers *before* the ACA, and the other showed the numbers *after* the ACA.

As seen in the photo section of this book, the difference in colors was staggering—in a quick glance, even critics could see how far along we were toward our transformative goal of providing affordable health coverage to every single Kentuckian for the first time in history.

Before the ACA, 75 of Kentucky's 120 counties were colored maroon and red, the colors signifying that more than 17 percent of their population under 65 had no insurance. Of the rest, 43 were colored gold or yellow (11 to 17 percent uninsured), and two were green (8 to 11 percent).

Not a single county was shaded light or dark blue, meaning 8 percent or less uninsured.

But the second map—showing the number of uninsured Kentuckians 18 months after the ACA was implemented—was dramatically different.

The red, maroon, and gold colors *totally* disappeared, and there was only one yellow county and one green county. Blue took over. In fact, 118 of Kentucky's 120 counties on the second map were shaded light or dark blue, representing 5 to 8 percent uninsured or less than 5 percent uninsured.

Those blue hues represented tens of thousands of Kentucky families who suddenly could afford to go to the doctor and be treated for health problems. And because of the link between access to health care and improved health, those colors also reflected families who were on their way to better health.

The maps were a great visual for an incredible fact: Kentucky ranked among the top states in reducing its uninsured numbers or was *the* top state, depending upon the survey and when it was put together.

But the maps were just one layer of the veritable mountain of evidence showing the success of Medicaid expansion and kynect, our state-created and state-controlled health benefit exchange.

See, I'm an evidence-based guy. I make decisions based on facts, figures, and analysis—not on some rigid ideology. If a program or initiative works and helps families, I implement it and maintain it, regardless of what some entrenched partisan political position tells me I'm supposed to be doing.

As I explain elsewhere in this book, that's why in 2013 I sought an independent evaluation of the effect Medicaid expansion might have on Kentucky even *before* I decided to go in that direction. I wanted to see the facts. I wanted to make sure it would be a good deal for our families and our state. Evidence-based research is also why I monitored the implementation and kept close tabs with month-by-month independent analysis of how the ACA was working in Kentucky.

What did this third-party analysis show? Clearly and convincingly, that Kentucky's embrace of health-care reform was improving access to health care, leading to better health, and providing a financial benefit to the state's economy and its budget.

The increased access to care was well documented and well publicized:

- In early 2016, a Gallup-Healthways survey measured Kentucky's uninsured rate at 7.5 percent, down from more than 20 percent before kynect and expanded Medicaid.

- Right about the same time, a report from the National Health Interview Survey showed that Kentucky led the nation with a 6.5 percentage point drop in its uninsured rate in the previous year alone.

As far as better health outcomes:

- A study by researchers at Harvard's School of Public Health published in *JAMA Internal Medicine* in August 2016 compared Kentucky to Texas, which didn't expand Medicaid. It found that low-income Kentuckians reported being in better health and were more likely to have a doctor, to have their chronic disease or condition treated, and to have been screened for things like high blood sugar and high cholesterol, which are important in treating heart disease and diabetes.

- Furthermore, the Foundation for a Healthy Kentucky has conducted quarterly snapshots of the ACA's impact since the beginning of 2015. These have shown increased screenings for things like colorectal cancer, hepatitis C, and breast cancer, as well as more people seeking dental care and treatment for substance abuse.

• The foundation's findings mirrored those in the final progress report in November 2015 of the kyhealthnow initiative, which showed dramatic increases in utilization, especially preventive care and screenings, as people began taking control of their health.

Health-care experts fully expect this higher utilization of care to pay off in better health for Kentuckians. Improved health isn't reflected yet in statistical measures of things like deaths and disease incidence rates because it takes several years to show up. That's an important point, because critics who want to roll back Kentucky's expansion suggest it's failing because current statistics don't show dramatic increases *right now*. They simply don't understand how health care works (or just don't want to understand).

Now, as far as economic impact and sustainability, there were myriad studies that showed the positive financial impact of health-care reform.

For example, the Kentucky Center for Economic Policy, using federal labor statistics, reported that in January 2016, 10,500 more people worked in the health-care industry in Kentucky than in January 2014, job growth that outpaced the overall economy.

The Robert Wood Johnson Foundation, in a March 2016 report, used data from Kentucky and 10 other expansion states to show that expansion would mean reduced state spending on programs for the uninsured, additional revenue from existing taxes on providers and insurers, job growth, and decreases in hospital uncompensated care costs.

But to me the most powerful evidence that Medicaid expansion was a good financial deal for Kentucky's economy, both now and long term, came from a study by Deloitte Consulting and the University of Louisville Urban Studies Institute.

See, even after we implemented the ACA, I remained intensely interested in whether the performance would back up the optimism of the 2013 analysis I had commissioned to guide my decision. So we hired Deloitte, an internationally recognized accounting and consulting firm, and U of L to look at actual performance data from the first year of Medicaid expansion and to project those findings through fiscal year 2021. Kentucky was the first state to take such a look. What we discovered was that, if anything, the 2013 report wasn't optimistic enough.

In the first year *alone*, Deloitte said, Medicaid expansion in Kentucky resulted in 12,000 new jobs and gave Kentucky providers $1.3 billion in new revenues—and almost $3 billion if you extended the time period out to 18 months. And providers were on the hook for substantially less uncompensated care.

Using first-year figures, the updated study predicted the creation of 40,000 new jobs and a $30-billion positive impact on Kentucky's economy over eight years because of expansion. Furthermore, speaking directly to affordability, the report said expansion also would create a $300-million positive impact on the state General Fund in the next two-year budget cycle. All told, it predicted a positive net impact of $820 million over eight years on state and local governments, even *after* the state match for Medicaid costs is phased in.

Those are the numbers, those are facts, and that is evidence.

However, critics continue to scoff at these numerous studies but offer nothing to contradict them. They simply continue to justify trying to undo Kentucky's progress by insisting that Medicaid expansion isn't sustainable or affordable. It's a tried and often effective political trick—if you repeat an erroneous conclusion over and over, soon people will start believing it.

Well, that isn't good enough. If you advocate pulling back on a transformative program that has made health-care coverage accessible to every Kentuckian for the first time in history, a program that has earned praise from every third-party analysis, then we can't play political games. Either make an evidence-based case for your decision or step aside and allow Kentuckians to continue to get healthier.

You see, facts and analysis do matter.

THE DOG HAS
CAUGHT THE CAR

Shortly after the 2016 election, I was asked to write a column for an online forum laying out what was at stake as Republicans in Congress, armed with a new majority, appeared to be rushing to do what they've tried unsuccessfully for years to accomplish—repeal the Affordable Care Act.

I used my 1,300-word essay to ram home the reminder that the issue of health care, first and foremost, needed to be about people, not politics.

"See," I wrote, "with all the ideological chest-thumping and rabid partisan rhetoric, with all the crowing about the political coup of gaining control of the White House and both chambers of Congress and what it will allow the GOP to do … not enough attention is being paid to the people who have the most to lose with this decision: the over 20 million Americans who currently have health coverage only because the ACA took an innovative approach to one of the most stubborn and damaging challenges in the modern era—the lack of access to affordable health care."

It's the same message I've been preaching for years in Kentucky, and I didn't stop just because my service as governor ended.

I had plans for life after leaving public office in December 2015.

I was going to play with my grandchildren, hit the golf course, read, and travel with Jane and our friends. In short, I was planning to ride off into the proverbial sunset and never look back.

But my conscience wouldn't let me do it.

We had worked hard to bring health coverage to hundreds of thousands of Kentuckians who needed it. It concerned me that during the campaign, Kentucky's incoming governor had vowed to eradicate the ACA and had pledged to both dismantle our state health benefit exchange (kynect) and roll back Medicaid expansion.

So, before I left office, I held a press conference about the status of Kentucky's health-care reform effort and encouraged the new administration to step back from the ideology-heavy rhetoric and study the data showing the progress we'd made and the sustainable nature of the new system. I laid out my vision for how better health would strengthen our state.

A leading health advocate who attended the briefing was quoted in the *Louisville Courier-Journal* the next day as saying she was optimistic.

"I think he really cleared up a lot of misinformation and misunderstanding," said Emily Beauregard, executive director of the advocacy group Kentucky Voices for Health. "I do think that the data Governor Beshear shared today will make a difference."

But she was wrong. It didn't make a difference at all.

Within days of taking office, the new governor took the first of numerous steps to begin unraveling Kentucky's nation-leading health reform program, canceling the federally funded advertising contract that helped Kentuckians understand how and when to sign up for insurance through the exchange. Soon thereafter, he formally notified federal authorities that he planned to disband kynect and move Kentucky to the federal exchange. And he continued to talk about pulling back on Medicaid expansion.

Around the nation, experts and observers were scratching their heads. "With Health Care Switch, Kentucky Ventures into the Unknown," read a headline in the *New York Times*. A headline in another publication read: "Kentucky Is Obamacare's Undeniable Success Story. This Man Is Trying to Burn It All Down."

Amid all the confusion, fear, and uncertainty, in February 2016, I launched a grassroots public education and advocacy campaign called *Save Kentucky Healthcare* to preserve Kentucky's dramatic success in expanding health insurance under the ACA.

One of the main goals was to embolden advocacy groups who had been working in the trenches for years to improve Kentuckians' health. These groups had celebrated the progress made through our aggressive approach and were quietly expressing outrage and dismay at the consequences of retreating from that commitment, but many were too intimidated to speak up against a new governor.

The campaign worked. Not only did numerous groups begin publicly voicing their concerns, but we also forced a public discussion of the negative impact of the proposed changes. As a result, many more Kentuckians now understand the issues and are supportive of the reforms we put in place.

However, despite warnings from the federal government about the high risk of user delays, gaps in coverage, and anticipated confusion as Kentuckians attempted to adjust to a more complicated system, the new administration moved to the federal healthcare.gov portal for private insurance, disrupting the one-stop-shop that kynect had provided for both qualified health plans and Medicaid signup. Canceling the kynect advertising campaign in December 2015 caused a significant reduction in enrollment during the 2016 re-enrollment period. It remains to be seen what negative impact the switch to the federal exchange will have during the 2017 re-enrollment period.

The new administration did back away from its promise to completely get rid of Medicaid expansion, but—despite hundreds of complaints from providers, advocates, and families—it formally applied for a Section 1115 demonstration waiver that would dramatically reduce enrollment and cut access to care. And administration officials continued to say that if the federal Department of Health and Human Services didn't approve the waiver as submitted, they would kill Medicaid expansion altogether—in the process stripping health coverage from 400,000 Kentuckians.

So as of this writing, the fate of health reform in Kentucky is uncertain. And it became even more uncertain with the results of the November 2016 election, which gave anti-ACA Republicans control of not only the White House and Congress but also both chambers of Kentucky's legislature.

We are at a seminal moment in US history, where our leaders are about to decide whether health coverage and good health—much like with education—is a basic right of all citizens or a privilege reserved for select groups. They are about to weigh in on whether they believe that the United States is stronger as a nation if its families and its workforce have access to affordable care and are healthy—or if those things aren't important.

In Kentucky, we know the answer to that question on a deep level—our experience over many generations has left no doubt. Long plagued with some of the nation's worst uninsured rates, our collective health before the ACA was among the worst if not *the* worst in the nation.

This has caused immense suffering among our people and devastating consequences for our state as a whole. There is a clear and direct line between poor health and almost every challenge Kentucky faces, whether that is poverty, unemployment, lags in education attainment, substance abuse, or crime.

So what is going to happen both nationally and in Kentucky?

As we go to press, no one really knows for sure.

Although the critics have advocated "repeal and replace" again and again, they've never given 10 minutes of realistic thought to what "replace" means. All at once, they are like the dog catching the car: "Oops, what do we do now?"

I do know one thing. It's time for Washington and Frankfort to adjust the lens through which they see health care. This is not about partisan power, ideology, or politics at all. This is about families, access to health coverage, better health, a stronger workforce, and our economy's competitive capacity. The folks in charge now need to pause, take a deep breath, let the reckless partisan fervor subside, and ask themselves: What is best for our families, and what will make our country stronger? What is to happen to those 20 million people who now have access to health care? If they start with those questions in mind, the rest will take care of itself.

The Beshear clan, when Mom and Dad were still living. In the back row are David Beshear, myself, Nancy Kweik, Bob Beshear, and Mary Ann Miller. Dad and Mom, Russell and Mary Elizabeth Beshear, are in front.

With Jane, Jeff (on Jane's lap), and Andy, back when I, then a
state representative, was running for attorney general

My wife, Jane, shown here speaking at a Celebration of Hope luncheon for cancer survivors, was reluctant to re-enter public life, but she quickly became one of the most active first ladies in Kentucky history.

The paralyzing 2009 ice storm was the worst natural disaster in Kentucky's modern history, but my visits to affected communities showed me that in times of crisis, people desperately want to know their leaders care. Here I am with McCracken County Sheriff Jon Hayden.

The town of West Liberty was all but destroyed on March 2, 2012, by a tornado that cut an 85-mile swath across Kentucky into neighboring West Virginia. Some 25 deaths were blamed on the 19 tornadoes that pummeled Kentucky that day. Touring the damage in West Liberty helped me get to know Robert Stivers, far left, who was later elected Senate president.

When my chief of staff, Mike Haydon, died suddenly in 2012, his wife, Lisa, lost the love of her life, and Kentucky lost a dedicated 30-year public servant and a truly unique character.

When a cargo ship ripped a 322-foot span off the piers of the Eggners Ferry Bridge on a cold winter's night, Kentucky had another bridge project on its hands. I made several trips to Western Kentucky to see the damage and monitor the progress of the repair.

Invited by President Barack Obama to sit in his box for the 2014 State of the Union, I was proud of the shout-out the president gave Kentucky and me (here in the bottom right corner) in his remarks.

Making the Affordable Care Act work was a daunting task, but we succeeded in Kentucky because of the quality of my top health advisers, including (left to right) Carrie Banahan, Audrey Tayse Haynes, and Sharon Clark.

With appearances on everything from the BBC to *Meet the Press*, I rode a publicity wave as a national voice for health care reform and one of the ACA's loudest defenders.

Percentage of the Population Under 65 that was Uninsured Prior to ACA

2012 Small Area Health Insurance Estimates

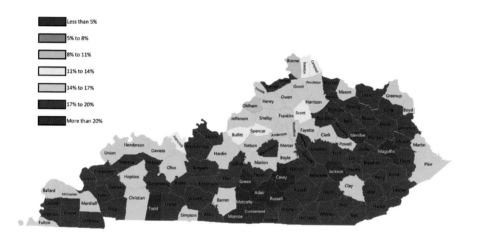

The dramatic reduction in the number of Kentuckians without health coverage led the nation and transformed the state.

Percentage of the Population Under 65
that is Uninsured

*Assumes 75% of New Enrollees previously uninsured /
KHBE 8-19-2015 Enrollment / Medicaid 2013 VS JAN - JUN 2015*

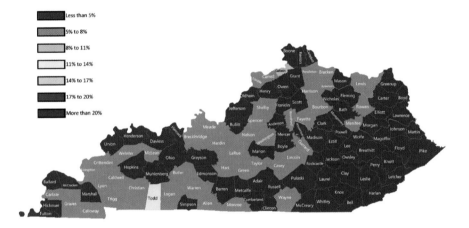

These color-coded "before" and "after" maps showed Kentucky's remarkable results in just 18 months.

Editorial cartoons published in the *Courier-Journal* (Louisville) newspaper acknowledged the history Kentucky was making with the implementation of the Affordable Care Act.

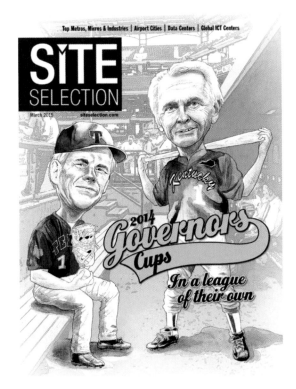

A record number of large economic development projects in 2014 put me on the cover of *Site Selection* magazine in March 2015, along with Texas Governor Greg Abbott.

When Kentucky won *Site Selection's* Governor's Cup for large-scale economic development per capita in 2014, I took the silver trophy on the road so local officials could share the honor. We won the Governor's Cup again for similar development in 2015.

When India-based UFlex Ltd. broke ground for a manufacturing plant in Elizabethtown in 2011, I participated in a traditional religious ground-blessing ceremony called a *bhoomi poojan*. My campaign opponent likened it to "idolatry."

An engagement ring I put on the hand of my wife, Jane (at left), in 1969 caught the attention of Tiffany & Co. officials as they made the decision on where to locate a \$2.75-million manufacturing facility. That personal touch, I believe, helped Kentucky "win" the competition, when Tiffany chose Lexington.

There is nothing like standing in the Winner's Circle at the Kentucky Derby. Here I am with my wife, Jane, and jockey Victor Espinoza after he had ridden Triple Crown winner American Pharoah to victory in 2015.

Kentucky landed a $360-million Lexus plant and 750 new jobs because Toyota Motor Manufacturing knew that Kentucky had its back. Here I am with Wil James, president of Toyota Motor Manufacturing, Kentucky (middle), and Larry Hayes, secretary of the Kentucky Cabinet for Economic Development (right).

Knowing that Kentucky needed to help all of its children get off to a better start in life, I made early childhood education and development one of my top priorities.

A former teacher, Jane was an absolute warrior on education causes, including helping to raise Kentucky's dropout age and supporting the annual Feed the Mind literacy celebration, which attracted 8,000 fourth- and fifth-graders in 2015.

A trip to the Middle East to see Kentucky troops in 2011 was an awe-inspiring experience and a highlight of my eight years. Whether they were overseas or back in Kentucky responding to natural disasters, service members in the Kentucky National Guard did the work of superheroes.

I campaigned with President Bill Clinton during my 1996 run for the US Senate. Between us in the background is the late US Senator Wendell Ford, the former majority whip who worked quietly but effectively to make Kentucky and America better places and made a name for himself as a leader who listened and cared.

Ohio Governor John Kasich and I worked together on a range of issues, including addressing prescription drug abuse. Here we are in Covington, Kentucky, discussing ways to move forward on expanding the capacity of the Brent Spence Bridge connecting our states.

Committed to working across party lines to improve Kentucky, I spent a lot of time with Republican Congressman Hal Rogers on SOAR, the ongoing campaign to diversify and energize Appalachia's economy.

Indiana Governor Mitch Daniels and I are of different political parties, but we worked together to build two bridges between Louisville and Southern Indiana.

When Mike Pence succeeded Mitch Daniels as Indiana's governor, I worked with yet another Republican governor in order to complete the Ohio River Bridges Project and finish the bridge between Milton, Kentucky, and Madison, Indiana. Pence is now the vice president of the United States.

The definition of panic? Getting invited to golf with Tiger Woods, and then at the last minute being forced to use borrowed clubs and new shoes. This was at the Greenbrier Classic in West Virginia.

Author Wendell Berry (wearing a suit at right) and other advocates protesting Kentucky's policy on coal came to my office expecting to get arrested, but I instead afforded them courtesy and a respectful ear.

Our older son, Jeff, is an equine veterinarian whose wife, Emily, is both a top-level event rider and a trainer. Small wonder that Nicholas, our oldest grandson, is already an accomplished rider.

Our younger son, Andy, is Kentucky's attorney general. His wife, Britainy, is a fantastic mother, and Jane and I are enthralled with our second and third grandchildren, Lila and Will.

My college sweetheart and wife for almost 50 years, Jane has been by my side through it all, including here, at the lively "political blood sport" spectacle Kentucky calls Fancy Farm.

Section IV
THE ECONOMY

THE BIG REBOUND
("ANYWHERE, ANYPLACE, ANYTIME")

"We need to go to India."

Economic Development Secretary Larry Hayes was on the phone. It was April 2011, and he had one of those classic good news-bad news scenarios.

The good news was that six months after I first traveled to India as part of a strategic effort to increase trade and investment opportunities between Kentucky and one of the world's fastest-growing economies, we were on the verge of landing a big company we had been courting.

But the bad news—or more accurately, the "catch"—was that we needed to get to New Delhi to close the deal.

Almost 8,000 miles away.

As soon as possible.

And right during the last few days of an important legislative session.

I didn't hesitate. Drop everything, I told Larry, and let's get going. Immediately. But let's try to do it over the weekend!

In no time at all, we were headed across the ocean on a trip that—to people not familiar with what's required to succeed in the high-stakes world of economic development—probably seemed ludicrous: All told, we were in the air for longer (36 hours) than we were on the ground (30 hours).

I'll write more about the details of that trip in another essay, but the experience was indicative of the personal touch and aggressive response that we employed to encourage investment and create and retain jobs.

Multiply our work in India by several hundredfold, and it explains how Kentucky was able to recover from the Recession of 2008 faster than many other states.

It also explains how we were able to cut Kentucky's unemployment rate from almost 11 percent during the depths of the recession to 4.9 percent when I left office; and how we led the nation in large-scale economic development per capita in both 2014 and 2015, winning the coveted Governor's Cup twice in the process. It also accounts for how we set records for exports five years' running; how we set a state record for economic activity in 2014, and then broke that record in 2015; and how we were able to attract nearly $21 billion in business investment in our eight years, creating about 90,000 new jobs.

Those are impressive numbers.

But progress like that doesn't happen by itself.

It requires vision, boldness, and aggressive implementation of carefully laid plans. It also takes the ability and willingness to collaborate. And it requires leadership in the right places. You have to have people who know what they're doing.

The need for those things was particularly urgent in Kentucky, given the economic maelstrom I inherited. Some governors are fortunate to come into office during a boom economy. I had horrible timing. I was sworn in for my first term at the leading edge of a global recession that the International Monetary Fund officially labeled the worst downturn since World War II.

The impact across the country was devastating: The unemployment rate skyrocketed. Housing prices plummeted. Stock market prices crashed. Wealth continued to concentrate in the hands of a few, but now at a quicker pace. And both household income and the net worth of households dropped.

In fact, the country was so precariously close to slipping into a deep depression that Presidents George W. Bush and Barack Obama and two Congresses were forced to approve and implement monstrous stimulus packages that bailed out both the financial and auto manufacturing industries.

Meanwhile, the impact in Kentucky was similar. Many businesses closed, while others cut jobs, product lines, shifts, and hours.

Families who lost jobs through no fault of their own struggled to keep a roof overhead, put food on the table, and pay for medicine. Those who were able to provide the necessities did so by cutting costs everywhere else: Turning down the thermostat, foregoing vacations and nights out, packing lunches every day to school and work, putting off trips to the doctor and repairs to the car, skipping college to go right to work, and wearing hand-me-downs instead of buying new clothes. Meanwhile, the savings that families spent their lifetime accumulating dwindled away.

Our families needed help. Unfortunately, the more that need increased, the less state government was equipped to provide it, given the corresponding drop in state revenues.

Overnight, the plans and promises made during my campaign gave way to one priority: putting our families back to work. In cities and small towns across the state, we needed to preserve our existing jobs and create new ones. The mission was desperate.

Now creating jobs was easier said than done. But we believed it *could* be done.

See, there's a common misconception about economic development. During presidential campaigns, incumbents and challengers alike are cautioned against assigning blame or taking credit for economic downturns or upturns because—as the conventional wisdom suggests—the economy is too big for one person to influence. That may be true on a national level.

But on a state level, that conventional wisdom is more nuanced. The economy certainly doesn't dance to one person's whims like a puppet on a string, but there are definitely things that a governor can do to help turn an economy around or keep it mired in the mud.

Critics also like to insist that it's the private sector, not government, that creates jobs. That's technically true. But that's too simplistic an assessment. Business investments aren't made in a vacuum. The underlying strengths and infrastructure of a state—everything from tax policies to its workforce, transportation network, economic incentives, roads, higher education institutions, energy costs, and logistics companies—play huge roles in executives' decisions. The factors are almost infinite. Government on both the state and local levels can do a lot to make a community a vibrant place to open a business.

Furthermore, the assistance that government agencies provide in navigating red tape, addressing concerns, and building infrastructure have huge impact on attracting prospective businesses and helping existing businesses succeed.

To say it another way, there was a direct line between Kentucky's economic success and the decisions we made during my eight years. That's not to say I deserve all the credit. I don't. Any specific economic announcement depended on the contributions of myriad officials and agencies, from local economic development boards to state recruiters to neighboring community colleges to legislators to regional energy providers.

But the tone was set at the top.

And I made it clear that Kentucky would do whatever it took to attract development.

The first decision I made was to get the right leadership in the state Cabinet for Economic Development, and I had only one man in mind: Larry Hayes. I came to know Larry well during the Collins Administration, when he was secretary of the Governor's

Executive Cabinet and I was lieutenant governor. Larry had a business background; he had a feel for what businesses needed; he knew how government worked; and he had helped Governor Collins land Toyota in 1984. In other words, he knew how to get things done. He also had my total confidence. I stepped back and didn't micromanage personnel decisions, and he, in turn, let me know when he needed me to wield the power and prestige of the Governor's Office to make calls, meet executives, and apply the personal touch. The 2011 trip to India was a perfect example.

As I told Larry, "I will go anywhere, anyplace, anytime."

One of our first big initiatives was to overhaul and modernize Kentucky's financial incentives program, which was both out-of-date and didn't do enough to help existing businesses looking to expand.

Another focus was international investment, also known as foreign direct investment.

The creation of Toyota Motor Manufacturing's massive car plant in Georgetown in the 1980s and the subsequent location of its North American headquarters in Northern Kentucky had drastically changed Kentucky's economy for the better. When I was lieutenant governor in the mid-1980s, Kentucky was home to a mere handful of Japanese-owned companies. Thanks to the vision and hard work of Governor Martha Layne Collins, the arrival of Toyota opened the floodgates for Japanese investment. The nurturing of that relationship between Japan and Kentucky by governors since that time became a foundation of our economy, especially in the world of automobile manufacturing. As of summer 2016, Kentucky was home to 179 Japanese-owned facilities with a total employment of more than 43,000 people.

I saw the Japanese-Kentucky relationship as a model to emulate, and we began an aggressive effort to both recruit international companies and find world markets for Kentucky products.

Knowing that if we created new markets for Kentucky goods,

then our Kentucky companies would have to hire more people to make those goods, we created the Kentucky Export Initiative in December 2010. As a result, Kentucky set export records for the next five years in a row, creating thousands of new jobs in the process.

In addition, we made an array of other strategic moves to grow our economy, both in the short term and over the long run. These include:

- We created a tax incentives program and the new Kentucky Automotive Industry Association to help our auto manufacturers and thus our more than 400 suppliers.

- We nurtured high-tech startups by creating the Kentucky Innovation Network and the Office of Entrepreneurship.

- We started a Build-Ready program that took the concept of "shovel-ready" sites a step further.

- We helped small businesses with new financing programs and tax credits, and we created the new Angel Investors Network to link entrepreneurs with private investors. Our efforts to help small businesses was such that in 2015, we were named a Champion of Small Business by the National Conference of State Legislatures, and both the Kauffman Foundation and Thumbtack.com gave Kentucky an "A" rating for small-business friendliness.

- We created the Kentucky Skills Network, which helps employers find, train, and prepare a tailored workforce, and took the concept of apprenticeship to a whole new level with an expanded dual-focus manufacturing work and school program. Students going through the KY FAME program work 24 hours a week at a participating company while attending class two days a week at a nearby community and technical college. They graduate with certification as an Advanced Manufacturing Technician *and* an associate's degree in applied sciences. Created in 2010 to help train new workers at Toyota Motor Manufacturing, KY FAME has grown to involve almost 140 Kentucky companies as of this writing, and it's still growing.

- To further the KY FAME initiative, we broke ground in April 2015 on a new Advanced Manufacturing Center at the new Bluegrass Community and Technical College campus in Georgetown. When it opened in January 2017, it began training workers for highly skilled jobs at Toyota and other companies.

- We also passed legislation and made highway improvements that enabled Kentucky Speedway in Sparta to attract a long-coveted NASCAR Sprint Cup Series race, beginning in 2011. NASCAR is the country's No. 1 spectator sport, and the economic impact of the race each year has been predicted to be more than $100 million.

- And, looking to the future, we began work on our farm team, so to speak, by creating the Governor's School for Entrepreneurs. Created to mimic the Governor's Scholars and Governor's School for the Arts programs, the summer school for high school students groomed a new generation of innovative and creative thinkers in the business world.

Again, it wasn't just me or Larry. It took a village working in a strategic fashion, aggressively and—above all—together. More than in any other sector, economic development requires partnerships across many boundaries.

The end result of these strategic planning efforts?

After hitting bottom during the recession, Kentucky's economy rebounded off that bottom and quickly reached new heights, setting state records in economic activity. And most importantly, it put our families back to work.

———

POSTSCRIPT: In the November 2016 election (almost a year after I left office), Republicans gained control of the Kentucky House of Representatives and now control the Governor's Office and both chambers of our legislature. Their agenda in 2017 includes preservation of our extremely low minimum wage and reductions in business taxes. They have repealed our prevailing wage laws and have passed their Holy Grail—the so-called Right to Work law. In spite of the fact that Kentucky was already No. 1 in the nation in 2014 and 2015 for attracting the most large-scale economic development per capita (finishing ahead of all of our neighboring right-to-work states), they have bemoaned our "terrible" business environment and promised to "turn things around" by passing this agenda. It will be interesting to compare the state's economic development performance over the next few years with our administration's highly successful track record.

THE PERSONAL TOUCH

I cannot overstate the value of developing personal relationships with decision makers in companies looking at a new location or expanding an existing location. When you're recruiting business, the secret to success is establishing a sense of trust. Companies need to feel that you really want them and that they can count on what you tell them. Most CEOs want you to be honest and upfront about what you can do, and more importantly, about what you cannot or will not do, instead of overselling and underperforming.

But it also helps to find that extra little something that takes a personal relationship to the next level.

Kentucky isn't as big as many states. We don't have the resources and advantages that some enjoy, and our reputation historically hasn't been as progressive and innovative as others. But during my time as governor, our Cabinet for Economic Development refused to let itself be out-worked and strived to build personal relationships with prospective companies and existing Kentucky companies—relationships founded on trust, listening, responsiveness, and attention to detail.

In fact, that personal touch was one of our best assets.

The battle for Tiffany & Co.'s new location in 2010 is a perfect example.

Tiffany, of course, is no ordinary company. It is a globally iconic company whose name has symbolized style, quality, and luxury to millions of people around the world for one and three-quarters centuries. Its unique designs of gold, silver, and precious stones have adorned the hands, wrists, and throats of celebrities, royalty, and those with a taste for class. If you want to see a woman's pulse race, simply mention the phrase "little blue box"—a trademarked company symbol, by the way—in the context of a present.

And if you want to see the pulse of a governor race, mention the prospect of locating a Tiffany & Co. facility in his or her state. And Tiffany & Co. was interested in investing $2.75 million in a new manufacturing facility outside of its traditional northeastern corridor, creating 125 new jobs. It was looking in the Midwest, and Kentucky was one of five or so states in the running.

Economic Development Secretary Larry Hayes had established a strong personal and working relationship with John Petterson, the senior official heading Tiffany's search.

One day Larry called to say that the company had narrowed its search to two or three states, and it was time to bring me into the process. We set up a meeting, and John and his group arrived at the governor's office. After introductions and pleasantries, John explained the project in detail and I expressed our strong interest in the company coming to Kentucky.

And then, with a touch of drama, I pulled out my secret weapon. I said, "John, I know that you are looking at several states, and I am sure that all of them can offer incentive packages similar to what Kentucky has on the table. However, I have one thing here in Kentucky that no other state has."

John and his group gave me a puzzled look and said, "Governor, what's that?"

I got out of my chair, opened a side door, and in walked Kentucky's First Lady, my wife, Jane.

After I introduced her around, I said, "John, take a look at that engagement ring on Jane's hand. I bought that for her at your Fifth Avenue store in New York City in 1969, and I just made the last payment on it last week." I then showed them the appraisal that Tiffany had given me at the time of purchase.

They were flabbergasted, amused, and impressed, all at the same time. They laughed, and each official in that room inspected Jane's engagement ring. We then went on with the meeting, but with a new feeling of warmth and connection. Here was a governor, they knew, who "got" their company.

In the end, Tiffany chose Kentucky. And when we had the groundbreaking ceremony in Lexington, John Petterson stood at the microphone and said, "Now let me tell you why we came to Kentucky." With that, he told the story of Jane and her Tiffany engagement ring.

Obviously, their decision was based upon much more than a 41-year-old purchase, but that personal touch just may have pushed Kentucky ahead enough to nose out all the other states at the finish line.

We cut the ribbon on Tiffany & Co.'s facility less than a year later—and less than three years later, the company announced plans for a $2-million expansion that would add an additional 75 jobs.

———

Let me give another example, one that involved Kentucky standing up to Congress, bucking public opinion, and proudly defending one of its top corporate citizens—another development in a 30-year relationship that contributed to us landing a $360-million Lexus plant and 750 new jobs.

The company, of course, was Toyota Motor Manufacturing. Kentucky is home to Toyota's Northern American manufacturing headquarters and its largest manufacturing plant outside Japan, and we have long enjoyed a relationship with Toyota that transcends business to involve personal friendships.

In early 2010, Toyota became the subject of safety recalls involving some of its vehicles, and all at once, all hell broke loose. Newspapers were writing accusatory headlines in 64-point type. TV stations were drumming up sound-bite outrage. Opportunistic lawyers were circling.

Politicians in Washington were posturing, and Congressional committees were gearing up to hold hearings. While safety was an important issue, what we were witnessing had all the tone and tenor of a 17th-century witch hunt.

So I reached out to governors of three other states that also had a large Toyota presence, and at my urging, we sent a letter to the secretary of the US Department of Transportation and the chairs of congressional committees that were to conduct the hearings. We demanded that Toyota receive responsible and fair treatment. We reminded them of Toyota's long history as a steward of safety and quality, its status as a valued employer in states across the nation, and the aggressive way in which Toyota had addressed the safety concerns.

A few weeks after he testified before Congress, I had the privilege of talking personally with Toyota President Akio Toyoda and Toyota Motor North America President Yoshi Inaba on their visit to Kentucky. They thanked me for stepping up so publicly on Toyota's behalf. "We weren't sure we had any friends left in America until we saw your letter," they said. I in turn thanked them for playing such a positive role in Kentucky's economy and reiterated my belief in the integrity and honor of the company.

Three years later, when Toyota was looking to establish the first-ever US production site for the Lexus ES 350 model, the top-selling Lexus sedan in the world, it chose to expand and retool its existing facility in Georgetown, Kentucky. The decision represented a total new investment of more than half a *billion* dollars ($531 million to be exact), including $360 million for Lexus, plus 750 new jobs.

Now, did Kentucky's public defense of Toyota back in 2010 have anything to do with its decision in 2013 to bring the production of the Lexus to our state? We'll never really know. Certainly, it helped that the year before the announcement I signed into law a bill that broadened the reach of the Kentucky Jobs Retention Act to give Toyota the same benefits that other automakers had received. But it also didn't hurt that—when the foreign-based automaker was under attack in Washington and across the nation—Kentucky stood up and very loudly had its back.

———

A third example of personal touch paying off involved Champion Petfoods, a premier pet foods company located in Canada.

On our first trade mission to Canada, in 2013, the US consul general hosted a small dinner for Secretary Hayes and myself at his home, and he invited several Canadian business officials to meet us.

During the course of sipping on and bragging about Kentucky bourbon, we met Tim Bowman, a principal with Bedford Capital. He advised us that the company owned Champion Petfoods and was looking for its first location in the United States. We, of course, told him about Kentucky and urged him to come visit the state. He agreed, and Secretary Hayes and the Cabinet began to work their magic. Tim's group visited several locations in Kentucky and were our guests for a day at the Kentucky State Fair.

One evening we hosted the group for dinner at the Governor's Mansion, where we introduced them to the First Dog of the Commonwealth Tory, as well as other dogs owned by the staff. The officials enjoyed getting to know everyone in our "kennel" and a few days later, sent a bag of food for each dog. All the dogs immediately "wrote" thank-you notes to Tim and his group and signed them with individual paw prints.

Not long thereafter, the company concluded that Kentucky was the place they wanted to be, and executives selected a location in a certain community. Here's where that level of trust and strong personal relationships paid off.

After first embracing the idea of a new company locating in their community, community leaders grew concerned about potential odors from the plant and changed their mind. The company, they said, wasn't welcome after all.

We couldn't believe it! Here was a company whose products were sold in 70 countries around the world, which wanted to invest $85 million in a community and create 147 jobs there, and after committing to Kentucky, they were being slapped in the face by the community they had selected.

We immediately sat down with Tim and his group and talked candidly about the turn of events. We apologized, told them we were embarrassed, and urged them to give us another chance to find an acceptable location. Because of the relationship we had established, Tim and his group never flinched.

"We want to be in Kentucky," he said. "And we will continue to work with you to find the right location."

Not every company would have been as understanding, but the folks from Bedford Capital and Champion Petfoods were class acts, and they knew we were committed to their success. They also knew they could trust both what we said and what we said we would do.

The story has a happy ending. We did find another site, in the small town of Auburn close to Bowling Green, and the company announced the project in July 2014. In May 2016, the company opened its facility, which by then had grown to a $122-million investment. In November 2016, the company announced an expansion that would take that investment to $178 million and its employment to 200. It also is buying most of the raw ingredients that go into its pet food from local farmers, giving a significant boost to the local agricultural economy as well. This is what people call a real win-win situation.

So the lesson of the Champion Petfoods story is simple: Honesty, sincerity, and reliability are still the principles that win the race, more often than not. If folks know that you care about them and their success, they end up going the extra mile for you. The thank-you notes from Tory and the rest of the dogs didn't hurt either.

ONE JOB AT A TIME

The landing of the Toyota Motor Manufacturing plant by Governor Martha Layne Collins in 1984 was certainly a home run in the economic development world (actually, most would call Toyota a game-winning grand slam). Thousands of additional jobs have been created in Kentucky because of that huge success.

But such home runs are few and far between, and smart economic development offices understand that. During my eight years as governor, we had a number of large successes, but most of the jobs we created came in relatively small doses. That's the way it usually happens.

Recognizing that fact and embracing a one-job-at-a-time philosophy helps shape economic development strategies, and sometimes it requires a change in vision and tactics. For Kentucky, that was especially true. In fact, when the historic recession hit at the beginning of 2008, we took that philosophy even further back to the basics and wisely focused our efforts largely on keeping the jobs we already had.

We understood that companies during a recessionary period look to cut expenses and consolidate operations. That posed significant danger economically, because Kentucky had a lot to lose. We had a number of companies who also had locations outside the state, and we knew that they would be looking to consolidate those locations in some way. Our goal was to make sure that any consolidation resulted in jobs coming into Kentucky, not in jobs leaving.

The potential for harm was magnified by the fact that we had a large number of companies that had been in Kentucky for a long time, and they were approaching the point where they needed to renovate, update, and revise their facilities and technology. Unfortunately, when they came to us asking for help with those renovations, we had to tell them there was no help available because they were already located here in Kentucky.

The problem was our economic development incentives programs. When first adopted, they were among the most progressive in the nation. But over time, their effectiveness had eroded, and they were now seen as obsolete, complicated, and inflexible.

A particular weakness was our treatment of existing businesses. Numerous CEOs had told me during my 2007 campaign that under our existing program, companies in Kentucky that wanted to add jobs got little financial assistance from the state, because our programs were all geared toward bringing new companies into the state. But if they moved their investment across the border to another state, they would get the red-carpet treatment there. In fact, many of these companies said they were looking to reinvest in their Kentucky operations, and that other states, promising all kinds of financial assistance, were actively recruiting them.

That was a problem, and we needed to fix it.

As I said at the time, "Our current economic tools are rusty. They're dull. They're missing parts. And some of them are outdated. We're using hand tools in a power-tool world."

Larry Hayes, who was the newly named secretary of the state Cabinet for Economic Development, put together a team that surveyed the country to find the most progressive economic development programs.

The result was a new set of development tools called Incentives for a New Kentucky or INK. It was proposed as part of a broader economic legislative package during the 2009 session, but time ran out before it could win approval. Undaunted, I made INK part of the agenda for a special legislative session that June, and with bipartisan support, it became law.

The legislation had many parts, including economic development incentives, tourism incentives, and a few other things. But the heart of it had to do with helping businesses, and it consolidated many of our existing programs into a single, more flexible program called KBI, for the Kentucky Business Investment program.

In addition to helping new businesses come to Kentucky, as most programs do, it also gave the cabinet the flexibility of granting incentive packages to existing Kentucky companies that wanted to expand and create new jobs, as well as the ability to grant incentives to encourage new investment, even if no new jobs were created at that moment. We knew that if a company made a $100-million investment in their facility, more jobs would likely follow down the road.

The way we looked at it, a job was a job no matter where it came from. And whereas it's always exciting to land a brand-new company, we also wanted to reward those companies that long ago had committed to the commonwealth.

Well, the impact was immediate and substantial. During the remainder of my eight years, INK-related incentives—which were performance-based, meaning companies were rewarded only if they actually followed through on their plans—were approved for 783 projects that came to fruition. Those INK-related projects represented more than $12.2 billion in new investment and the potential for more than 63,000 new and retained jobs.

It goes to show that whether you add jobs by the hundreds, the dozens, or a few at a time, if you have the right tools, you can get to some pretty big numbers.

IT'S A BIG WORLD

During my years as governor, I made 33 trips to recruit international companies and find markets for Kentucky products, including visits to 18 different countries—among them Taiwan, Singapore, China, Japan, Germany, England, Italy, Austria, Spain, France, Sweden, Canada, the United Arab Emirates, and India.

Having been involved through the years with building Kentucky's strong ties to Japan and its business community, I saw India as an opportunity to begin building a similar relationship.

In October 2010, I became the first sitting Kentucky governor to visit India, meeting with business and government officials in New Delhi and Mumbai. What I found was a country yearning to expand to new markets. I wound up taking three trips to India, including the April 2011 trip to land New Delhi-based UFlex Ltd., a global leader in the flexible packaging industry.

The 30 or so hours Larry and I spent in New Delhi on that trip were packed with activity.

Immediately upon landing, after almost 20 hours in the air, we headed to a hotel to shower and shave, then to a temple to meet with a Hindu priest and pay our respects, and then—with a truck full of armed guards following—to a gated community and the home of UFlex Chairman Ashok Chaturvedi.

There we met the chairman's family, had drinks, toured his estate, and had dinner—all part of the traditional get-to-know-you-personally introduction to Indian business negotiations. And then, dressed in native clothing and marked with the traditional and symbolic red dot called a *tilaka* on our foreheads, we proceeded to his office for the signing ceremony, the formal finalization of a memorandum of understanding.

As a UFlex executive told us, Kentucky's agreement with the company was "like an Indian marriage. This is forever."

The next night, the deal was celebrated in a reception attended by a large crowd of Indian business folks and government officials at a large hotel in New Delhi.

Make no mistake: Kentucky's chief executive traveling to India in person was a sign of respect and commitment. And our host recognized it.

As a result, a few days later in Kentucky, we held a press conference to announce that UFlex was locating its first US manufacturing plant in Hardin County. The project, called Flex Films USA, was initially cast as a two-phase development that would bring 250 jobs and a $180-million investment, but it eventually grew to a $250-million investment.

UFlex had considered locations in a dozen states, narrowed the search to Ohio and Kentucky, and then chose the Bluegrass State.

How did little Kentucky win the competition? With personal attention, enthusiasm, and lightning-fast responsiveness to the company's concerns and questions.

Financially speaking, Ohio was the better option, according to Anantshree Chaturvedi, the director of Flex Films USA, who talked to the *Lane Report*'s Mark Green for a magazine article published in January 2015. But "we felt really wanted in Kentucky," Chaturvedi told Green. "I would write an e-mail at 3 a.m. Kentucky time and get a reply at 3:05."

And when decision time came in April 2011, and UFlex called both Kentucky and Ohio to see about a top state official traveling to India, Kentucky's interest was obvious.

Chaturvedi told Green, "Ohio said, 'We'll let you know,' and Steve [Beshear] said, 'When do we leave?'"

In the beginning, the media in Kentucky would try to make an issue out of my trips, as if we were taking vacations. In fact, coverage in one paper of my first trip to Japan ran with the banner headline that spoke of luxurious trips being "a Frankfort tradition." I wish one of those media outlets had sent a reporter to accompany us on these trips. I doubt they could have kept up. We ran ourselves ragged, running from town to town, meeting to meeting, event to event, both selling Kentucky as a place to do business and marketing its products.

You see, we didn't visit only big cities and stay in swank hotels. Sure, in Germany, for example, we met business officials in Berlin, Munich, and Hamburg. But we spent much more of our time in little vans, driving two and three hours into old towns of 15,000 or so people, where we visited the small- and medium-sized family-owned businesses that supplied the big auto manufacturers. We'd tour the facility, immerse ourselves in the history of the company, eat lunch in the home of the people who had started the company, and, above all, listen. In short, we met people where they were, and we invested time in finding out what made them tick and what they aspired to.

Typically, they were astounded that a governor from the United States had crossed the ocean and was standing there in their offices in their hometown. But for all their excitement, there was nothing glamorous about our strategy. It was time-consuming and exhausting. But because of that personal commitment, those companies that decided to invest in Kentucky knew that the day of their announcement was not the last time they'd see us. We were committed to making their business succeed.

That approach paid off. And as we began announcing new investments and new jobs, the media stopped being so cynical about the relatively minor costs of these trips, because the return on investment was phenomenal. In one two-year period late in my term, 35 percent of new investment and 27 percent of new jobs in Kentucky were created by companies based in places like China, India, Japan, Germany, France, and Canada.

I can draw a direct line between those trips and dozens of projects in Kentucky. For example, visits to Germany helped us recruit the Bilstein Group, iwis, and Dr. Schneider Automotive Systems. A trip to Japan helped us land Taica North America Corp. Meanwhile, Zotefoams Inc. decided to expand after my trip to the United Kingdom, as did L'Oréal US after my trip to France.

By 2015, of the nearly 400,000 full-time manufacturing, service, and technology jobs in Kentucky, more than one in five came from foreign-owned businesses.

We also used these foreign trips for another purpose: to help develop markets for Kentucky products, another part of our job-creation strategy. As I describe in another essay in this book, those efforts resulted in some interesting experiences—and some big numbers.

Folks who are uncomfortable with people who don't look like them, live like them, or worship like them need to understand that in the economic world, borders are transparent. Relationships bridge differences in culture, language, and ethnicity. Kentucky is competing in an international marketplace and must think globally.

Kentucky's success will continue only so long as the commonwealth presents itself to the world as a welcoming place for all peoples and cultures. Narrow-minded and partisan views on things like immigration and religion may appeal to someone's political base, but such positions will shut down our ability to attract and keep foreign companies in Kentucky, losing thousands of jobs in the process.

ACCUSED OF IDOLATRY

Here I was, locked in the middle of a tough re-election campaign against a formidable opponent, and I was suddenly confronted with a campaign manager's nightmare, times 70.

Just a week and a half before the 2011 election, I was invited in my role as governor to a *bhoomi poojan*, a formal and elaborate Hindu religious ceremony. Traditional in India's business community, this ceremony is designed to inaugurate or cleanse the ground before construction.

It was taking place in Elizabethtown, Kentucky—by all accounts for the first time in the state—and I was proud and excited.

The ground was being blessed so that a global firm based in New Delhi called UFlex Ltd. could build its first-ever manufacturing facility in the United States, a project that turned out to be a $250-million investment. I had traveled to India twice to recruit UFlex, and I hoped that its arrival would signal the start of a strong and harmonious relationship between Kentucky and the Indian business community, much like the lucrative bond Kentucky enjoyed with Japan and many Asian-based companies.

While in India, we had been treated with respect and hospitality, and I intended to return the favor for our Indian visitors. After all, long-term relationships are founded on and nurtured by the enthusiastic and respectful exchange of ideas, traditions, culture, and commerce. And Kentucky has a long history of accepting and integrating others' business customs.

Nevertheless, I recognized the political danger of the moment.

As governor, I routinely attended groundbreakings as a personal touch that strengthened relationships. And while I didn't know exactly what a Hindu ground-blessing would entail, I knew that my political opponents would misconstrue my participation in a highly stylized religious ceremony. The issues of immigration and terrorism had given birth throughout the United States to anxiety, anger, and fear—sometimes to an unhealthy and excessive degree—toward other cultures, religions, and traditions, especially those that originate in India's part of the world.

Some politicians like to feed that fear and then tap into it for political gain.

The timing of the ceremony was tied to the Hindu calendar, so I didn't even consider asking UFlex officials to delay the ceremony a few days until after the election. I also had no intention of skipping the ceremony or refusing to participate.

So, on that day, I kicked off my shoes, applied a red dot called a *tilaka* to my forehead, and climbed down into a "pit" to sit cross-legged on white cushions, surrounded by Indian officials in traditional garb. Arrayed before us were a ceremonial fire, burning incense, dishes of food, drink, flowers, and a shovel lying on several concrete building blocks. As a Hindu priest moved through the ceremony, an Indian official quietly explained to me the significance of events.

It was a beautiful ceremony, and I could tell my hosts were deeply into the moment. (And frankly, the longer it went on, any worry about political consequences in my mind gave way to worry about whether my cramped old legs would let me even stand up.)

After it was over, I was glad that I had participated, even though my opponent in the gubernatorial race likened my participation to "idolatry" a few days later.

"He's sitting down there with his legs crossed, participating in Hindu prayers with a dot on his forehead with incense burning around him. I don't know what the man was thinking," David Williams was quoted as saying in an article in the *Lexington Herald-Leader*. "To get down and get involved and participate in prayers to these polytheistic situations, where you have these Hindu gods that they are praying to, doesn't appear to me to be in line with what a governor of the Commonwealth of Kentucky ought to be doing."

The remarks were disappointing if not surprising. Tapping into the intolerance and prejudice that lurks beneath the surface in many parts of America (and *on* the surface in many parts, judging from the 2016 presidential campaign)—is a page right out of the national GOP political playbook.

And it didn't go unnoticed.

Political observers called it the sign of a desperate campaign, and religious leaders across the country condemned my opponent's reaction.

The national Hindu American Foundation said the reaction "conjures up the lowest sentiments of exclusion and bigotry." And, interestingly, my campaign immediately received donations from 50 or more Americans of Indian descent.

Many business officials, like me, disagreed with his premise, thinking instead that showing respect to other cultures as a way of welcoming international investment is *exactly* "in line with what a governor of the Commonwealth of Kentucky ought to be doing."

The fact is that international companies are a pillar of Kentucky's economy, and recruiting them requires thought, effort, and mutual respect. You can't expect executives to invest millions of dollars in Kentucky and send top-ranking people here if we don't make it a welcoming place.

Kentucky is richer not only financially but also culturally and intellectually because of the work of governors throughout history to build relationships in other countries. Participating in symbolic and ceremonial traditions is what is required of Kentucky's top business recruiter.

HOUSEBOATS AND
ASIAN CARP

In Dubai, I cruised around the harbor on a Kentucky-made houseboat owned by an Indian businessman.

In Wickliffe, Kentucky, I ate Asian carp taken from Kentucky Lake and processed by a Wickliffe processing plant started by a Chinese native who left a seafood business in Los Angeles to sell fish to the Far East.

And in London, England, I watched in amusement as Britons visiting a Kentucky bourbon booth hand-dipped their own miniature bottles of Maker's Mark in a vat of red wax to create that iconic, individualized seal. Unable to resist, most got only a few steps away from the booth before they broke open the seal in order to sample the famous brown liquid.

So what do those experiences have in common?

They all came about because of our aggressive and strategic effort to develop new markets for Kentucky products.

When many governors think of job creation, their attention automatically zeroes in on recruiting a new business to locate in their states, investing money in a new facility that needs workers to operate. That obviously is one piece of the puzzle, but there are many others that some states overlook.

One of those often-missing pieces is growing the exports of

a state. How does that relate to job creation? When you think about it, it is pretty simple. If you are successful in creating a new market for the goods of a Kentucky company, that company will eventually need more people to make more of those goods to sell. So, more Kentucky jobs.

After successfully overhauling our business incentives program, we turned our attention to this piece of the puzzle. In 2009, Kentucky ranked sixth in the nation in exports per capita. For a small, non-border, non-coastal state, this was a huge achievement. But we saw a significant opportunity to improve our performance.

In December 2010, under the leadership of Larry Hayes, secretary of the Kentucky Cabinet for Economic Development, we devised the Kentucky Export Initiative, a new program designed to help small- and medium-sized businesses sell goods in other countries. We brought together our leading international trade organizations including the state cabinet, the Kentucky World Trade Center, the US Department of Commerce, the Kentucky Chamber of Commerce, the Northern Kentucky International Trade Association, and the US Chamber's TradeRoots program.

More than anything, this was an educational process, because many of the small- and even medium-sized companies who thought about exporting were intimidated by the prospect. They didn't know how to locate new markets; how to assess their viability; how to gain entrance into those markets; how to identify potential distributors, agents, and end users; how to navigate issues related to compliance, logistics, and legalities; and how to obtain sometimes necessary financing to make it all happen.

So KEI had many pieces, including technical help, trade fairs, loans and grants, and state-sponsored trade missions that brought Kentucky companies to Canada, Mexico, and the United Kingdom. After recruiting Kentucky companies to visit those markets, we set up meetings there with officials in those industries who had an interest in Kentucky products. State officials, meanwhile, got to know the leaders of that country or province and began building relationships that might benefit us in the future.

Turns out, these export assistance efforts in Kentucky fell on fertile ground, resulting in a sort of show-them-how-and-they-will-go phenomenon.

Thanks to KEI, we wound up setting export records for the next five years in a row, from 2011 through 2015. In 2010, we exported $19.4 billion. That grew to $20.1 billion the following year and eventually to $27.6 billion in 2015—a 42 percent increase since the implementation of KEI.

By far, Kentucky's top export was aerospace products and parts, followed by motor vehicles and parts, pharmaceuticals and medicines, rubber-related products, and basic chemicals. Canada was our biggest destination for goods, followed by the United Kingdom, Mexico, China, and France. In a five-year period, automotive exports rose 163 percent, exports of bourbon and other distilled products rose 113 percent, and aerospace exports rose 65 percent.

But the stories of lesser-known Kentucky products finding markets were endless, diverse, and incredible. We helped a Louisville brewery sell beer in Canada, a Hart County company that made grilling tools get into Wal-Mart Europe, and a Wayne County company that manufactured houseboats make connections in Dubai.

The houseboat story is a good example of thinking outside the box.

The houseboat building business was on the rocks because of the historic recession that hit us in 2008. People were simply unwilling or unable to spend money on luxury items such as these large houseboats. As a result, several of our Kentucky companies went bankrupt, and the rest were in serious trouble.

Then suddenly, an Indian businessman operating out of Dubai in the United Arab Emirates contacted a houseboat company located near Lake Cumberland with a proposition: Make him houseboats that he could sell to wealthy people in the UAE. Our Kentucky company was faced with an exciting but daunting task: figuring out how to ship houseboats to Dubai and how to be sure that they got paid.

Enter our Economic Development Cabinet, which worked with the Indian businessman and the Kentucky company to overcome obstacles and set up a deal.

The net result? About a year later, while I was on a trade mission to Dubai, Larry and I had breakfast on a Kentucky-made houseboat in the Dubai Harbor with the Indian businessman, who then took us on a tour around the harbor to see much bigger boats.

Who would have ever thought that a Kentucky governor would get to have such a surreal experience?

Another exotic example of thinking outside the box to create jobs from exports involved the Asian carp. This invasive species (actually three species) has infiltrated our Western Kentucky lakes and rivers and has created a threat to other aquatic life. The carp reproduce at alarming rates, grow to prodigious size, and consume food sources usually eaten by our domestic fish population, including game fish like bass.

In addition, they pose a danger to fishermen, recreational boaters, and water skiers. The noise and vibrations of boat motors agitates one of the species—the silver carp. Fish by the dozens jump out of the water right in front of a moving boat or water skier. Can you imagine being hit in the chest by a 40-pound fish while you are moving at 15 to 20 miles per hour?

We turned this bad situation into a win-win solution. A couple of startup companies in Western Kentucky began to process Asian carp and market them to the Far East, where they're used for food and food products, including imitation seafood, fishmeal, fish oil, minced fish, and fillets.

We helped them get on their feet and establish their business model. Today, they are hiring local anglers to provide them with a steady supply of Asian carp, which they dress, fast freeze, and ship overseas.

One company almost immediately became the nation's biggest exporter of the fish, with sales throughout Asia and in places like Bangladesh and the Middle East.

So we are better managing the Asian carp population and creating jobs in the process.

All because we made it our mission to export Kentucky products—no matter what they were.

BOURBON AND HORSEPOWER

When I gave speeches in other states, I had a standard intro I often used to break the ice.

"Most of you probably know very little about Kentucky. You have probably heard of the Kentucky Derby. Thoroughbred horses. Kentucky Fried Chicken. College basketball. And hopefully, most of you have sipped some of that brown liquid called Kentucky bourbon! Folks, we have 4.3 million people in the commonwealth. Right now, we have more than 5 million barrels of bourbon aging in warehouses. So that's one for each Kentuckian, and then we share the rest with the world."

Then I would immediately segue into what I was invited to talk about: how Kentucky was building a new reputation as a leader on issues like health care, education reform, or job creation.

Well, the references to alcohol and fast horses were always good for smiles and a few laughs. But the glibness belied a serious point: The equine and bourbon industries are two of Kentucky's signature industries for more than symbolic reasons—they also represent multi-billion-dollar sources of jobs, tax revenue, business investment, and tourist attractions.

In other words, here in Kentucky, bourbon isn't just a classy drink and horses aren't just animals that prance in an arena or run fast around a track. That's why we invested so much time, money, energy, and attention into keeping both of those industries strong, and why both industries enjoyed unparalleled periods of growth in impact and prestige during my administration.

Jobs don't just come from manufacturing or the service industries.

Kentucky's tourism industry, for example, generated $13.7 billion in economic impact during 2015, an increase of 5 percent over the year before. Altogether, the industry supported more than 186,000 jobs, as Tourism, Arts, and Heritage Cabinet Secretaries Marcheta Sparrow and Bob Stewart often reminded me.

Much of that had to do with the state's natural beauty and features like lakes, caves, cliffs, and rivers. It also had to do with our many cultural attractions. But those numbers also had to do with bourbon and horses.

As governor, I attended so many groundbreakings and ribbon-cuttings related to the bourbon industry that I used to joke that I was going to have to create a separate Cabinet for All Things Bourbon.

According to a 2017 report from the Kentucky Distillers' Association (KDA), the industry saw $485 million in capital construction from 2011 until 2015, including new and expanded distilleries, warehouses, bottling facilities, and tourism centers. New projects worth a total of $620 million were planned for 2016 through 2020.

At one such groundbreaking in 2015, I noted how in the time it takes to age a Kentucky-distilled bourbon—about two years—the industry had nearly doubled its workforce, tripled its number of distilleries, and set modern records for exports and barrel inventories.

The KDA-generated economic impact study reported that the bourbon industry in 2016 had an $8.5-billion economic impact; generated up to 17,500 jobs, either directly or indirectly; and created $190 million in state and local tax revenue.

Thanks to an array of new single-barrel and small-batch boutique bourbons, barrel production had increased from 455,000 barrels in 1999 to 1.9 million in 2015.

Meanwhile, distilleries on the Kentucky Bourbon Trail and Kentucky Bourbon Trail Craft Tour reported more than one million visitors in 2016. More than 70 percent of those visitors came from outside the state, the KDA said, and they each on average spent $1,200 during their stay.

Oh, and the number of barrels of bourbon aging in Kentucky? That had climbed to 6.7 million in 2016.

When I was recruiting jobs in countries like Japan, India, or France, it always stunned me how many executives wanted to talk about bourbon. That led to another oft-used talking point: "Ninety-five percent of the world's bourbon is made in Kentucky … and all of the rest is counterfeit!"

From the state's economic development standpoint, we went out of our way to use incentives, infrastructure investment, export marketing help, and changes to state law where needed and appropriate to encourage and facilitate development of the industry. And I made sure I attended as many announcements, groundbreakings, and ribbon-cuttings as I could.

As for horses, well, they're part of our heritage, too. In fact, you could say they're part of our very identity.

Kentucky's home to about a quarter of a million horses. We ride them for fun, we work them, we show them, and most of all, we race them and we bet on them. Let me tell you, when you're standing in the winner's circle at the Kentucky Derby with millions of people watching and you hold that trophy in your hands and you present it to the winning owner—as I had the privilege to do eight times—it's difficult not to get overwhelmed by the history, euphoria, glory, and magnitude of the moment.

There's a reason that Kentucky is called the Horse Capital of the World.

We're proud of that title, and we worked hard to maintain it. Again, the title wasn't just symbolic. A 2012 study of the equine industry measured its economic impact in the commonwealth at almost $3 billion and said the industry generated more than 41,000 jobs here.

Under my predecessor, Governor Ernie Fletcher, Kentucky won the right to host the 2010 Alltech FEI World Equestrian Games. It was the first time the games—a sort of Olympics for horse riders—were held outside Europe, and the first time all eight equestrian disciplines were held in the same location, in this case, the Kentucky Horse Park. It was a massive undertaking, but Kentucky's performance was—in the words of the FEI president—"nothing short of miraculous."

Tickets were sold or given to nearly 420,000 visitors from 63 countries and all 50 states. Millions around the world watched on TV. The total economic impact of the games on the commonwealth was more than $201 million, with $128 million of that in direct visitor spending.

A $45-million indoor arena and a $25-million outdoor stadium built for the games have greatly increased events that can be held at the Kentucky Horse Park, including the prestigious National Horse Show beginning in 2011. As I explain elsewhere in this book, I had to reallocate state park funding to make this happen.

But then Kentucky is used to hosting world-famous horse events. Not only do we put on the Kentucky Derby and the Rolex Three-Day Event every year, but we also hosted the Breeders' Cup three times during my administration: in 2010, 2011, and 2015.

But being Horse Capital of the World isn't only about showy events. Through the work of the Kentucky Horse Racing Commission and the Kentucky Equine Drug Research Council, the commonwealth during my administration was at the forefront of addressing the crisis of trust caused by the use of performance-enhancing and performance-affecting drugs. This included both tangible steps taken within the state and lobbying on a national level for broadbased reform that included not only uniform medication rules but also common testing rules and procedures.

There was a reason I was invited to Saratoga, New York, in August 2015 to speak before the Jockey Club on this issue. I told the Roundtable Conference on Horse Racing, "There is no state in this nation with more at stake, both economically and emotionally, as our industry wrestles with the issue of medication and its impact on safety, integrity, and trust."

I then laid out the steps Kentucky had taken within the state and the steps we were urging the nation to take. Because when you're a leader in an industry, you're expected to come up with solutions.

The way I looked at it, Kentucky was the international home for bourbon and fast horses, and we weren't about to give that up.

———

Another thing we weren't about to give up related to horsepower of a different sort—our status as one of the nation's leading auto manufacturers, another of Kentucky's signature industries.

In 2011, Kentucky ranked fifth in the nation in production of cars, light trucks, and SUVs. In 2012, we were fourth. And by mid-2013, we became No. 3, behind only Michigan and Ohio. On a per capita basis, Kentucky was No. 1 and remains so as of the writing of this book.

According to the Kentucky Automotive Industry Association, which we created in 2014 to pull together the industry in Kentucky, more than 1.3 million vehicles were made in Kentucky in 2015. Lined up end to end, those cars would stretch from Seattle to Miami. These include well-known brands like Ford's Escape, Expedition, and F-250 Super Duty pickup; Lincoln's Navigator and MKC; GMC's Chevrolet Corvette; and Toyota's Camry, Camry Hybrid, Avalon, Avalon Hybrid, and Lexus ES 350.

Kentucky is home to more than 480 automotive-related manufacturing, service, and technology establishments, including four major auto assembly plants. Altogether, the industry employs almost 90,000 people in Kentucky.

We were proud of those numbers, and we worked hard to make them grow. The KAIA says that since January 2010, more than 330 motor vehicle-related projects have been announced in Kentucky, adding more than 20,000 jobs and $4.5 *billion* in capital investment.

During my years as governor, major expansions and/or retooling were announced at all four of our major assembly plants: Ford's Kentucky Truck Plant and Louisville Assembly Plant; Toyota's Georgetown production plant, the company's largest outside of Japan; and the General Motors Bowling Green Assembly Plant, the only place where Corvettes are made.

My staff and I took an array of steps to smooth the way for those projects and to make sure our automakers knew how much we valued them.

When Ford was consolidating across the country in 2010 because of the historic recession, we flew to Detroit on more than one occasion to push the case for keeping its Louisville plants, including the one that began in 1913 by making Model Ts. When Congress targeted Toyota over safety recalls, we stood up and insisted the hearings be fair. We helped broker agreements between labor and management when necessary, and we partnered in investments made by all three manufacturers.

And we kept working to the very end. Just seven days before I left office, the banner headline in the *Courier-Journal* touted Ford's announcement that it was investing $1.3 billion and would create 2,000 new jobs at its truck plant in Louisville.

Simply put, whether it came to horses, cars, trucks, or bourbon, we in Kentucky recognized the value of our signature industries, and we worked to keep them strong.

THE *I* WORDS

Kentucky doesn't have the reputation of California's Silicon Valley or North Carolina's famed Research Triangle, but the activities and research occurring outside the public eye in offices and laboratories across the commonwealth could change the world.

I'm talking about things like manufacturing miniature satellites and selling space for experiments on the space shuttle.

I'm talking about things like solar cells, simulated electronic warfare, drug-delivery systems, potential cures for cancer, and control of space vehicles.

Each year, I learned more about some of that cutting-edge work when I either attended the BIO International Convention in places like San Diego and Boston or announced the newest recipients of Kentucky's unique version of a high-tech grant program.

As the largest global event for the biotechnology industry, BIO is the ultimate place for networking, partnering, and promoting, and each year, Kentucky hosted a governor's reception that was the longest-running such get-together of all the states.

One of the reasons the Kentucky "booth" got so much traffic was because the state had an aggressive program to match grants given to companies through the federal SBIR-STTR programs. Short for "Small Business Innovation Research" and "Small Business Technology Transfer," these programs are designed to foster high-tech entrepreneurship and commercialization.

Through 2015, the end of my second term, Kentucky's SBIR-STTR program had—in its nine years—awarded almost $58 million in matching grants to support 116 companies, which had also received more than $104 million in federal grants. Because of those matches, 42 innovative companies—the kind of companies every state wants to land and brags about when it does—had moved to Kentucky or were planning to do so.

So, what do I mean by cutting-edge research?

Let me give you examples of companies that received awards, and the types of work the grants were helping to fund:

- Bexion Pharmaceuticals was testing a treatment for one of the most common and aggressive brain cancers in humans.

- TiER1 Performance Solutions was working on software to support NASA in designing space vehicles and mission control centers.

- Gismo Therapeutics, Inc. was developing a new way to disrupt the inflammation cycle of rheumatoid arthritis.

- Lakota Technical Solutions was developing a software-based tool to more accurately simulate electronic warfare scenarios.

- Advanced Genomic Technology LLC of Louisville was developing a blood test to diagnose Alzheimer's before people notice symptoms.

- Innovative Diagnostics Inc. of Lexington was creating a device to determine periodontal health using saliva.

- And Mercury Data Systems Inc. of Lexington was working on an inertial measurement unit to make missile systems more accurate.

I could go on and on, because this was amazing stuff. Whether you call it "cutting edge" or "pushing the envelope" or "thinking outside the box," these companies epitomized what I referred to in speeches as the *I* words: imagination, innovation, invention, intellect, ingenuity, ideas, and inspiration.

Companies in the SBIR-STTR program put the lie to the backward image that Hollywood and others have created for Kentucky. Instead, they serve as inspiration to those Kentucky children who are conditioned to embrace an inferiority complex that keeps them from having the courage to reach for the literal stars.

And they also serve as a lesson for leaders making decisions that will dictate the future of this state: Kentucky is founded on agriculture and manufacturing, and those will forever remain core parts of our economy. But the sophisticated farms and factories of the future will be scarcely recognizable to those of us making decisions here today. We need to not only encourage and foster the use of new technology and practices in these traditional sectors, but we also need to nurture the growth of Kentucky's burgeoning biotech community. If we don't, we will be left behind.

WE'RE NO. 1

When I found out in early 2015 that Kentucky had finished first in the nation in large economic development projects per capita for the year 2014, I felt like college basketball coaches John Calipari and Rick Pitino.

And the news was too good not to share.

So I took the championship trophy, the Governor's Cup—a large silver cup awarded by *Site Selection* magazine—on the road to celebrate with the folks largely responsible for Kentucky's No. 1 showing: business and government officials in our cities and small communities.

Everywhere I went, folks were full of excitement and momentum, and above all, fiercely proud of the progress we'd made together in recovering from the recession.

In Owensboro, the winner of the 2009 Emerging Ventures business plan competition—Dalisha's Desserts—baked a cake in the shape of the cup.

In Erlanger, the Brainy Bots robotics team from Ryle High School had their robot deliver the cup to the speakers' platform.

In Bardstown, the Stephen Foster Singers serenaded us with "My Old Kentucky Home."

And in many other towns, themed gifts reflected pride in local attractions and features: a goodie basket in Mount Sterling, a T-shirt in Danville, a quilt in Ashland, and a picture of Maysville's downtown.

And the picture-taking: It seemed that everybody wanted their photo taken with the cup—especially in those communities that also made *Site Selection*'s list of top-performing metropolitan and micropolitan areas.

In all, I visited about a dozen and a half communities with the Governor's Cup trophy.

At each stop, I called attention to the economic development announcements we had made in that community since 2008, and I bragged about Kentucky's overall numbers: In 2014 alone, for example, Kentucky announced more than 350 new industry location and expansion projects worth $3.7 billion in investment.

As these projects announced in 2014 came to fruition, they stood to create nearly 15,000 jobs.

That was the most yearly business investment in Kentucky since the state started keeping track nearly 30 years ago.

Site Selection counted only projects that had one or more of these characteristics: capital investment of $1 million or more, 20 or more new jobs created, and 20,000 or more square feet of new space. In 2014, Kentucky attracted 258 such qualifying facilities.

Per capita, those numbers were the highest in the nation.

Site Selection—whose magazine cover carried the headline "A League of Their Own" and depicted me as a baseball player holding a bat—praised Kentucky for a "state and local economic development infrastructure that is short on bureaucracy and long on getting businesses operational quickly."

But the incredible thing is that, the very next year, we blew that number away. For the year 2015, Kentucky attracted 285 qualifying projects, according to the magazine. That also topped the nation on a per capita basis.

And so Kentucky won the Governor's Cup for the second year in a row, my last year in office. When the award was announced in early 2016, I, of course, was out of office by then, and so I couldn't take the cup on tour. But I wanted to, because

Kentucky's local business and elected officials deserved to share in the glory. And they deserved gratitude. They had worked hard alongside us to create vibrant environments in which businesses wanted to invest, and together we had succeeded. That was fact, and no one could argue with it.

You see, the Governor's Cup wasn't based on popularity, opinion, or potential. It was confirmation and recognition of facts, figures, and performance—development that had actually happened.

Winning the cup not just once but two years in a row demonstrated that by working together, by not worrying about who got the credit, by creating a thoughtful strategy, and by bringing a personal touch to negotiations, we had been able to turn Kentucky's economy around and become a national leader in job creation.

And we had the shiny silver trophy to prove it.

Section V

EDUCATION

LOOK HOW FAR
WE'VE COME

At one time, Kentucky's collective school experience was cause for embarrassment, plagued by low test scores, high dropout rates, weak curriculum, falling-down buildings, and political corruption.

No longer.

Over my eight years as governor, our state education system significantly improved its national reputation for innovation and reform. When our educators attended conferences, more often than not they were asked, "How did you do it?" and "What is Kentucky working on these days?"

The answer to the second question from 2007 to 2015 was "a lot."

After all, during that time, Kentucky was the first state to adopt Common Core State Standards and the second state to adopt the Next Generation Science Standards, we doubled our college and career readiness rates, and we leapfrogged many other states with massive gains in our graduation rates.

Consequently, I received the "Greatest Education Governor Award" in 2011 from the National Education Association, and in summer 2015, the Education Commission of the States selected the Kentucky Board of Education as the winner of the Frank Newman Award for State Innovation.

And we did this with a budget squeezed almost to suffocation by the tight vise of a national recession.

I'm intensely proud of these accomplishments. On some basic level, every governor wants to be known as the "education governor." But for me, the value of education was ingrained in me from the earliest age growing up in tiny Dawson Springs.

My father completed about a year and a half of college before quitting to work. My mother never went to college at all. But for them there was never a question that my two brothers (Bob and David), two sisters (Nancy and Mary Ann), and I would pursue some form of higher education. Our parents pushed us hard in high school, so much so that four of us were the valedictorians of our classes and one was salutatorian.

My sisters went to Murray State University and the University of Minnesota. My brothers and I went to the University of Kentucky, which for folks like us was like going to Harvard. To pay for college, we took out loans, we worked, and our parents mortgaged and re-mortgaged their house.

Education was that important.

I went on to earn a law degree, and I married a woman who became a teacher.

Jane entered the profession a little naïve and with idealistic notions, but she was shocked at how shaky the academic foundation was for many of her high school students. Some struggled even to read.

Kentucky has made significant and measurable progress since those days, beginning with the transformative Kentucky Education Reform Act of 1990. With KERA, Kentucky took a stand against failure. Pushed by a court ruling and energized by widespread community support, we raised taxes and created from scratch a system whose goal was to give all children in the commonwealth a chance at a quality education, regardless of income, race, or geographic location.

But when I ran for governor in 2007, it was clear that more work needed to be done. We'd made progress, but the world had continued to change dramatically. The fundamental foundation of knowledge and skills that our graduates needed to function—and succeed—had expanded far beyond what we could have possibly imagined during the education reform effort of 1990. And as the world grew increasingly sophisticated, other states weren't standing still. Kentucky's competitive position was slipping, and we were at risk of being left behind once again.

We needed not only new energy but also new strategies.

My campaign material featured an array of aggressive plans—particularly for expanding access to preschool and kindergarten for Kentucky's most vulnerable children—but unfortunately, I walked into office just as the global recession hit with all its fury.

It cost me focus and resources. Of necessity, my focus shifted to helping our families and businesses survive and our economy recover. And our budget went south in a hurry. Rather than invest, I had to cut. Deeply. In fact, I was forced to cut spending some 15 times during my eight years (a total of about $1.6 billion). But I'm proud to say I never cut funding for teaching in our classrooms. I just refused to do it.

It wasn't easy. To protect K–12 classroom funding, I had to cut many other agencies even more deeply, and I'm sure even some of my cabinet secretaries resented it. My desire to protect education became an issue in the 2011 gubernatorial election when my Republican opponent—the sitting Senate president—set up a legislative showdown over my refusal to make cuts across the board.

I won that showdown, thanks to firm conviction and support from House Speaker Greg Stumbo and a Democratic-controlled House. A few years later, in 2014, I persuaded the general assembly to approve a two-year budget proposal that enabled us to increase per-pupil K–12 funding to its highest level ever; to reverse damaging cuts to funds for teacher training, textbooks, school safety, and Extended School Services; and to expand preschool services to potentially more than 5,100 more children.

"We must answer a fundamental question," I said in my budget address. "Does Kentucky march aggressively into the future, or do we cower under the covers as the world leaves us behind? Do we lead, or are we too afraid to even follow? ... This budget proposal clearly gives my answer: We can and we must build a more vibrant Kentucky."

See, that's where I don't understand the strategy of governors like Sam Brownback in Kansas. He worked with Republican legislators to make massive tax cuts in 2012 and 2013 despite warnings that, unfortunately, came true. At the same time Kentucky was increasing money for education, Kansas was reducing funding for its schools, requiring many to cut programs and shut their doors early for the summer in 2015.

I felt the same disappointment and puzzlement when I heard that Kentucky's new governor, despite inheriting a budget surplus, was proposing 9 percent cuts to K–12 education programs in his first budget in order to free up even more money for public pensions. The cuts would have meant reductions in critical things like preschool, textbooks, family resource centers, school safety, teacher training, afterschool programs, and career and technical education. The proposed cuts were so draconian that a longtime administrator from the Kentucky School Boards Association called them "probably the most severe across-the-board proposal for K–12 that I can recall," according to the *Lexington Herald-Leader*.

If that's what Kansas wants, so be it. But that's not what Kentucky needs. The path to a brighter, more competitive future requires *investing* in schoolchildren, not walking away from them. Thank goodness, the Democratic-controlled state House opposed the education cuts and ultimately preserved the K–12 budget.

But money was only one of the challenges in education during the early years of my first term. While we worked to improve Kentucky's economy as a way to boost state revenues, we also took aggressive steps to improve the effectiveness of our schools.

Twenty years after Kentucky's heralded education reform act, I brought together the education community and its stakeholders for an in-depth discussion called Transforming Education in Kentucky, billed as a revisit of KERA. After a year of forums and research, the TEK task force published 35 recommendations in February 2011 on how Kentucky could better prepare its students for success in the 21st century. They included an emphasis on kindergarten readiness, expanding access to preschool programs, raising the dropout age, expanding dual-credit programs in high school, and creating better career and technical education.

By the time I left office, we had made significant progress on every one of those issues.

But to do that, we needed good leadership to oversee the education of our roughly 675,000 public schoolchildren in Kentucky.

When the Kentucky Board of Education hired Terry Holliday in July 2009, fortune smiled on the state. Holliday—who had been named Superintendent of the Year in North Carolina—was a progressive and aggressive leader, and we saw issues in much the same way. He also wasn't afraid to shake things up. (Holliday later won a couple of big-name awards for his work in Kentucky. In 2014, the National Association of State Boards of Education named him Policy Leader of the Year, and in 2015, the National Board for Professional Teaching Standards gave him its prestigious James A. Kelly Award.)

Holliday came to Kentucky on the heels of the passage of Senate Bill 1 in 2009, which created urgency by establishing an aggressive agenda focused on student readiness and accountability.

I worked with Holliday and leaders in the Education and Workforce Development Cabinet to bring resources, structure, innovation, and urgency to Kentucky's education system. We also worked to harness the energy of Kentucky's veritable army of education warriors, an army made up of concerned parents, business officials, civic leaders, social service agency workers, some dedicated legislators, policy experts at the Kentucky Department of Education, and the administrators and teachers themselves. One of those unsung heroes working alongside Holliday at the Department of Education was my sister Mary Ann Miller, who began there as a policy adviser in 1987, later also served as executive director of the Kentucky Board of Education, and is currently chief of staff for Holliday's successor, Stephen Pruitt. She proved invaluable to both Holliday and me in this effort.

We also benefitted from unprecedented cooperation between our K–12 system, led by Holliday, and our postsecondary system, headed by Bob King.

Most importantly, when the communities themselves engaged, great things happened.

Commissioner Holliday loved to hold up the school district in Floyd County as one such shining example. The district had a troubled history. As Holliday pointed out in a blog post in October 2014, the state had taken over management of the district in 1998 because of horrendous test scores that ranked it among the lowest performers in the state. The state ran the district for seven years.

But with leadership, a vision, strong support from the community, and a new attitude that did not tolerate excuses, the district began to turn things around. Still, as recently as the 2011–12 school year, Floyd County's accountability scores ranked it in the 41st percentile in the state.

As of the writing of this book, it's in the 98th percentile and holding, and as Holliday pointed out, its graduation rates and college and career readiness rate were among the highest in Kentucky.

When the new scores came out in 2014, Holliday wrote of attending a major celebration in a high school gym filled with students, parents, school staff, cheerleaders, and bands. "I have never seen a celebration of academic achievement like I saw in Floyd County," he wrote.

To help districts like that, we tried to set the tone at the state level with innovative policy, new laws, and investments. As I've described in other essays, we made early childhood education a priority and became the first state to answer President Obama's call to join the 21st century by raising our compulsory school age from 16 to 18, changing a standard that had been on the books since before the Great Depression.

But those were just two of many large initiatives. Others included:

- Spurred by the requirements of Senate Bill 1, we became the first state to adopt and implement the Common Core State Standards (known here as the Kentucky Academic Standards) for English/language arts and mathematics in 2010, and three years later, became the second state to adopt the Next Generation Science Standards. (When a legislative panel rejected the science standards partly out of concern over the teaching of evolution and climate change, I overrode its decision.) Despite critics who conjure up all sorts of crazy descriptions about Common Core, these initiatives simply created a set of academic guidelines designed by states to clearly describe what students need to know before they complete each grade level. They bridged the disconnect between student learning in the K–12 system and expectations in higher education and the workforce. Kentucky teachers were heavily involved in designing and implementing training materials related to core content and local curriculum. Here at home, Kentucky's Academic Standards promote creative and critical thinking (rather than memorization), communications skills, and collaborative problem solving—exactly the type of skills that today's jobs require.

- We increased Kentucky's high school graduation rate to rank among the nation's leaders. It's impossible to compare Kentucky's past with its present, since a few years ago, we began using a new federally required definition of graduation rates called the cohort rate, which was developed by the National Governors Association. But it's clear that Kentucky has made great strides and that the improvement has continued to be steady. Using the cohort rate, Kentucky's 2013 graduation rate was 86.1 percent, above the national average of 81.4 percent. Kentucky's class of 2014 reached an all-time high graduation rate of 87.5 percent. In 2015, that had increased to 88 percent and in 2016, 88.6 percent.

- We more than doubled college and career readiness rates. When the state first started measuring college and career readiness in 2009, only 30 percent of Kentucky's high school graduates were ready for the next step—whether that was entering the military, finding a job right out of high school, or going to a two- or four-year college. By 2014, that rate was 62.5 percent. By 2015, 66.9 percent. And by 2016, 68.5 percent.

- We implemented a new model of career and technical education (CTE) that emphasizes innovation and integration of core academic areas, 21st-century skills, and full-time CTE classes. Today's CTE classes are no longer the shop classes of yesteryear, but viable alternative pathways that prepare them for the technical world of advanced manufacturing and other highly skilled jobs.

- We also embraced dual-track apprentice-style programs that allowed students to earn work experience and pay while also going to school.

- We rolled out a new teacher evaluation system called the Professional Growth and Effectiveness System. Unlike the old system, which focused on evaluation and punishment, the new system emphasizes continuous improvement in teaching skills. By the way, as of this writing, Kentucky ranks ninth in the nation in the percentage of teachers who are nationally certified.

- We pushed for and signed into law transfer credit and dual credit initiatives. The first smoothed the transfer of credits from two-year community and technical colleges to four-year institutions, and the second let more students in high school earn college credit for approved high school courses. The effect of both was to smooth the path to a college degree at a lower cost to families.

- We created an online School Report Card to give parents and others access to data and information on the school level for things like test performance, teacher qualifications, student safety, finances, and parent involvement. This is transparency like never before, and it helps answer whether a particular school is doing the job it's supposed to be doing.

- And we strengthened the program that gives aggressive and effective support to struggling school districts with the use of on-site personnel, including planners called educational recovery leaders and educational recovery specialists who bring expertise in math and literacy.

How do Kentucky and its students compare with other states? Quite favorably and a lot better than we used to.

In the national Quality Counts annual report card put together by the publication *Education Week*, Kentucky ranked as high as 10th in the country during my years as governor. The evaluation tracked dozens of indicators in areas like K–12 achievement, school finance, the teaching profession, and students' chance of success.

Within the area of K–12 achievement, on the National Assessment of Educational Progress, Kentucky students outscored the nation as a whole at most levels in the subjects of math, science, and reading. In fact, a 2013 Harvard University study ranked Kentucky eighth in the nation in improvement in student performance over the previous two decades. And Kentucky was called "a beacon to all other states" in the 2015 "Building a Grad Nation" report because we had all but closed the gap in graduation rates between low-income students and all other students.

Now, is there work still to be done? Yes, lots of it. A 68.5 percent college and career readiness rate might be more than double what it used to be, but that means that still almost one-third of our graduates, according to this measure, aren't prepared for what comes next. Even an 88.6 percent graduation rate means that more than 1 in 10 kids aren't getting a high school diploma. And according to the Common Kindergarten Entry Screener, 50 percent of our children entering kindergarten still aren't ready for that work.

Nevertheless, Kentucky has come a long way. Such a long way that many people still don't believe it. Skeptics and naysayers—most of whom live *in* Kentucky—read about our progress and give some version of "Yes, but ..."

To them I say, "But *what?*"

There was a time when Kentuckians, disheartened by their state ranking near the bottom of many education measures, would say "Thank God for Mississippi" or whichever state happened to be below us. Today, however, I think we should start comparing ourselves to the *leading* states in the nation, because we are becoming one of them.

EVERY CHILD DESERVES
A CHANCE

Imagine two kindergarten classes.

In one class, the kids are bright-eyed and healthy. They know the alphabet, their numbers, and a little rudimentary math (basic addition and subtraction). They can even read a little bit, and are able hold a conversation with adults. They're confident, curious, creative, and energetic. In short, they *want* to learn.

In the other class, the kids are just the opposite. Several have health problems, like toothaches, asthma, and lingering sickness caused by poor nutrition. They've never been read to, and they don't know their letters or numbers and can't spell their names. They're either aggressive with their classmates and teachers to the point of being out of control, or they're too timid to interact, showing little interest in anything around them. To summarize, they're completely unengaged in the process of learning.

You don't have to be a kindergarten teacher to predict the outcome of the year: One class will spend the year learning, the other will struggle. When the students enter first grade the following year, the same gap will exist, only it'll be wider. In later grades, the gap will be wider still. By the time they graduate, the difference between the students will be shocking.

Barring aggressive intervention, the kids who begin their school careers behind are likely to remain behind the rest of their lives—and I'm referring not only to things like GPAs and ACT scores but more far-reaching things like career potential. When they enter the workforce, the quality of the job opportunities available to the kids who were engaged throughout their school careers will be far superior to those for the kids who struggled from the start.

I used the image of these two classrooms in early 2012 to make the case for expanded preschool funding as part of a broader education initiative in my proposed two-year budget. Kentucky's kids didn't get the funding that year, partly because the budget continued to be tight and partly because some legislators just refused to grasp both the importance of investing in education and the science of learning.

However, two years later, I was able to convince enough of those legislators to invest in our kids, including allocating $18 million more a year to expand preschool services to give us the potential to reach 5,125 more four-year-olds whose family income was below 160 percent of the federal poverty level.

A piece of historical trivia provided interesting context for that discussion.

The pictures on the cover of my proposed 2014–16 budget document marked the 100-year anniversary of the construction of the current Governor's Mansion, which began under the watch of Governor James B. McCreary.

Out of curiosity, I went back and read some of the papers of Governor McCreary. The parallels were startling.

Like me, Governor McCreary also served two terms as chief executive, although his terms came 36 years apart. And like me, he fought for education. Thanks to his budget and legislative proposals that year, Kentucky increased its spending per pupil by 25 percent, created a Textbook Commission, lengthened the school year, and made school attendance mandatory. In 1914, in his biennial message to the general assembly, Governor McCreary argued that these ideas would represent "a long step toward bringing our school system to that state of efficiency that would make it equal to the demands of a more enlightened and intelligent public opinion."

Ironically, I was pushing for similar things—increased funding and mandatory attendance to a later age.

In some ways, I found this depressing.

How disappointing, how utterly shameful, I thought, that in the 21st century—100 years later—we were still having to make the case for investing in education. How depressing it is that we are still articulating the need for Kentucky to catch up. How mind-boggling that some leaders still failed to see the direct link between school and a competitive economy.

You see, that's where some leaders just don't get it.

My vision, I often said as governor, was to "create a Kentucky where every child—regardless of whether he or she is born in the inner city, in a mountain hollow, on a farm, or in the suburbs—*every child* is guaranteed the potential for a life of promise and meaning. A Kentucky where every child is given the opportunity and the ability to succeed."

That vision represents a moral obligation. But it also defines the most direct path to a stronger Kentucky, because the very best thing Kentucky can do for its future is to build a healthier, more educated population and workforce.

College is much too late to *start* doing that. So is high school. So even is grade school. The seeds of learning are planted much earlier in life: Scientists say that some 90 percent of physical brain development occurs from birth to age three.

So the best time to start developing a talented workforce is in the earliest days of a child's life, and we need to continue to build off that development during preschool to prepare our children to hit the ground running in kindergarten.

That's why I worked so hard to get our youngest children access to health care, and it's why I created both the Governor's Office of Early Childhood and, in February 2009, the Governor's Task Force on Early Childhood Development and Education. I wanted to signal that the issue was going to be a priority for me. In November 2010, the task force released its final report, and over the next five years, we worked to implement many of its recommendations and make other changes designed to get our children off to a better start in life and school.

The steps we took included:

- We created and funded both community early childhood councils and the Early Childhood Advisory Council to collaborate with other groups to ensure a strong start for our children on a local level.

- We worked to have all parties—including educators, school community providers (both public and private), and community leaders—coalesce around a new shared definition of kindergarten readiness.

- We implemented a screener to gauge whether children were arriving at school ready to succeed, the results of which are used to both guide the programs of early childhood care providers and provide schools with the strengths and weaknesses of each child. In 2013, we began screening every child as they entered kindergarten to gauge their cognitive development, i.e., whether they were prepared to hit the ground running on the first day of their school career.

- In the same year, we published our first "Early Childhood Profiles," a compilation of county-by-county data about kindergarten readiness, preschool and kindergarten attendance, and similar measures.

- We secured a $44-million federal Race to the Top grant to support parents and improve early learning programs.

- We passed the All STARS plan to add accountability and transparency to all of our early child-care facilities by building on our successful quality rating system. Way back in 2001, we became the third state in the nation to implement a voluntary quality rating system for licensed child-care programs called STARS for KIDS NOW. The changes implemented by the All STARS plan greatly improved the rating system's effectiveness and reach by, among other things, making participation mandatory for all early childhood programs that received public funding.

Furthermore, when I was elected to my second term as chairman of the Southern Regional Education Board in June 2014, I named pre-kindergarten education as the board's focus for the year. In so doing, we not only shared what Kentucky was doing but learned from other states.

Now, several themes should stand out here.

One is the word "early." The key to kindergarten readiness—kids starting their school careers eager, ready, and able to learn—is high-quality child care and support for families at the earliest possible time in a child's life. Studies show that the earlier the intervention, the greater the chances of success in making a difference. That's why studies show that every dollar invested in early childhood development pays off in some multiple of itself down the road.

And the second theme is "collaboration." It takes communities working as partners to ensure kids are ready for kindergarten. Parents can't do it alone. Schools can't do it alone. Child-care agencies can't do it alone. And government's role is and should be limited.

It takes all of us working together to get children off to a good start—and by "all," I mean not just the whole village but the whole state.

DON'T MESS WITH
THE FIRST LADY

Sometimes even a small financial reward can have a big impact.

In the case of Kentucky raising its so-called dropout age, the lure of $10,000—an amount that, relatively speaking, represented just a handful of pennies compared to the budgets of most schools—changed the future of education in Kentucky.

But I'm getting ahead of myself.

When I signed Senate Bill 97 into law on March 18, 2013, I called it "one of my most satisfying acts as governor."

The bill raised the compulsory school attendance age from 16 to 18 and was designed to put teeth into Kentucky's fight against a historic challenge—too many kids dropping out of school before they picked up the knowledge and skills needed to succeed in today's world.

Letting students leave school at age 16 was a relic from 1920, an era that barely resembled the world we live in today. Back then, parents needed kids to work on the farm or in the family business, or just to bring in income. And for many years, the job market didn't punish those without a high school diploma. Many teens left school and got high-paying jobs at a factory.

Today, however, options are much more limited for dropouts. We had a study that said by the year 2018, nearly 89 percent of

Kentucky jobs would require a high school diploma *or above*.

Unfortunately, it was estimated that 6,000 students were dropping out every year in Kentucky, and studies confirmed the negative financial impact of their leaving school. Statistics show that high school graduates are more likely to be employed, earn higher wages, live longer, and raise healthier, better-educated children. They're also less likely to be teen parents, commit crimes, and rely on government health care or other assistance.

Requiring students to stay in school long enough to get a diploma sounds like a no-brainer, but even educators had legitimate concerns about whether schools were prepared to engage students who wanted to drop out but were forced to stay.

A new rule—in essence, a law enforcement approach—by itself wasn't enough to fix the problem. Kids abandon school and lose hope for a reason. Many have serious personal issues that involve things like drugs, poverty, poor health, and lack of family support. Kids with problems like these need schools and teachers to be flexible, to work with them to address their challenges. Education is not a cookie-cutter program. To succeed, at-risk students needed wrap-around services, individualized attention, and tailored education programming—not just aggressive truant officers. And they needed to see the direct connection between education and a career.

The Graduation Bill required school districts to certify that they had programs in place to both identify potential dropouts and to keep them in school. The new approach to alternative programs included innovative paths, digital learning (virtual programs and courses), dual-enrollment programs that emphasized career and technical education, and other alternative means to create effective learning environments that promoted student engagement, achievement, and success.

We first proposed this legislation in the 2009 legislative session, picking up on previous proposals. Another Beshear led the charge—First Lady Jane Beshear, the former teacher for whom education was and is a passion. She was assisted by a whole array of people, including Education Commissioner Terry Holliday, state Representative Jeff Greer, state Senator Jimmy Higdon, other legislators, numerous educators, child advocates, and others. In addition, every education group supported the legislation, and surveys revealed that 85 percent of parents favored it as well.

However, although the Democratic-controlled House passed the measure, the Republican-held Senate refused to consider it. Fortunately, for the children of the commonwealth, the Republican Senate had no idea whom they had just taken on! Jane simply looked them in the eye, smiled, and said, "I'll be back."

And back she came. To build awareness and galvanize support, in 2009, Jane and others solicited the help of American's Promise Alliance—the national group created by General Colin Powell and Alma Powell—to put together a two-day dropout prevention summit in Frankfort. This summit was followed by regional summits around the state. The summits yielded a comprehensive list of recommendations for keeping students in school, of which the dropout bill was one.

Support for the issue grew, and in 2013—after *five* legislative sessions—Jane's persistence finally paid off. Even then, however, we couldn't pass the bill outright. Senate Bill 97 didn't mandate the new standard, but allowed school districts to adopt it on a voluntary basis. However, it said that once 55 percent of districts—or 96 of them—made that choice, all remaining districts would have to follow suit within four years.

But we had to get to 96.

Commissioner Holliday, Jane, and I met in the governor's office at the end of the session to plan a campaign to persuade local school districts to adopt the change. We knew that many of them would leap at the opportunity, but how to get to 96? That's when Commissioner Holliday had a brilliant idea: In announcing our "Blitz to 96" initiative later that week, Holliday also announced that the Kentucky Department of Education would award planning grants of $10,000 to help with the implementation of the bill—but only to the first 96 districts to sign up.

In the grand scheme of multi-million-dollar budgets, $10,000 isn't much. But you'd have thought we were offering pots of gold.

Within two days, 58 districts made the change. Within a week, 75. And within two weeks, we had more than the required 96.

At that point, every one of Kentucky's 173 districts was required to adopt the Graduation Bill within four years and keep students in school until they turned 18 or had a diploma. By January 2015, all districts had already done so.

Kentucky had finally stood up for its youth and entered the 21st century. And all because of a First Lady's persistence.

SOW'S EAR INTO
A SILK PURSE

When it comes to proposed legislation, it's not where you start, but where you end up. Every once in a while, a situation arises in politics where a group of folks who want to take a step backward propose legislation which, by the end of the process, takes us instead several steps forward. Such was the case with educational testing and accountability measures in Kentucky in 2008–2009.

During the first decade of the 21st century, Kentucky was one of the nation's leaders in developing a fairly progressive evaluation process for its schools and students. However, this area was also becoming more politicized, with conservative legislators wanting to pull back on our standards by implementing simple, quantitative testing rather than a qualitative approach.

In the 2008 legislative session, Republican senators introduced accountability and testing legislation for Kentucky schools that most experienced educators felt would take us significantly backward in our efforts. However, senators argued that too much time was being spent testing our students in the classroom and that simple multiple-choice testing was sufficient. Although the Senate passed this bill, called Senate Bill 1, I announced my opposition and a majority of the House of Representatives refused to pass the bill. We, too, wanted to change our current system, but we wanted to replace it with an even more progressive qualitative evaluation system.

As I said in a press conference in March 2008 urging that the bill be defeated, "This proposal alters the underpinnings of Kentucky's education improvement effort at a critical point. ... Now is not the time to retreat. Now is not the time for needless disruption. Now is not the time for trying to assess student achievement on the cheap."

In the 2009 legislative session, Senate Bill 1 was resurrected with much of the same simplistic so-called reform. However, this time we were more prepared with an alternative developed after months of collaboration among legislators, educators, state officials, parents, and education partners such as the Prichard Committee for Academic Excellence, the Kentucky Association of School Superintendents, and the Kentucky Education Association. Led by Representative Carl Rollins, the House Education Committee prepared a committee substitute for Senate Bill 1 that would take us to the next level of testing and accountability and sent it back to the Senate. In a conference committee, the House stood firm on its proposal and the Senate finally relented.

As passed, SB 1 mandated a new testing and accountability system that moved beyond merely measuring student proficiency to focusing on student readiness and whether students were prepared to succeed at the next level. The accountability model included a variety of measures of student learning (including achievement, student growth, college/career readiness, and graduation rates); educator effectiveness; and support systems. It also enabled officials to look at the performance of schools and districts.

Specifically, the revised legislation required high schools to increase graduation rates and the Department of Education to collaborate with higher education officials to introduce new content standards aligned with postsecondary expectations (the genesis of the later Kentucky Academic Standards). It also required college/university teacher preparation programs for the new standards, and remediation, so our colleges and universities had standards for introductory and basic courses.

I signed the bill on March 26, 2009, with President Williams and others standing with me.

I acknowledged the fierce debate that had gone into the bill and admitted that even the final product wasn't perfect. But it represented another step in the ongoing transformation of Kentucky schools that started with the renowned reform effort of 1990. "I believe that great forces of change *are* coalescing in Kentucky, coalescing around the need to re-energize and reinvigorate our commitment to education," I said.

So, Senate Bill 1 became law, having started as a retreat from testing and accountability and ending in real progress for Kentucky's schoolchildren. All at once, Kentucky became a leader in the nation in this area on the K–12 level. Indeed, we had taken a sow's ear and turned it into a silk purse.

NO NEED TO RETREAT

I probably wasn't on the Christmas card lists of too many university presidents my first year in office.

Because of the historic recession, I entered office in late 2007 with a two-headed financial challenge. Not only did I have to immediately fill a $434-million end-of-year shortfall, but I also had to put together a two-year budget using revenue projections that fell almost $900 million short of current year spending. It meant I was cutting a lot of budgets, and since I was determined to protect K–12 classroom spending and Medicaid, it meant bigger cuts for everyone else. (Unlike at the federal level, Kentucky's Constitution *requires* a balanced budget.)

Given the importance of higher education in creating a stronger workforce, I cut it less than I cut most other areas of state government, but reduced cuts were about the best I could do.

University presidents, administrators, and board members howled in protest—publicly and privately—and I didn't blame them. At a time when Kentucky should have been investing *more* in education at all levels (and believe me I wanted to), we were unable to do so.

Funny thing was, after about a year, many of those same presidents came to me and quietly thanked me for protecting them to the point I did. They had spent that first year of the recession watching what was happening around the country and talking to their colleagues in other states, and they realized that many of the universities outside Kentucky were being forced to absorb much bigger blows than institutions in Kentucky.

I appreciated their realization and their willingness to work within the budgets they had. Higher education has many sources of funding, and they were able to shift funds around to replace public funds that weren't available. As a result of their hard work and flexibility, the quality of our institutions increased even in the face of some budget cuts. At the same time, I recognized that our presidents had to delay investing in programs and people, and that was unfortunate. I also realized that reduced state funding pushed tuition higher for our students, although again, we put limits in place that held those increases to less than they might have been otherwise. We also protected student financial aid from cuts that were made in other areas of higher education.

Over my first three biennial budgets, it was estimated that General Fund support for the universities had been cut 15 percent. In many ways, I was a little proud that we had kept that number so low. Many state agencies by that time had been cut 30 to 40 percent.

I was also proud that, while we couldn't increase state allocations, we were able to eventually invest in physical infrastructure through both General Fund-supported bonds and by letting the universities tap their own revenue streams to pay off new borrowing, a process called "agency bonds."

In 2013, for example, the general assembly and I authorized our public universities to fund 11 major construction projects with $363.3 million in agency bonds, including dormitory renovations, new student centers, and athletic facility improvements—all at no cost to Kentucky taxpayers. The following year, in 2014, we passed a budget that included both $419 million in General Fund-supported bonds and $451 million in agency bonds.

That same year, we authorized—for the first time in Kentucky history—the use of agency bonds for one high-priority project at each of the 16 two-year schools in the Kentucky Community and Technical College System (KCTCS). The authorization was also unique in that it involved the use of a sort of public-private partnership. The $145.5 million in agency bonds supported by the schools' own revenue streams would be matched on a 75/25 basis with almost $50 million raised from the local communities through public and private sources. This public-private financial collaboration was particularly fitting given the close relationship between these two-year colleges and local businesses. In many ways, these colleges are economic development tools in their communities in that they supply a large portion of the workforce for many of the local businesses and industries. This unique funding mechanism strengthened those ties.

Projects included renovation of existing buildings, construction of new classrooms, and the second phases of ongoing projects.

Together, this represented the single largest investment in the KCTCS system since its formation, and it indicated our recognition of its importance. At the time, more than 92,000 students were accessing education through the two-year system and its 16 colleges and 73 campuses. There was a reason the system's tagline was "Higher education begins here."

During the eight years of my administration, the total bond-funded capital investment in higher education was more than $2.7 billion. Agency bonds represented almost $1.9 billion of that, meaning taxpayers weren't responsible for paying those bonds back. That figure—$2.7 billion—represents a lot of bricks and mortar.

But money wasn't the only thing we invested in our higher education institutions.

We also invested a lot of time and energy into improving the efficiency and effectiveness of the higher ed system.

The most fundamental and often overlooked improvement (because it was accomplished on the K–12 level) was in the quality of the students entering our higher education institutions. It's just common sense: You can do a lot more with energized and educated 18-year-olds than you can with those needing extensive remedial help.

So we made an array of changes during every level of a child's development and education career that improved their chances of succeeding. As a result, we more than doubled the college and career readiness of our high school graduates, better preparing them for the work involved in college and decreasing the need for remedial classes.

I also created the Higher Education Work Group that met from fall 2008 through November 2009 and issued two sets of recommendations related to access and affordability. These recommendations included things like student financial aid, transfer from two-year to four-year schools, operating efficiencies, cost containment, and college readiness.

Several significant initiatives emanated from those recommendations, including legislation in 2010 that made it easier for KCTCS students to transfer credits to the state's four-year institutions.

We also took steps to allow students in high school to earn college credit for approved career and technical education courses and general education courses, speeding a student's path to a certificate or degree and reducing their costs in college.

A few months before I left office in December 2015, we looked at the state performance scorecard put together as part of the Kentucky Council on Postsecondary Education's "Stronger by Degrees" initiative, and it was clear that we were making significant progress:

- The number of degrees and credentials awarded had increased 18.8 percent over five years.

- Student transfers from KCTCS to four-year institutions had increased 31.4 percent.

- Our graduation rate for bachelor degree students had gone up 2.2 percentage points.

- Degrees and credentials in STEM+H fields (science, technology, engineering, mathematics, and health) had increased 24.5 percent.

- Online learning had risen 5.8 percentage points.

- And overall education attainment for adults ages 25 to 44 had risen 4.9 percentage points.

I also felt good about funding for higher education going forward. With the economy and state revenues recovering, it appeared as if the next governor would have much more money to work with than I did, and would be in a position to catch up on higher education funding.

About two months before I left office, I conveyed that optimism to university administrators and trustees at the annual Governor's Conference on Postsecondary Education Trusteeship. "I encourage every leader and institution in this room to be vocal in working with the new governor and with legislators to make the case for more investment in higher education," I said. "I think Kentucky can do it. And frankly, I'm looking forward to seeing it."

As I describe elsewhere in this book, a few days after I left office, the state Consensus Forecasting Group (the same experts whose projections provide the basis for every governor's budget proposal) released numbers that backed up that optimism. The CFG predicted that Kentucky would end the 2015–16 biennium with a $223-million surplus. It also projected that revenues for the coming two-year budget cycle (fiscal years 2017 and 2018) would grow 3.2 percent and 2.4 percent, respectively.

Little did we all know what was in store.

Announcing that putting every available dollar into our troubled public pension system was his highest priority, the incoming governor hit higher education with two body shots right off the bat: One, in his proposed two-year budget that would take effect July 1, 2016, he asked for 9 percent cuts to higher education. And two, he ordered immediate mid-year cuts of 4.5 percent—or about $41 million—to university budgets in the waning months of the then-current biennium, bypassing the legislature altogether. (He later reduced his "order" to 2 percent, about $18 million, which he withheld from the universities.)

Kentucky State University warned that it would have to close, Morehead State University announced that it was furloughing workers, and KCTCS predicted further tuition increases.

Fortunately, neither of the governor's proposals stood. Because of pressure from the Democratic-controlled House, the general assembly reduced the two-year cuts from 9 percent to 4.5 percent. And Attorney General Andy Beshear, my son, challenged the immediate mid-year cuts. He argued that the unilateral action exceeded the governor's authority and violated state law. In September 2016, the Kentucky Supreme Court agreed with the AG and ruled that the governor overstepped his authority in trying to wrench away the budget-setting power of the legislature.

Nevertheless, the universities had to absorb a (in my view needless) 4.5 percent cut in the 2017–18 biennium and, given the new governor's priorities, face a financial future even more uncertain than it was during the recession.

It's imperative that elected leaders always remember the critical role of higher education in our economy, which is to improve our intellectual capital and competitive capacity. An investment in our colleges and universities is an investment in Kentucky's economy. I'm proud that during my eight years—despite tight budgets caused by a devastating global recession—university leaders, legislators, and I found ways to strengthen our institutions.

Section VI
POLITICS

GETTING PAST THE RANCOR

Elections are a big physics experiment. Candidates and ideas crash together in a collision of discussion and debate that, ideally, produces the best leaders and focuses them on the most urgent issues. Elections are also a useful tool for holding incumbents accountable for their policies, votes, and words.

Of course, the process can get heated because partisan politics has always been rough and tumble. And that's okay. Political combat serves a purpose. Distinguishing yourself from your opponent lies at the heart of the American political system.

But that system breaks down if—after the heat of the campaign is over—leaders with differing philosophical beliefs are unable or unwilling to put aside the partisan fighting and collaborate for the good of the people they serve.

In a nutshell, there is a time for campaigning, and there is a time for governing.

In the not-too-distant past, a majority of our elected officials were able to put the rancor behind them from time to time to find common ground on decisions that moved the country forward.

Unfortunately, in our nation today we are increasingly unable to leave the vitriol and venom behind when the election results are known. Too many people right now are guided 24/7 by a rigid ideology that leaves no place for collaboration and favors rabid, personal attacks over civil discourse.

Daily headlines are filled with conflict and controversy stemming from reckless words designed to fit within sound-bite parameters. We're told it sells newspapers and boosts ratings.

Outside the mainstream media, inflammatory rhetoric is at an even higher premium. Places like talk radio and social media thrive on disrespect, insults, intolerance, and downright hatefulness. Dignity—and truth—are in short supply. It's an increasingly ugly world, full of venom that is dividing this country into "us" and "them." And the rise of so-called fake news—deliberately false stories that are published and re-published recklessly across the Internet—is further poisoning the atmosphere.

And it's getting worse. As Max Ehrenfreund wrote in the *Washington Post* in November 2015, "It isn't just that Democrats and Republicans agree on less and less these days. It's that they hate each other's guts."

Our families are suffering because of it.

Of all people, Richard Nixon spoke poignantly on this topic in his first inaugural address. The late president, in the minds of most Americans, isn't remembered for his consensus and collaboration. But his words about a country "ragged in spirit" are poetic.

"In these difficult years, America has suffered from a fever of words; from inflated rhetoric that promises more than it can deliver; from angry rhetoric that fans discontents into hatreds; from bombastic rhetoric that postures instead of persuading. We cannot learn from one another until we stop shouting at one another ..."

Nixon gave that speech almost 50 years ago. But his warning resonates today.

Whether you're a voter or an elected leader, it's easy to get caught up in this negative dialogue, to believe that rancor is mandatory, and to conclude that consensus and collaboration are cardinal sins.

But move outside the political realm, and people are frustrated.

Our families are focused on putting food on the table and keeping a roof overhead; getting up every day and working until quitting time; wishing for safe neighborhoods and good schools for their children; and just trying to get ahead and wondering why they can't. They are weary of the bickering and the hate.

They want leaders who build bridges, not dams. Leaders who are motivated by the common good, not ideology. And leaders who reject the politics of division and intolerance.

Rank partisanship doesn't put a single meal on the table. It doesn't educate a single child, and it doesn't create a single job. It doesn't lead to better health, and it doesn't nurture opportunity.

In short, this nation is being ripped apart by partisan rancor and rigid ideology. We are polarized and we are paralyzed. Washington, DC, is broken, and the political systems in many of our states are not far behind.

But in Kentucky during the eight years I was governor, we fought hard against becoming another voice in Washington's acrimonious shouting match, and by and large, we were successful. In fact, during my two terms, Kentucky was one of the relatively few places in the country where democracy still worked.

During my first election, in 2007, I liked to say that I didn't care "whether an idea was a Democratic idea or a Republican idea, so long as it was a good idea." And I governed with that mentality.

I strived to make Democracy work in Kentucky partly because I had to.

We had a divided government the entire time I was governor. Republicans controlled the Senate. Democrats controlled the House. In Washington, those are the ingredients for gridlock.

Yet in Kentucky:

- We passed balanced budgets, even during a recession, that protected core priorities—like education—while cutting spending.

- We raised Kentucky's dropout age and consequently its graduation rate.

- We expanded substance-abuse treatment and addressed addiction to prescription painkillers.

- We protected unemployment benefits for people who lost their jobs and preserved tobacco fund money for farmers.

- We took significant steps toward reforming the public pension system.

- We expanded preschool access.

- We invested in our community college campuses.

- We created about 90,000 new jobs and attracted nearly $21 billion in new investment.

- We twice won a coveted trophy for finishing No. 1 in large-scale business activity.

How? What was the secret?

First, I knew that the "real" Kentucky wasn't to be found in my office, on the floor of the general assembly, or in the tweets of a partisan hack. It was out there in homes, on farms, in classrooms, on assembly lines, and along the Main Streets in our 120 counties.

So as governor, I got out of Frankfort as much as I could. During weather crises, I toured affected communities, served food, and reassured people whose homes and businesses were damaged or destroyed. I visited factories and construction sites to personally announce expansions and new locations. I dropped by schools, crisis centers, and health clinics. I welcomed home National Guard units. And when I signed new legislation into law or announced policy changes, I did so at places where those laws and changes would have the biggest impact.

And before and after events, I tried always to take time to mingle with people in the crowd, to hear their stories and their concerns. I wanted to hear what was on their minds.

See, I grew up in a small town, where my father was a preacher and a funeral home director, and I learned by watching him that a compassionate and friendly ear is at the heart of true service. My mother worked at the funeral home and was the consummate volunteer, so I understood that meeting people's needs should be the core priority of any program or initiative.

It also helped that I am a son, a husband, a father, and a grandfather. I find it easy to share the pride, worry, hopefulness, enthusiasm, and fear of constituents, because I know where they're coming from.

Getting away from Frankfort reminded me why I was elected.

It taught me to look not at the political impact of a policy, decision, or a speech but at the people impact. And when discussion devolved into partisan bickering, it kept my eyes focused on the big picture.

Second, you can't do this by yourself. It takes relationships, partnerships, and collaboration based on trust. So I worked hard to build that trust: with thousands of state employees, many partners in the private sector, educators, doctors, and prosecutors. And it took leaders whose politics were often at odds with mine. Republicans.

Let me give you three examples.

In late 2011, Kentucky was stunned to learn that the number of people killed by drug overdoses had surpassed the number killed in accidents on the state's highways. For years, Kentucky communities had been ravaged by addiction to prescription painkillers. But the suggestion that medicine cabinets had become more dangerous than reckless drivers was too horrifying to ignore.

The result was House Bill 4, a landmark piece of legislation that brought medical oversight to the all-but-unregulated use of pain pills, drove reckless doctors and rogue profit-focused pain clinics out of business, and expanded help for patients who had accidentally become addicts while seeking relief from injuries and chronic medical problems.

The fight to pass HB 4 in the 2012 legislative session was long, tense, and bitter. In fact, at one point, lobbyists for the medical industry sat in my office and told me flat out, "We're not going to let you pass this bill." Well, they succeeded, but only temporarily.

I immediately ordered legislators back into a special session. And in the end, concern for Kentuckians and the need to fix a broken system trumped the complaints of lobbyists, the medical profession, the pharmaceutical industry, and partisan ideologues.

Moments after the legislation (now called HB 1) passed, one of the legislators who had played a pivotal role in its passage came into my office: Republican Senate Majority Leader Robert Stivers. He had gone against other GOP leaders at great political risk because he knew that many families in his district were caught in the horrendous cycle of addiction and desperately needed help.

With the television in my office still tuned to KET's coverage of the session, I rose from behind my desk and shook Robert's hand, thanking him on behalf of beleaguered Kentuckians for his courage.

Senator Stivers and I were supposed to be political enemies. In fact, Robert later became president of the Senate, and he and I had several disagreements. He's a strong leader. But on critical issues, we could put the rhetoric aside and work together for the good of families. I respected that.

To say it again, there is a time for political combat and a time for governing.

Outside of Frankfort, I enjoyed the same collaborative relationship with many Republican leaders.

My second example concerns the Ohio River Bridges Project.

Officials in Louisville and Indiana had talked for decades about the need for new bridges across the Ohio River, but the project was stalled. Then I got together with Indiana Governor Mitch Daniels, and we created a plan to put the project back on track. We talked regularly by phone to guide our staffs through hurdles and challenges, primarily related to cost and funding. The weekend before I left office, the ribbon was cut on the Downtown Crossing, and the East End Crossing was completed and opened to traffic in late 2016.

Now, Governor Daniels is a Republican. I, of course, am a Democrat. But we ignored partisan differences and worked closely together because we knew how badly that region needed new bridges. (I shared a similar working relationship with Governor Daniels's successor, Republican Mike Pence.)

Likewise, and this is my third example, I worked closely with Republican Congressman Hal Rogers, then chair of the House Appropriations Committee, to address challenges in Eastern Kentucky. The precipitous downturn in the coal economy had exacerbated generational problems in Eastern Kentucky, including poverty, unemployment, low educational attainment, poor health, and lack of economic opportunity. Representative Rogers and I decided to tackle the problems head on, creating the Shaping Our Appalachian Region (SOAR) initiative.

At first, there was a lot of mutual suspicion, given that we belonged to different political parties, and we had our own ideas on the best strategies for SOAR. But Hal and I had known each other for a long time, and he's obviously a strong advocate for that part of Kentucky. And I knew that Kentucky can't be strong if it leaves a region behind. So gradually, we learned to trust each other and work through our differences.

SOAR was built on several principles:

One, government didn't have all the answers. This couldn't be a top-down effort driven by Washington or Frankfort; it had to be one whose answers came from the people who live and work in Appalachia.

Two, this would be a *process*, not a one-time event designed to produce a magic formula. We put in place a framework to sustain the effort long after Hal left Congress and I left the Governor's Office.

Three, we weren't reinventing the wheel. Similar efforts have occurred before, and we wanted to build off that work while accounting for changes in the marketplace, employment trends, technological advances, and decreases in available government funding.

And four, we weren't writing a plan—this region has been studied and planned to death—but a framework for action.

When I left office, SOAR was helping Eastern Kentucky move forward on a wide array of projects. These included building a high-speed broadband network, widening and extending the Mountain Parkway to create a four-lane highway into the heart of the mountains, setting up an office to nurture innovative new businesses and the framework for private-sector funding, expanding job training, providing low-cost home loans, improving dental access, and offering more substance-abuse treatment options.

The work isn't finished—as a process, SOAR will never be completely finished—but there has been measurable progress. And none of that would have occurred if the congressman and I had remained entrenched in our ideological positions or had worried about grabbing credit for ourselves and our party.

The point is, sometimes politics, and by that, I mean the stereotypical notion of parties working to undercut each other, just gets in the way.

For Kentucky to succeed, leaders in both parties need to know when to put the heated campaign rhetoric aside and govern. Whether it's health-care access or funding for preschool, they have to be willing to make decisions based on what will help Kentucky's people, not on what will sound good on the campaign trail. They have to stop worrying about the next headline and the next election.

In Washington, the national discourse suggests that only two opinions exist: Democratic and Republican. But in Kentucky, we know better. Here, we are more than our political loyalties. Our state is richly populated with people who identify themselves by other names first. Titles like Mom or Dad. Sunday school teacher. Farmer. Police officer. Student. Nurse. Autoworker. Professor. Miner. Coach. Volunteer.

For this state—and this country—to thrive, we need to focus on that which unites us instead of that which divides us.

That's not easy. Kentucky is not a homogenous state, by any definition. Someone who lives in a hollow in Owsley County has a much different life than someone who rents an apartment with no yard in Louisville, or someone who lives in a subdivision in Edgewood.

As leaders, we could focus on income strata, our various ethnicities, the blue-collar vs. white-collar divide, the fact that some of us are Baptists and some are Catholics, and our registration as Democrat, Republican, or Independent.

Or we could remember that most of us want similar things: a steady job, a safe neighborhood, good schools, economic opportunity, and enough money to enjoy a vacation, a sports game, or a cultural event.

Rational and respectful conversation also helps us leaders recognize that Kentuckians' views aren't as strident as we try to make them be. For example, despite the claims of party slogans and sound bites, Kentuckians actually aren't anti-tax. They are against unnecessary taxes. And they're not anti-spending. They oppose wasteful spending. And they're not anti-government. They are against poorly run government.

Nuances are important, because they help us build consensus.

When talking about unity, a lot of politicians like to cite Kentucky's "United we stand, divided we fall" motto. It's almost expected that we do so. So it's become a cliché.

But if you look closely at the official state seal, you get a stronger understanding of the strength of that motto. It's been 225 years since Kentucky adopted that seal, so the buckskin jacket and the swallowtail coat pictured in that image are out of date. But the symbolism of the two men clasping hands is as relevant as ever.

If the frontier woodsman and the formally educated landed gentry could look past their striking differences more than two centuries ago, then we in 2017 are capable of doing the same. In fact, we must.

As I said to anyone who would listen, "Our elections are partisan, and we all enjoy the give and take of a good campaign. But when the elections are over and the votes are counted, the people of Kentucky expect us to remember that we are Kentuckians first and Democrats and Republicans second."

When and if the politicians in Washington get the same message, this country will start moving again. However, left to their own devices, I'm not sure that will happen anytime soon. I am reminded of that question out of the Bible: "Can a leopard change its spots?" In the end, it will be up to voters to demand a change in attitude. Because about the only thing most of these politicians respond to are threats from the ballot box.

THE PEW AND
THE BALLOT BOX

I come from a family of preachers. My father, grandfather, and uncle were all lay preachers in the Primitive Baptist Church, one of the many Baptist denominations around the country.

The church doesn't pay its ministers a set salary, and therefore, my father and uncle were also partners in Beshear Funeral Home in Dawson Springs. (You can imagine what a great combination being a preacher and a funeral director was.) Washing one another's feet was a part of the yearly communion celebration, and there was no instrumental music allowed, only a cappella singing. (As a small child, one day I asked my father why we didn't have an organ or piano in the church, and he said it was because they didn't have organs or pianos during Jesus's time. I then asked him why we had light bulbs in the church since they didn't have those in Jesus's time either, and as I recall, he just ignored me.)

The church and the Bible were daily and integral parts of my childhood. My dad preached at several churches during the month, and we were usually in the car with him on those trips. He also loved music and taught all of us to sing as soon as we were old enough to carry a tune.

In fact, one of my most vivid and endearing memories from my childhood was gathering in the funeral home basement with my two brothers, Bob and David, and my father, where we would record gospel songs that would serve as the introduction for his 30-minute show on the radio station in Madisonville. And when we sang at funeral services, we tried to sing the departed all the way to heaven.

So yes, I understand deeply the vibrant importance of faith in people's lives. But as a Baptist, I was brought up with a very strong belief in the separation of church and state. In fact, history tells us that Baptists played a very important role in the development of the Bill of Rights in our US Constitution, because they had experienced persecution at the hands of the "official" church in several of the colonies. Sadly, some Baptists today have forgotten their heritage and now advocate for a government that will give preferential treatment to their particular brand of Christianity.

As an elected official, I felt I had an obligation to all people, including those with various religious beliefs as well as those with no beliefs at all. That obligation was to uphold a shared vision of freedom, equality, and a good quality of life for everybody. It is a concept that is colloquially known as the common good.

Having grown up in a community surrounded only with people who thought and looked like I did, I can understand others who live in similar circumstances when they voice concerns about civil laws and practices that appear to conflict with their religious beliefs. What they tend to forget is that there is a big world out there: *billions* of people who look different, think different, speak different languages, and have different religions. America is blessed with the same diversity. And we Christians must realize that those folks have just as much right to be American citizens as we do and that our Constitution guarantees that all of us can think and believe as we please. As Americans, all of us are entitled to life, liberty, and the pursuit of happiness, as long as we abide by a common set of rules that maintain a peaceful society.

Given the current political climate and the undercurrent of intolerance that flowed through the 2016 presidential election, this message is more relevant today than ever before. It appears that religious freedom will be a fiercely debated issue in the months and years ahead. We need to step away from our own prejudices and fears and remember the ideals upon which this country was founded.

My belief in the separation of church and state caused me political problems more than once. An early test of that approach came when I was Kentucky attorney general. The US Supreme Court in 1980 struck down a state law requiring the posting of the Ten Commandments in public schools. I was asked for an advisory opinion on whether that meant that existing displays would have to be removed from the schoolhouse walls. They do have to be removed, I wrote in that opinion issued in 1981. The law was absolutely clear, and the highest court in the land had spoken.

That opinion created a firestorm in more conservative circles, and within a week, a billboard went up on Interstate 65 in Jefferson County that said "Keep the Ten Commandments, remove Steve Beshear!" The fact is, I obeyed the law. Besides, as my father often told me, it's not so important where the Ten Commandments hang, but it sure is important that you live by them. More on that later.

Once I became governor, religion became part of the discussion of many issues, sometimes unexpectedly.

In 2009, the Kentucky Finance and Administration Cabinet issued a press release that I hadn't seen announcing a search for an evergreen tree that would be put up on the Capitol grounds and decorated with lights, as is the annual custom. Only the release called it "a holiday tree."

Oh my goodness! I was immediately accused by some of declaring a "war on Christmas."

So we sent out a subsequent e-mail making it clear that while the tree celebrates a tradition that is enjoyed not only by people of many religions but also by those without religion, for me *personally*, the tree had always been a Christmas tree. That tamped down some of the outrage.

The intersection of religion and government came to the forefront again in 2010, when the group Answers in Genesis applied for state tourism tax incentives for what it said would be a $150-million, 160-acre theme park in Grant County.

Because the park was to be based on events in the Bible (it was to include a life-sized replica of Noah's Ark), many people assumed that the project would not be eligible for incentives.

However, as long as it was a tourist attraction and not a church, it met the requirements of the Kentucky Tourism Development Act, even though the project had a religious theme.

Personally, I was focused primarily on the jobs the theme park would create in that rural area of Northern Kentucky. As the commonwealth continued to claw its way out of the recession, I needed to put people back to work, and if that work was sweeping up after animals or selling tickets to see the Tower of Babel, I didn't care. As I was quoted saying at the press conference announcing the project, "The people of Kentucky didn't elect me governor to debate religion. They elected me governor to create jobs."

Naturally, the news created a furor. Some didn't understand why the state would endorse and promote religion (we weren't) or would be spending state money on such a project (we weren't doing that either). The incentives were performance-based, meaning they would apply only if the park created the jobs and investment. And contrary to what some people were saying, they represented a credit on future tax payments, not an upfront payment.

Eventually, however, we felt compelled to reverse course and deny the incentives. Although the group first indicated in its written agreement that it would not discriminate in hiring on the basis of religion, it later became clear from job advertisements that religious beliefs would be used as a litmus test when hiring, moving the project from a tourist attraction into the realm of a religious ministry in the state's opinion. In my mind, the state shouldn't be giving tax incentives to an organization that was going to base hiring decisions on religious beliefs. Our decision brought a lawsuit from Answers in Genesis, and a conservative US district judge appointed by President George W. Bush ruled against us.

Although in my opinion, his decision would have been reversed on appeal, my successor declined to appeal the ruling. So, as of this writing, the Ark Park is open to visitors, complete with its 510-foot boat, animal sculptures, and nearby Ark Encounter zip lines and zoo.

In 2013, the role of religion burst into the news in an even bigger fashion with the general assembly's passage of House Bill 279, the so-called religious freedom bill (alternately called the discrimination bill by its critics).

Proponents claimed that the removal of prayer from schools and other such things warranted a new law "protecting" people's right to practice their religion. Cynics, on the other hand, recognized correctly that our Constitution and Bill of Rights already provide such protection.

The wording in the legislation was extremely vague, broad, and imprecise. Dozens and dozens of organizations—including churches, social workers, and civil rights groups—called my office with concerns about the wording in the bill, which could hamper enforcement of laws and conceivably justify child abuse, for example. Plus, there were no exceptions for the protection and safety of the general public, such as public health standards.

Because HB 279 had the potential to invade and harm the civil rights and constitutionally guaranteed freedoms of numerous populations in Kentucky, I vetoed it.

As I said in a formal statement, "I value and cherish our rights to religious freedom and I appreciate the good intentions of House Bill 279 … [but] I have significant concerns that this bill will cause serious unintentional consequences that could threaten public safety, health care, and individuals' civil rights."

I knew my veto would be overturned, and it was. The possibility of unintended consequences—and the need to separate church and state—weren't enough for legislators to risk being perceived as anti-religion in an election year. The vote to override my veto was 79–15 in the House and 32–6 in the Senate.

Blurring of the line separating civil laws and religious beliefs played a huge role later in another issue, gay marriage, that earned Kentucky a lot of scorn on a national level, but that's a story worth a separate essay.

The point is, faith and religion are important elements of many people's daily lives and a core part of how we identify ourselves. We pray, we attend services, and we try to live according to our beliefs. Faith gives us strength, inspires us to do good works, and fills us with love and compassion.

My family was grounded in such an atmosphere, and Jane and I raised our boys, Jeff and Andy, the same way. So I personally know the good that religion brings to society.

But in a country where religious freedom, by historical precedent and by law, includes both the freedom to choose our own religion and the freedom to choose no religion at all, elected officials need to be able at appropriate times to separate the pew from the ballot box.

HYPOCRITES IN OFFICE

Virtually every religion that I have studied to any degree is based on a desire to live in peace, be kind to your neighbors, and do the right thing. Every one of those religions has thousands if not millions of devout followers around the world. And since the beginning of time, some of those seeking power have understood the influence that religion has on people and have used that knowledge to gain political control.

That's not to say that every politician is a hypocrite utilizing religion for his or her own political benefit. I know many folks in political life who have sincere religious beliefs. However, religious hypocrisy abounds in America's political world and has become one of the primary tools utilized by some office seekers to get elected and then to stay in office.

When I first came to Kentucky's capital, Frankfort, as a new state legislator in 1974, I saw firsthand how some so-called leaders used the religious angle to pander to the folks back home. It was particularly disturbing because I saw how some of those same leaders—ironically, usually those who talked loudest about their faith—failed to both *live* and *lead* according to that faith.

I say "live" because Frankfort has long had a reputation for improper behavior. That's not new information, and most folks don't behave that way. But I saw and heard enough that the word "hypocrisy" came through loud and clear.

And I say "lead" because too many leaders talk about concern for the poor and the vulnerable and then wash their hands of them when it comes time to act. They talk about the Golden Rule and then abandon the use of it when the opportunity arises. These leaders go to church on Sunday and then on Monday vote against health care for the working poor. They work to cut the cords of the safety net that helps people during vulnerable times of their lives. They deny voting rights to people who broke the law, paid for it, and are trying to rebuild their lives and find redemption. These leaders vote to deny physical protection for unmarried women beaten by their boyfriends. They campaign on a right-to-life platform for the unborn and then turn their backs on those kids and their mothers once birth occurs.

They advocate loving their neighbor but then attempt to destroy any neighbor who disagrees with them. To them, the "truth" is simply a flexible tool to be twisted in any way that accomplishes their goal.

In other words, these so-called leaders talk the talk, but don't walk the walk. They preach like prophets, but they govern like Pontius Pilate.

These modern-day Pharisees wrap themselves tightly in the shroud of faith, knowing that if they shout "Judeo-Christian values" loud enough and often enough people will vote for them—no matter how much their policies and positions fail to back up those Christian beliefs.

The Apostle best described them in the First Epistle of John, chapter 2, verse 4: "He that saith, I know Him, and keepeth not his commandments, is a liar, and the truth is not in him."

It's time for voters to wake up and quit being played for suckers. It's time for people to again separate the pew from the ballot box when it comes to hypocritical politicians and to hold those politicians accountable for the beliefs they profess to hold and then don't act upon.

SECONDS IN COMMAND

An ear, nose, and throat surgeon who previously represented one of Kentucky's poorest areas in the state Senate.

A charismatic and gregarious attorney who had led Kentucky's largest city for so long that he was deemed "Mayor for Life"—and was stolen away from Kentucky by President Obama.

And a descendant of two governors whose aggressive work as a two-term state auditor of public accounts and gubernatorial adviser had earned her a sterling "white hat" reputation as an enemy of fraud, waste, and bad government.

The three people who served as lieutenant governor during my administration brought unique skills and a lot of experience to the job. That's a good thing, because the job, by law, was basically whatever we made of it.

I served as lieutenant governor in 1983–87, alongside Governor Martha Layne Collins, but the job had changed significantly with the 1992 constitutional amendment approved by voters. The lieutenant governor now ran on a ticket with the governor, no longer lived in the Old Governor's Mansion, no longer presided over the Senate, and no longer became the acting governor when the governor was out of state.

With the office stripped of many of its constitutional duties, it was left to individual administrations to create new ones.

I had to do that three times. I think I was the only Kentucky governor to ever serve with three separate lieutenant governors.

I picked Dr. Daniel Mongiardo as my running mate in 2007 because of his political popularity, his ties to Eastern Kentucky, and his health-care expertise.

As a physician, his focus on improving health care in Kentucky laid the groundwork for our later embrace of the Affordable Care Act. In particular, he helped Kentucky become an early leader in the move toward electronic health records. The creation of the Kentucky Health Information Exchange in 2010 was a big step toward developing and using technology to help providers better coordinate care, deliver care more efficiently, and improve patient care and health.

Early in 2009, Dr. Mongiardo announced plans to run for the US Senate in 2010. So in July 2009, when I announced my plans to run for re-election in 2011, I also announced a new running mate, Jerry Abramson, who was in his 20th year as mayor of Louisville, then the nation's 28th largest city.

I had known Jerry for almost 30 years, beginning when I was attorney general and he was general counsel for Governor John Y. Brown Jr. Jerry was the only person I approached about being my new running mate.

"To me, there is only one test for a lieutenant governor nominee—is he or she qualified to be governor?" I said at the announcement. "Jerry easily passes that test."

Of course, I easily won re-election, and Jerry settled in to become a significant part of my administration.

Among many other things, he chaired the Governor's Blue Ribbon Commission on Tax Reform I created in February 2012, beginning a yearlong analysis that exposed structural weaknesses in our outdated tax system, and then he wrote a plan to fix those weaknesses. Unfortunately, the general assembly had no appetite for comprehensive tax reform, and the changes passed in the 2013 and 2014 sessions were small in number.

I also tapped Jerry to chair a multi-pronged initiative called kyhealthnow that attacked seven of Kentucky's most stubborn, long-standing health problems, including obesity, smoking, dental decay, and heart disease. It was an aggressive effort that set tangible five-year goals like reducing Kentucky's rate of uninsured to less than 5 percent and reducing our obesity and smoking rates by 10 percent.

When he joined my team, Jerry announced his intention of becoming the most active lieutenant governor in modern Kentucky history, and he certainly made a run for that title. Among his many other initiatives was launching a statewide version of "Close the Deal," a program he started as mayor that helped high school graduates move on to college. He also advanced the cause of career and technical education through the "Career Craze" program and traveled around the country to market Kentucky to site consultants, bringing jobs and investment to the Bluegrass.

His wife, Madeline, became sort of a super volunteer, serving as chairwoman of the Kentucky Commission on Women, the Red Cross Regional Volunteer Services Advisory Committee, and the Kentucky Center for the Performing Arts, among other things.

So Jerry was a true partner and a vocal advocate, short on patience, but long on enthusiasm and drive. He was a strong believer in government's ability and obligation to make the world better for our families, and he knew how to make government—especially local government—work for its people. So it wasn't a surprise when President Obama hired him away from me in November 2014 to become deputy assistant to the president and director of intergovernmental affairs.

It was a huge loss, but I had a historical surprise waiting in the wings.

During the same press conference announcing Jerry's departure, I also announced Crit Luallen as his replacement.

It was a huge coup—especially during the point in my administration when most governors are traditionally considered lame ducks.

Crit had served two terms as state auditor of public accounts, where she wasn't shy about investigating local officials who had mishandled money and where she had uncovered millions of dollars in government fraud and questionable expenditures. Having worked for six governors in roles like state budget director and secretary of the Governor's Executive Cabinet, Crit had toyed with running for governor several times, and many people in the state thought she *should* be governor.

As with Jerry, my search had begun and ended with one person.

"There are few issues in which she is not well versed, and few challenges that she has not had to address," I said then. "In this era of cynicism and scorn, her motivation to some people seems almost quaint: Crit believes—*with all her heart*—that public service is an honorable calling."

Well, Crit stepped in right where Jerry had left off, and we didn't lose a beat. If anything, her leadership of the kyhealthnow initiative was even more aggressive, and its results—as I describe elsewhere in this book—were impressive.

She wound up being a steady and intellectual presence in the office that helped keep us focused and ambitious during my last year. Her appointment also signaled something to Kentuckians and the legislature about my plans for the rest of my time in office, and I made sure that point was clear in my announcement remarks.

"Some governors coast their last year in office," I said that day. "But my second-in-command will soon be a West Wing adviser whose office is literally directly above the president's. And that adviser's replacement will be one of Kentucky's most venerated public officials of all time. With these appointments, I am sending a strong message to the people of Kentucky that I intend to continue to use every second of my time as governor to energize and elevate this state."

And with Crit by my side in Frankfort and Jerry just a phone call away in the president's inner circle, I did exactly that.

GOOD-BYE TO GRIDLOCK

The departure of David Williams as president of the Senate after 12 years—and the rise of Robert Stivers—represented one of the most momentous changes in modern Kentucky legislative history. That's true whether you measure it by the fate of individual proposals like the Graduation Bill or by the radical shift in the overall demeanor of the general assembly.

It also marked a significant turning point in our ability to move forward on the challenges confronting Kentucky during my eight years as governor.

Why?

Because Senator Stivers and I could work together; Senator Williams and I couldn't.

The reasons were rooted in history, leadership styles, and personalities.

Senator Williams had ruled the Senate with an iron hand for 12 years. Supporters praised him for fiercely protecting Republican priorities and helping the GOP take over the Senate in Kentucky. But many others felt that Senator Williams had a combative my-way-or-the-highway style of leadership, micromanaging every aspect of the GOP caucus and tending to take disagreement as a personal affront.

Although I knew that the path to legislative success required building relationships with legislators, including those of the opposing party, my overtures to GOP senators mostly failed. Several of them told me early in my term that they weren't allowed to meet with me to get acquainted or discuss issues or pending bills without a chaperone from GOP leadership. And I was told by more than one Republican committee chairman that he couldn't pass an important bill out of committee—even one he himself supported—because "David won't let me." To me and others, it seemed that many GOP senators were so intimidated by the Senate president that they had lost any appearance of independence.

The bottom line is that without trust between us, Senator Williams and I had no relationship on which to work through differences on important issues. (In fact, he would later run against me in the 2011 governor's race.)

It didn't help our personal relationship when, in the opening weeks of my first term, I had to rearrange some funding across the state, including in Senator Williams's district.

At issue was a controversial $11-million expansion of a road project, the widening of KY 90 and KY 61. I actually supported the original $50-million-plus project. But the expansion was authorized via a change order approved by the outgoing Fletcher administration not long before midnight on the day before I became governor, even though engineers on the project had declined to approve it. The size of the change order was almost unprecedented, and because it added an extra section of road to the original plan, Kentucky Transportation Cabinet officials said it amounted to an entirely new project.

Misuse of the change-order process was problematic, and given limited dollars in an over-programmed state Road Fund, I did not believe this was the best use of our money because we had other roads in much greater need of safety improvements.

Noting the road was in Senator Williams's district, my staff bluntly asked me, "Do you really want to pick this fight?"

My response was equally candid: "Is it the right thing to do?" I called to tell Senator Williams of my decision and, needless to say, the conversation didn't go well.

A second issue involved preparing the Kentucky Horse Park for the 2010 World Equestrian Games. The games—which represent an Olympics of sorts for eventing, dressage, show jumping, and other equestrian disciplines—had never before been held outside of Europe, nor had it ever been held in one location.

In winning the bid in 2006, the outgoing administration had promised to make several improvements to the Kentucky Horse Park, including the construction of a new indoor arena and the complete renovation of the outdoor arena. But when I took office in December 2007, no steps had been taken to fund and fulfill our obligations, and time was running out.

Kentucky's reputation—and its status as the Horse Capital of the World—were at stake. We needed money quickly, so I decided to divert funding from 13 pending improvements within the state park system to the Kentucky Horse Park, amounting to a little less than $29 million.

It so happened that three of the 13 projects (representing more than half of the $29 million) were to have benefited Dale Hollow State Park in Senator Williams's district, and he was not pleased. I understood his irritation, but the WEG was an international event that would focus millions of eyes on Kentucky. We *had* to keep our word and put our best foot forward. And as reporters noted, I had not targeted his district but had swept away funding from *all* the projects that had not yet started. So, in my mind, the accusations of "politics" were groundless.

The stunning success of the games—and the Kentucky Horse Park's use of the facilities years afterward to greatly expand the number and scope of events it hosted—proved the long-term wisdom of my strategy.

Nevertheless, it didn't win me favors with a man who held the keys to the locked gate through which bills had to move through the Senate.

As a result, bills such as the Graduation Bill and the authorization of agency bonds for state universities remained stuck, session after session. So did a host of minor bills that state cabinets and agencies needed to go about their daily business, bills that in the past were approved as a matter of routine. The Senate president and I clashed repeatedly in the media on issue after issue.

I tried to get around President Williams by working with both Democrats and Republicans in the House and Democrats in the Senate, and Senator Williams and I did agree on a few limited issues. So I was able to build consensus on things like balancing the budget, pension reform, the economic incentives overhaul we called INK, and other issues. In addition, we agreed to raise the cigarette tax, which created much-needed revenue and had some positive effect in reducing people's smoking habits. And it helped when, in August 2010, I promoted the head of my legislative office, Mike Haydon, to chief of staff. Haydon had spent more than 30 years working in state and local government, and he and Senator Williams had a decent working relationship. That left more of Haydon's work in the legislative office to the very capable Roger Thomas, Kate Wood, and Robin Morley.

But the progress we made wasn't nearly what it could have been and needed to be, given the historical challenges facing Kentucky.

When Senator Williams decided to run against me in the 2011 governor's race, the angry rhetoric intensified and our relationship deteriorated further. The short session that year was particularly unproductive, and it was readily apparent that partisan politics had infiltrated every decision and vote.

My pleas to put campaigning aside to focus on governing went unheeded.

When he adjourned the Senate that spring without addressing a plan to fix the budget and fill a Medicaid shortfall, I called a special legislative session with a fervent speech that held him accountable for "holding the future of Kentucky's families hostage to his political games and aspirations." All told, I would be forced to call five special sessions while Senator Williams was head of the Senate.

Well, we got the budget proposal through the legislature, and in the election that fall, I won the governor's race by 170,000 votes. Kentuckians showed that they preferred my bipartisan approach to governing.

Then Circuit Judge Eddie Lovelace unexpectedly died in mid-September of the following year, and I began hearing through the grapevine that Senator Williams was very interested in the post. When his name was one of the three forwarded to me by the local judicial nominating committee, I appointed him to the bench in October 2012, and he accepted.

And so, with a stroke of a pen, we changed the course of Kentucky legislative history, and a new era—one I hoped would be much different than the one before it—was about to begin.

I had reason to be optimistic. Senate Majority Leader Robert Stivers was selected by his Republican colleagues to fill the void, and I couldn't have been more pleased. Senator Stivers had been my first choice and that of my staff, but we had been careful to stay out of the process, knowing any sign of endorsement from me could very well kill his chances.

I'd gotten to know and respect Senator Stivers while working with him to pass House Bill 1, the comprehensive bill attacking prescription painkiller abuse, during the special session earlier that year. I had admired how he stood up to top Republicans and medical industry lobbyists to get the bill through the Senate, and how throughout the fight, his focus had never wavered from families in his district who had been devastated by addiction.

Through our joint work on this legislation, we began to develop the most important and necessary ingredient for successful bipartisan governing: *trust*.

Senator Stivers and I shared a pragmatic and long-game approach to governing. Whereas we often started out on opposite ends of issues, we could sit in a room, just the two of us, and talk frankly, identifying the hurdles and the holdups, and working through them to find common ground. I also knew that when he left my office, the conversation would be confidential.

As soon as Senator Stivers was elected president, we met to develop a process for regular communication. From that point on, before every session, Senator Stivers and I would meet for candid and matter-of-fact discussions of our respective legislative priorities, figuring out areas in which we could build consensus and those on which we were unlikely to bend.

With Senator Stivers as president, the Senate kicked off the 2013 session with a bipartisan luncheon, which I attended, and thus was born a new atmosphere of civility and dignity in Frankfort marked by the willingness to engage in respectful dialogue and seek consensus, even amid deep philosophical differences.

The impact was immediate. In the 2013 session, I worked with the legislature to pass bills that addressed a number of priorities, including:

- raising the compulsory school attendance age from 16 to 18 (after years of trying);

- strengthening the regulatory framework of the landmark prescription painkiller legislation passed in 2012;

- authorizing public universities to fund 11 major construction projects worth $363 million, using campus revenue streams to pay off so-called agency bonds;

- helping Kentucky children by creating better infant health screenings, increasing protections against child predators, and formalizing a panel to investigate cases of death or serious injury due to neglect or abuse;

- taking more steps to stabilize our pension systems, including raising revenue to fully fund the annual increased estimated state obligation, creating a hybrid cash-balance plan for future employees, and improving transparency and legislative oversight of the Kentucky Retirement Systems; and

- taking small steps in the direction of a larger tax reform effort.

For an odd-year session, which lasted 30 days instead of 60, this represented an unbelievable collection of legislation. The new tone of the session didn't go unnoticed, either, as reporters fell all over themselves to write about it.

"President Stivers proved to be a trustworthy and reliable partner in the legislative process—willing to look at policy first and politics second," I told the *Lexington Herald-Leader* for a piece published on March 27. "We didn't always agree, but we could always have honest and open dialogue about any issue."

Senator Stivers praised our ability to communicate, saying I had "played a big part in several major pieces of legislation, especially the pensions. He was on the phone a great deal with us. He held many meetings. … From my perspective, he was more active and involved than I've ever seen him."

Despite celebrated differences on some key issues, we were able to maintain that cordial and cooperative relationship in the years ahead.

In 2014, we agreed on a $20.3-million General Fund budget. Among many other things, the budget increased per-pupil classroom funding, raised teacher pay, expanded preschool to make it available to as many as 5,125 more four-year-olds, and funded high-priority building projects at each of the state's 16 KCTCS campuses. We also set aside money to subsidize child care so low-income parents could work, and funded major initiatives like high-speed broadband access across the state, an advanced manufacturing training center in Georgetown, and the Breathitt Veterinary Center in Hopkinsville.

The legislature also created the adult abuse registry, developed new job incentives, reformed the juvenile justice code, and banned the sale of electronic cigarettes to minors.

In 2015, we passed a comprehensive attack on the growing heroin crisis, reset the floor for the gas tax to stabilize the Road Fund, modernized booster-seat requirements to protect more children, and expanded domestic violence protection to dating couples. We also created the All STARS program to add accountability and transparency to all of Kentucky's early child-care facilities, established a funding mechanism for the SOAR renewal initiative in Eastern Kentucky, created an oversight board to monitor the Kentucky Teachers' Retirement System, and protected tobacco settlement funds.

Top to bottom, it was one of the most productive sessions in modern history, and many of the biggest successes came on bills that had been stuck in the Senate for numerous legislative sessions under the previous Republican leadership.

There was much more to be done, of course. We failed to win approval for smoke-free legislation, legislation to expand Kentucky's ability to enter into public-private partnerships (P3s), a constitutional amendment vote on a local option sales tax, and a long-term funding plan for the Kentucky Teachers' Retirement System. But even some of those issues moved further along in the process than ever before.

I'm confident that had I been around for the 2016 session, we would have made progress on these and many other issues important to the future of Kentucky. That's how optimistic I was in working with the new Senate leadership.

Before the start of the 2015 session, which was my last, President Stivers summed up for Kentucky Educational Television what it was like to work with me:

"Where [Governor Beshear] has committed, he has delivered. When we've needed to have the private discussion about how things would play out, he's never broken any confidence," Senator Stivers said. "And if you're going to move government forward and the state forward, you're going to have to have those types of conversations and I give him a lot of credit for being able to do that."

That's how divided government (or any government for that matter) is supposed to work.

However, the toughest test lies ahead.

In the November 2016 election, Republicans seized control of the Kentucky House of Representatives for the first time since 1921, gaining 18 seats to win not only a majority of the 100 seats, but also a supermajority, with 64 seats. Now with control of both chambers of the general assembly and the Governor's Office, Republicans have unfettered ability to enact their conservative agenda.

What will that agenda mean for Kentucky families?

During my eight years as governor, the Republican Senate leadership and I were able to work on many issues together, but at the same time, they never hesitated to disagree with me on other items. Now that there is a Republican governor, the question becomes: Will they and the new Republican House leadership speak up when they disagree with him, or will they simply become followers, afraid to speak up even when they think the governor's wrong?

So far, the outlook is not promising.

Republican leadership in the Senate wholeheartedly had supported our long-term solution to the public pension issue in 2013 and more investment in education in my last budget.

However, in early 2016, when the new Republican governor proposed cutting K–12 education programs 9 percent a year in order to put additional money into the pension system, they never blinked, following along in lockstep with him. Fortunately, the Democratic House refused to go along with those cuts, and the governor and the Republican Senate backed off.

To help me pass House Bill 1 (the major prescription drug abuse bill), President Stivers stood up to top Republicans in the legislature because he knew that numerous families in his district—some of whom he knew personally—were being devastated by addiction to prescription painkillers. Many of his Republican colleagues felt the same way. To them, at that time, people were more important than politics.

But the same circumstances exist today in connection with the Affordable Care Act and expanded Medicaid. Before the ACA, more than 20 percent of Kentuckians lacked health coverage because their employers didn't offer it or they couldn't afford it. Thanks to the ACA, we reduced that number to 7.5 percent. In Clay County, where President Stivers lives, the uninsured rate was measured in late 2015 at 0.6 percent—down from 17 percent before we implemented the ACA. That incredible drop in Clay County came because almost 8,700 people signed up for health coverage through kynect as of January 2016. Similar numbers mark the districts of his Senate colleagues.

The new Republican governor, however, is now doing all he can to undo the ACA and erect barriers to expanded Medicaid, making it more expensive and harder to get. And so far, President Stivers and other Republicans representing these rural areas are again marching along in lockstep with him, even though most of their constituents will be devastated by the withdrawal of access to affordable health care.

Furthermore, while I and others felt that President Stivers's predecessor, Senator Williams, allowed rank partisanship to unduly interfere with governing, President Williams did strongly believe in the separation of powers between the legislative and executive branches, as set forth in Kentucky's Constitution. He challenged both Democratic and Republican governors when he felt they had infringed on those legislative powers. However, current Senate leaders have acquiesced to the new Republican governor's seizure of legislative authority on at least two occasions without so much as a whimper, requiring Attorney General Andy Beshear to have to challenge the constitutionality of the governor's actions in court. (Incidentally, the Kentucky Supreme Court sided with the attorney general in one case, while the other is pending as of this writing.)

Obviously, it takes courage to stand up to a governor of your own party when you think he is wrong or when his proposals hurt Kentucky's families. For the sake of those families, I hope President Stivers, newly elected House Speaker Jeff Hoover, and other Republican leaders in the House and Senate will find the courage to do so.

DESERT SAND
AND BLUEGRASS

The first thing that struck me about Iraq in the summer was the heat.

It wasn't just hot. It was oppressive, almost unbearably so. The sun and dry terrain seemed to draw every drop of moisture from every cell of my body and then whisk it away, leaving me feeling like a piece of bread being toasted again and again and again. And every breath in the 120-degree-plus temperatures was a gasping effort.

Looking around, my respect for our soldiers, many of whom were from Kentucky, grew immensely. The only extra gear I was wearing was a flak jacket and a helmet. They typically wore that protection and carried 60 to 80 additional pounds of gear.

Suffice to say that the Middle East was a hostile place, and the atmosphere in which they were expected to function was unbelievable.

It was August 2011.

I had been invited across seas by the US Department of Defense to visit soldiers born or trained in Kentucky who were defending freedom and protecting the vulnerable in the nation's War on Terror.

I was accompanied by the governors of Tennessee, Nevada, and Utah, states like Kentucky that had significant contingents of soldiers deployed in dangerous areas.

I was thrilled at the invite and jumped at the chance to go.

It didn't matter that it came in the last 100 days of my re-election effort and would take away precious time and energy. Politics could wait. This was important for a variety of reasons.

One, I was a veteran myself. I had served in the Army Reserves during the Vietnam War. My unit had never been called to battle, but I had plenty of friends who had fought. Some came back scarred physically and psychologically. Others came back in coffins. Those soldiers and my military experience were very much on my mind as I made plans to fly overseas.

Two, as governor I wanted to show support for our men and women. Sure, many would likely have preferred a visit from a professional athlete, a comedian, or a model or actor, but as governor, I spoke on behalf of 4.3 million Kentuckians, and I wanted to make darn sure our soldiers knew how proud we were of them.

See, Kentucky has a long and honorable tradition of military service—so long, in fact, that our contributions to this nation's defense actually predate our statehood.

That's historical fact. The account is well known to any student of Kentucky history, but the late historian Lowell H. Harrison tells it as well as anyone in his *Kentucky's Governors* compilation.

Back in 1780, a British major named Ferguson, who commanded England's forces in the western Carolinas, was tired of frontiersmen coming across the mountains and harassing and killing his troops. So he sent a warning: Any more raids from the "back-country men," he said, and he would send an army to wipe them out.

Well, one American officer from the Kentucky area, who had gained fame in Lord Dunmore's War for his fighting spirit, was infuriated by Ferguson's attempt at intimidation. So that officer gathered volunteers and marched east with other patriotic contingents. In October 1780, they met Ferguson and his troops atop a piece of land known as King's Mountain. It took charge after charge, but in the end, this Kentucky officer helped knock Ferguson off that hill and severely damaged the British effort on the southern front of the American Revolution.

That officer—thereafter known as "Old King's Mountain"—was Isaac Shelby.

A few short years later, in 1792, he became the first governor of the new Commonwealth of Kentucky. He served as governor again two decades later and led Kentucky during the War of 1812, a war in which the young state supplied some 25,000 men for the nation's defense. In the War of 1812, more Kentuckians were killed than soldiers from all other states combined, even though the state was never invaded. That's also historical fact.

Those are telling stories. They illustrate that from the early days of the Bluegrass State—in fact, even before Kentucky *was* a state—Kentuckians have understood and treasured the courage, commitment, and sacrifice required to protect our great nation.

We wear this tradition as a badge of honor as we have sent our sons and later our daughters to fight wherever required—in the trenches on the Western Front, the beaches of France, the rugged terrain of Korea, the jungles of Vietnam, the desert sands of Iraq, and the mountains of Afghanistan.

I wanted to pay testament to that history—and whereas governors no longer lead troops into battle, we are still called to support our troops using the powers of our office.

The third reason I was in the Middle East was to remind Kentuckians back home that we remained a nation at war, and we had soldiers in danger.

For all the fear inspired by the 9/11 attacks in 2001, and for all the "shock and awe" inspired by the colorful explosions that played out on network TV when the United States began its 2003 invasion of Iraq, the War on Terror had largely slipped out of the American consciousness in the decade and a half since.

During World War II, war hit home every day with the rationing of everything from gasoline to tires to hosiery to sugar. During Vietnam, body counts made the nightly news. And during the Persian Gulf War, yellow ribbons and bows attached to trees, doors, telephone poles, and lapels served as a daily patriotic homage to our men and women overseas.

But aside from families of soldiers, by 2011, many Americans seemed to have largely forgotten that the United States was still actively engaged in fighting in the War on Terror.

Part of that had to do with the shifting objectives of a war where the goal was not to conquer a land or a people, but it also had to do with short attention spans. I hoped that media coverage of my trip and my talking about it after I returned would help change that.

Even so, I was unprepared for the emotional impact of the trip. Simply put, it was one of the most moving experiences of my life.

First, the itinerary:

After Pentagon officials briefed us in Washington, we flew to Kuwait, where I visited Kentucky troops at Ali Al Salem Air Base and Camp Arifjan. Then I flew by C-130 to Iraq, where I met with troops at Joint Air Base Balad, Taji Air Base, Camp Victory Baghdad, and Baghdad International Airport.

At the time, more than 2,600 Kentucky servicemen and women were deployed to Iraq and Kuwait—about 1,000 from Fort Campbell, 140 from Fort Knox, and nearly 1,500 from the Kentucky National Guard. The Guard troops included the 149th Maneuver Enhancement Brigade from Louisville and Southeastern Kentucky, whose deployment represented the largest mobilization of Kentucky National Guard troops since World War II—just one more sign of Kentucky's commitment to the War on Terror.

The next day, I flew to Afghanistan, where I visited troops in Kabul, Kandahar, and Bagram. We also went to a forward operating base in Kunduz, where we rode in an MRAP—a mine-resistant, ambush-protected armored vehicle.

At the time, more than 9,600 Kentucky troops were deployed in that country: 6,000 from Fort Campbell, 3,600 from Fort Knox, and 79 from the Kentucky National Guard. Among them were members of the Kentucky Guard's AgriBusiness Development Team, handpicked soldiers who taught villagers in remote areas how to farm and how to turn that farming into a successful business.

I got to meet many of these soldiers. I shook their hands, posed for pictures, chatted with them, and conveyed my admiration. It wasn't surprising how, in this hostile place, their thoughts turned to family and activities back home.

One soldier sent his love back home to his pregnant wife in Louisville. Another soldier talked about his grandparents in Western Kentucky. Several groups of soldiers posed with me in front of the Commonwealth of Kentucky's flag. And another group spent an afternoon with me predicting the outcome of the annual football game between the University of Kentucky and University of Louisville.

In all, more than 75 soldiers gave me personal messages to deliver to family members they had not seen in quite a while. I wished that along with those messages I could have brought the soldiers themselves back home, to keep them safe.

Too soon, the trip was over. On that Friday, the other governors and I returned home, they to their states and I to Kentucky.

Tired as I was, I returned bursting with the need to talk about what I had seen, felt, and heard. I wanted to share my immense pride, to convey the anxiety I felt. Kentuckians *needed* to know about the soldiers' sacrifice and service on their behalf, many thousands of miles away.

Fortunately, I had a great forum for that message, the very next day.

Fancy Farm.

With Election Day just months away, the annual church picnic in Graves County once again would bring together candidates, elected leaders, and thousands of rabid partisan supporters in a too-close-for-comfort spasm of political speechifying. As the incumbent locked in a re-election struggle against Senator President David Williams, a Republican, and the late Gatewood Galbraith, an Independent who was a perennial candidate, I was considered a headliner for the event. A lot of ears would be listening, both at the event and on statewide TV.

Now, I have a love-hate relationship with Fancy Farm.

The non-political part of the event—a picnic that benefits St. Jerome Parish—is a great cause. As a native of Dawson Springs, I get to see a lot of my Western Kentucky friends. The barbecue is the best there is. And the energy surrounding the event is a great reminder of the magnetic appeal of American politics.

But there's a lot of negativity, as well.

When you speak, you have to scream to be heard. Audience members are encouraged to be disrespectful and rude, to interrupt and yell. Speakers are encouraged to ridicule and be mean. Taking potshots is expected.

As reporter Joe Sonka wrote in the publication *LEO Weekly* that year, the audience comes "to witness a political blood sport, where both sides roast and heckle one another into submission. It is a verbal cockfight, where basic rules of human decency are seen as a sign of weakness."

In the weeks leading up to Fancy Farm, I had prepared myself to give such a speech, one that would play to the crowd. I'd done it before, several times. But after spending the week with Kentucky's soldiers and witnessing firsthand their service and sacrifice, partisan bickering just seemed petty and pointless.

My heart and mind were thousands of miles away.

I wanted to testify about what I'd seen. To *not* do so, to *not* put Kentucky soldiers front and center, would be disrespectful. Sacrilegious even.

I figured some of the more partisan people would fault me for not bowing to the tradition of insults, but I didn't care. My visit changed me. It was a reminder that there were more important things than slinging mud and throwing barbs.

So that's what I did. I used my time on stage to talk about the soldiers I'd seen and the sacrifice they and their families were making for our country. The grandparents of one of the soldiers I met were in the crowd, so I introduced them as well. And I asked the crowd to salute the military.

Needless to say, my approach didn't go over well with many there. They wanted their blood sport, not praise for Kentucky soldiers overseas. Galbraith followed me to the mic and called it "the worst darn speech I've ever heard" and said he was "highly offended" by it. Senator Williams said I was avoiding my record.

A columnist for the *Lexington Herald-Leader*, perhaps feeling cheated, noted that I had silenced the jeering section, but complained that I had "gone on and on" about our soldiers.

But others weren't so critical.

A lot of military families thanked me. Joe Sonka of *LEO Weekly* got it right, noting wryly that "there aren't many places in America ... where an eight-minute tribute to troops fighting overseas is panned as rude, offensive, cowardly, and inappropriate."

And to be truthful, I really didn't give a damn.

The commonwealth has more than 300,000 living veterans and countless war casualties. Too many times during my administration, we had to lower the flag to honor a Kentucky soldier who had died. And at any given moment, Kentuckians are serving their country both statewide and across the globe.

Like I said time and again as governor when signing a military-related bill or instituting a new policy, we can never fully repay our military men and women and their families for their service and sacrifice to this great country. But we can act to lessen the hardship that military service sometimes creates. We can support our military installations, help our veterans and active service members take advantage of opportunities as they provide for their families, and provide deserving recognition. And we can provide nursing facilities to care for our veterans in the waning days of their lives and military cemeteries to honor their service in a respectful way.

In 2011, the Department of Defense and the hundreds of soldiers I met in Iraq and Afghanistan reminded me of the true meaning of service.

I haven't been the same person since.

This country would be better off if more leaders in Washington stepped back from their focus on partisanship and thought more about what our soldiers and their families are doing for all of us.

BACK TO THE BASICS

The mid-term elections of 2014 were a disaster for Democrats on both the national and state levels. The GOP gained nine seats in the US Senate, 13 seats in the US House, two governorships, and control of 10 additional state chambers. That left Democrats in control of the smallest number of state legislatures since 1860.

But in Kentucky, they ran into a brick wall.

In Kentucky, Republicans failed to take over the state House—despite a decade of trying, despite publicly proclaiming it as a top goal, despite support from the Koch brothers and other national groups, and despite Republican US Senator Mitch McConnell winning 110 of 120 counties in an easy victory over challenger Alison Lundergan Grimes.

In fact, Kentucky Democrats didn't lose a single seat in the House and were actually only 200 votes short of gaining a seat.

Observers were astonished and impressed.

In fact, the national Democratic Party was so impressed that I was asked to serve on the national task force set up to analyze the 2014 elections to figure out how to get Democrats back on track. And I was subsequently picked to deliver the task force's preliminary recommendations in February 2015 to a huge crowd of state party chairs, consultants, and other leaders in Washington, DC.

I began my remarks that day with a short statement of fact: "The Democratic Party has lost its way …" I then proceeded to explain how we were able to hold back the national Republican tsunami in Kentucky. It wasn't magic, I told the crowd. We just talked to families about things they care most deeply about: jobs, health care, and education. And we did it in a way that engaged them, excited them, and demonstrated in clear terms how Democratic leadership was making their lives better.

In other words, I said, "When you take care of the people, the politics takes care of itself."

That was the lesson not only for party leaders but also for elected officeholders. See, for me, that axiom wasn't just words— it represented a core belief. Focusing on education, jobs, and health care wasn't just a *political* strategy. It was a *governing* strategy. Throughout my eight years, my focus was on helping our families and businesses survive the recession in the short term and on strengthening our economy, our workforce, and our people to make Kentucky more competitive in the long term.

Families in Kentucky recognized that, and voters responded.

They knew I cared about them, and they knew I was working aggressively not to garner cheap headlines on the media-anointed issue du jour but on challenges and goals that would have deeper and lasting impact, things such as health coverage and creating jobs.

In national political circles, there's a lot of talk about "family values," "small-town values," and "social values." Those are usually code words for things related to moral standards or personal beliefs. I chose to focus on priorities that were more basic, whether I was sitting behind the governor's desk or on the campaign trail.

Whether we're white, black, Hispanic, or Asian; whether we're male or female; whether we're Baptist, Catholic, Muslim, Jew, or atheist; whether we live on a farm or in a city; or whether we're gay or straight, we all want certain basic things. We all want stable jobs with a decent income. We want good schools for our kids and safe neighborhoods to live in. We want a chance to have fun and relax, and we want a sense that we're inching closer to the proverbial American Dream. We want to believe that this is *still* the land of opportunity, and that if you work hard and play by the rules, you *will* create a better life for yourself and your children.

So my message to national Democrats worried about the future, and my advice for every elected officeholder, was and is simply this: Get back to the basics. Stop getting distracted by extraneous issues and letting our response to them define us as a party. Those are good for buzz on social media, but they don't help people put food on the table and keep a roof overhead.

The fact is, too many people *don't* think they're getting ahead. Instead, they feel like they're falling behind. They're frustrated and they're disillusioned. And unfortunately, there is a basis for their frustration. We now live in an era in which the privileged few are grabbing a larger and larger share of wealth, power, and hope. And those vulnerable by birth or health or circumstances have found themselves powerless and voiceless. In fact, even those who enjoy a little more financial security, those in the so-called middle class, are convinced that society is passing them by, and that those who run this country have bent the rules to favor the powerful.

Whether voters belong to the Tea Party on one end of the political spectrum or the Occupy movement on the other, at heart they share these feelings.

And in search of quick answers and a place to vent, these voters are easily led astray by negative narratives that play on fear, frustration, and bitterness, and too often they vote against their own self-interest, supporting candidates who tap into their rage, but whose initiatives actually hurt instead of help them.

It's no wonder that in 2015 and 2016, voters lashed out at those with political experience and turned to perceived outsiders. In Kentucky in 2015, voters elected as their new governor a businessman with no government experience. And in 2016, voters picked as president Donald Trump, another businessman who built his brand on sneering at current leaders and whose strategy focused on undercutting the public's trust in government, the courts, schools, science, and the core principles of this country. The backlash in Kentucky against Trump's Democratic opponent— longtime public servant Hillary Clinton—ricocheted down to statehouse elections, where straight party voting defeated many good leaders who had long worked on behalf of the people.

How bad was the down-ticket reverberation in the Bluegrass State in fall 2016? One of those newly elected to the state general assembly was a Republican candidate who was harshly denounced by his own party for a series of racist Facebook posts and pictures and who remained unapologetic about the posts even after *his own party* suggested he withdraw. Despite these posts and his complete lack of experience, he was elected by voters who threw out the incumbent simply because she had experience and was a Democrat.

Look, I understand frustration. I became governor on the leading edge of a global recession that drove unemployment levels into double digits and cost many people their homes, jobs, savings, and health care.

But a real leader's answer to this smoldering resentment and frustration is to address the issues that caused them. However, we now have an entire generation of politicians—not just candidates but also consultants, fund-raisers, staff, and volunteers—whose view of politics and public service is skewed by the emphasis on winning elections instead of service. Too often today, "win at all costs" and "whatever it takes" serve as both political philosophies and motivation for getting involved. To them, anything is acceptable, because they believe that the end justifies the means.

This new generation grew up hearing Kentucky Senator Mitch McConnell proclaim on behalf of Senate Republicans that the single most important thing they wanted to achieve was to make President Obama a one-term president. They also heard the late Ohio Senator George Voinovich and other senators similarly describe the GOP marching orders: If the president was for it, they had to be against it.

With candidates and campaigns always looking for a political edge instead of a policy success or a way to improve people's lives, it's no wonder that public discussion focuses on inflammatory issues that divide us instead of fundamental needs around which we can all coalesce. And it's no wonder that truth, facts, accuracy, honesty, and integrity have fallen by the wayside. The rise of "fake news"—deceptive stories created to mislead that are published in the unregulated free-for-all realm of social media— is indicative of this.

This is a serious problem going forward in this country. If people can't separate fact from fiction, if they accept outrageous stories and memes simply because their messages reinforce previously held beliefs and prejudices, then this country is in real trouble.

What's important for Democrats going forward is to recognize that this election cycle was not a repudiation of our values and our priorities but simply a measure of the frustration of the American (and Kentucky) people.

How do I know this? Because at a time when Kentucky was rapidly moving even further red, I won election to the governorship twice and helped hold off the Republican takeover of the Kentucky House for a couple of election cycles by focusing on health care, education, job creation, and helping our families survive. I made it clear that I was willing to work with anybody at any time on any issue, provided only that they leave the partisan politics at the door. And I backed up that promise by working with both Democrats and Republicans on a range of high-profile issues. Non-partisanship became part of my brand. Not surprisingly, voters of all persuasions appreciated that I put families first—far ahead of partisanship for its own sake.

Don't misunderstand me. I campaigned hard for Democrats during election season. But when it came time to govern, the *D* or *R* behind somebody's name was irrelevant to the issue at hand.

Again, *take care of the people, and the politics takes care of itself.* That's why I didn't get too worried about governing in a state in which President Obama, the leader of my party, was so unpopular. I simply opposed him when I thought he was wrong, and supported him when I thought he was right. And my decisions were made on a case-by-case basis, depending on the issue and its impact on Kentuckians.

Voters respected that.

When Kentucky embraced the Affordable Care Act and created its own state-based health benefit exchange, called kynect, I urged people who needed coverage to check it out.

"You don't have to like the president, and you don't have to like me," I told Kentuckians. "Because it's not about the president, and it's not about me. It's about you. It's about your family. It's about your kids. So you owe it to yourself and to your family to get on the kynect website and see what the ACA can do for you. And I guarantee you'll like what you find."

I made it about the program and the people, instead of partisan considerations. The conventional wisdom was that the ACA would hurt me politically. But it didn't. I spent my last two and a half years as governor talking about health care every chance I could. About three months before I left office, a SurveyUSA poll said 50 percent of voters approved of my performance, while 32 percent disapproved. That's a plus-18 percent rating for a Democratic governor in a state where the head of my party, President Obama, had a negative-30 percent rating. And a separate poll, just weeks before I left office, gave me a plus-26 percent rating, with 57 percent of voters approving of my job performance and 31 percent disapproving.

That's "really remarkable considering many of the controversial things Gov. Beshear has done in the state," *Herald-Leader* political writer Sam Youngman was quoted as saying in an article published by WKYT. "I think President Obama would ask Gov. Beshear, 'What's your secret?'"

But to me, there was no secret. I simply was able to convince voters that I cared about them by the way I talked—constantly—about how my policies and decisions would improve their lives and strengthen our state. They saw me put campaigning aside and focus on governing. They saw me work with Republicans. They saw me fight for them even at the risk of my political career. They understood in clear terms that I was putting people over politics. As a result, in an era where voter disgust with government might be at a historical high, I earned their trust.

Section VII

MEMORIES

MEETING A BEATLE

Governors get to meet a lot of famous people.

During my eight years, for example, Jane and I got to meet or mingle with an array of celebrities, sports stars, and international leaders, including famous people like golfers Tiger Woods and Phil Mickelson; NBA greats Earvin "Magic" Johnson and Julius "Dr. J." Erving; singers Cyndi Lauper and Tom T. Hall; ambassador Caroline Kennedy; Broadway performer Billy Porter; actors Ashley Judd, Renée Zellweger, and George Clooney; Presidents Obama, Bush, and Clinton; Prince Charles of England, and yes, Queen Elizabeth herself.

But for Jane and me, a couple who attended both high school and college in the 1960s, the night of June 2, 2010, was on a whole different level. It was our chance to meet not only a Who's Who list of musical artists but also an actual Beatle.

It was during my re-election campaign, and Jane and I somehow ended up together one evening at the Governor's Mansion (a rare occurrence at that point). We were sitting on the sofa opening mail when we came across an envelope from the White House. It contained an invitation to an event honoring Sir Paul McCartney—yes, *that* Paul McCartney—with the Library of Congress Gershwin Prize for Popular Song.

"This really looks like fun," Jane said, picking up the invitation.

"Well," I replied, my brain focused on the long and heated

campaign ahead, "we've got a fund-raiser that evening, so we can't go."

Jane just looked at me. "Well, *you* may have a fund-raiser that evening," she said, "but *I* am going to the White House to see Paul McCartney."

Needless to say, I came to my senses and asked my running mate, Jerry Abramson, to substitute for me at the fund-raiser. And Jane and I headed to Washington for the gala hosted by President Obama and First Lady Michelle Obama.

At the appointed hour, we entered the White House and were escorted to a short, pre-event reception. We were surprised to see that it was a somewhat small gathering, with only about 200 people, and to my knowledge, I was the only governor present.

Once we entered the East Room for the event, we found seats—at the very back, next to the aisle, and in front of a closed door. These, we thought, were the "cheap seats," with the best seats reserved (as they should be) for various celebrities and Washington dignitaries. But much to our surprise and delight, all the entertainers and artists who were to perform that evening were gathered in the room behind that closed door—and as each one waited to be announced and walk to the stage, they came out and stood right beside Jane and me.

And what an incredible lineup!

We got to see singers Emmylou Harris, Faith Hill, Elvis Costello, Jack White, David Grohl (of Nirvana and the Foo Fighters), Corinne Bailey Rae, and the Jonas Brothers, as well as concert pianist Lang Lang and jazz pianist-composer Herbie Hancock. Jerry Seinfeld did a great comedy routine. Stevie Wonder performed "Ebony and Ivory" with Paul McCartney, and of course, McCartney himself performed.

At one point during this magical evening, I turned to Jane and said, "Isn't it amazing that two kids from Bowling Green and Dawson Springs, Kentucky, are sitting in the White House with the president and First Lady of the United States listening to Paul McCartney sing? Only in America!"

As the event ended, we walked down to the front and introduced ourselves to the guest of honor, the former Beatle himself. When we said we were from Kentucky, McCartney looked at us and said with a twinkle in his eyes, "I hope *y'all* enjoyed the evening!" As an added bonus, we then went to a reception in the Lincoln Room, where all of the performers gathered for a few minutes and we were able to meet each one personally.

Man, am I glad Jane made me miss that fund-raiser!

A PRIVATE TAKES OVER

As the state's chief executive, a Kentucky governor serves many roles, but not one of them is a bigger honor than being commander-in-chief of the Kentucky National Guard.

During my eight years, these dedicated men and women went over and above the call of duty time after time in their unique dual missions, both in fighting the war against terror in the Middle East and in protecting our citizens in the face of ice storms, tornadoes, floods, and other natural disasters.

The public has no clue just how active our men and women in green and blue are.

In addition to scheduled call-ups to provide security and support for annual events like the Kentucky Derby, I mobilized Guard units on an emergency basis on 16 different occasions to bring help in major weather disasters during my term.

"Superman's not available," I often said only half in jest, "so I'm sending in the Kentucky National Guard."

And then, as part of federal missions directed by President Obama, the Kentucky Army Guard mobilized more than 4,700 soldiers during my eight years, and the Air Guard deployed more than 3,000 troops to 46 locations, albeit for shorter tours. The Kentucky Guard did everything from fighting in Iraq to teaching agriculture in Afghanistan to providing security in Djibouti and helping earthquake victims in Haiti. In fact, the mobilization of

1,363 soldiers from the 149th Maneuver Enhancement Brigade was the largest Kentucky brigade mobilization since World War II, and these soldiers were some of the last to depart from Iraq.

I felt a special bond with the Guard, particularly the enlisted men and women, because I had served my country as an enlisted man in the United States Army when I was in my early 20s. I knew what it was like to be in their position and know that everything related to my future—from where I would be sleeping that night to possibly where I would spend my next year—was in the hands of someone else.

So one day, when I was asked to address a room full of enlisted men and women with the adjutant general and an array of other high-ranking officers (major generals, brigadier generals, and the like) seated behind me, I decided to have some fun.

I started by thanking all of them for their service to the people of the commonwealth. Then I looked out over the audience and said, "All of you enlisted men and women, take heart, because you never know what the future holds. I rose to the rank of specialist 4th class in the United States Army, and today I am commander-in-chief of the Kentucky National Guard. And that means I get to tell all these generals sitting behind me what to do!"

The room erupted in laughter, and I noticed a lot of smiles on the faces of those enlisted men and women sitting in front of me. (I couldn't tell if those behind me had the same reaction.)

A HUG FROM
GEORGE CLOONEY

Jane found the job of First Lady extremely rewarding in terms of what she could accomplish to better the lives of people in our state.

But her desire for her privacy and a quieter life stayed with her, and from time to time, she really missed the solitude of our farm, instead of living in the fishbowl of politics in the Governor's Mansion in Frankfort. We all need a place where we find peace and tranquility, and for her, that place was in a saddle on the back of a horse, not behind a desk or a microphone.

During that first year or so, she wrestled with finding that balance to her life that would bring her the most happiness, and I found myself looking for ways to help her find it.

One such occasion arose when the producers of the movie *Leatherheads* announced that they would premiere the show in Maysville at the Washington Opera House. The movie starred George Clooney and Renée Zellweger, and Clooney—a native of that area of Kentucky—wanted to do something for the place where he grew up.

That evening we drove to Maysville, picked up our friends, Bob and Judy Vance, and headed to the opera house. We walked the red carpet, gave a few interviews, and went inside.

I was asked by our tourism people to present gifts to George and Renée on stage before the first showing of the movie, and those gifts were brought to me as we took our seats. I told Jane I wanted her to go on stage with me to present the gifts, but she demurred, saying I should go alone. I insisted. "I'll give the gift to Renée, and you give the gift to George," I told her.

Well, those were the magic words. After all, George Clooney is a two-time winner of *People* magazine's "Sexiest Man Alive" award.

At the appointed time, we went up on stage together and joined George and Renée. I said a few words, handed the gift to Renée, and gave her a hug and a kiss on the cheek. Jane followed my lead, presented the gift to George, and gave him a kiss as well. As for the hug, I wasn't sure if she was going to turn loose!

After the movie, we went upstairs in the theater and visited with the two stars for 15 minutes or so before leaving. When we got in the car, I turned to Jane and said, "So, are things getting a little better about this First Lady job?"

She laughed and said yes, things were looking up.

THE ULTIMATE
IN RECYCLING

Call it an innovative recycling project times 10.

For 32 years, Kentucky State Police had been training new recruits on a floor of the agency's headquarters in a converted hotel. The facility lacked adequate space for both classroom work and physical training, wasn't equipped with modern technology capabilities, required cadets to travel to other locations for some activities, and backed up to residential areas, making outside training difficult. As KSP Commissioner Rodney Brewer said, we had been "training 21st-century troopers in a 20th-century facility."

But the cost of a new facility was estimated at about $35 million, money we simply didn't have.

Then in early 2011, came an off-the-wall suggestion from the man I'd picked to lead the Justice and Public Safety Cabinet, Secretary J. Michael Brown: Why didn't we turn a nearby sparsely populated state prison into a training facility?

On its face, the idea seemed outlandish. But once Brown made the case with the help of Brewer and Corrections Commissioner LaDonna Thompson, they got my attention.

For one thing, we no longer needed the prison, a 205-bed minimum-security facility called the Franklin Career Development Center.

Whereas over the previous few years, Kentucky had led the nation in the rate of growth in our prison population, careful management by Brown, Thompson, and their staff had reversed that trend and the inmate population actually dropped between 2008 and mid-2011. (In fact, thanks to that management and later legislation that stressed treatment instead of incarceration for low-level drug offenders, we were able to end all contracts with private prison companies during my term.)

For another thing, the setup was perfect: The prison had a huge campus, lots of classroom and dormitory space, a cafeteria that could feed more than 100 people at a time, laundry facilities, meeting rooms, and exercise areas, as well as a running track, basketball court, and softball field. And there was plenty of room to grow, as funds became available.

So after announcing the project in May 2011, we moved what few inmates remained at FCDC into other facilities and began Phase I of the renovation.

We all recognized the irony of transforming a facility designed to house criminals into a facility that trained people to catch them. But adding to that irony was this: Much of the $4.5-million cost of Phase I was funded using money seized from drug dealers.

"Even with the accomplished reality sitting here for all of us to see, it sounds a little far-fetched, doesn't it?" I said at the dedication in April 2015.

Far-fetched or not, just a month later, 64 recruits reported to the repurposed Kentucky State Police academy to begin 23 weeks of training that—if they made it to graduation—would qualify them to join the "thin gray line" protecting the public from harm.

To my knowledge, no ghosts of the former residents who may haunt the facility in any way interfered with that training!

RUSHING TO VIRGINIA

It was the type of phone call that all parents dread, even after their children are grown.

Our oldest son, Jeff, who is an equine veterinarian, had been hurt in a horse-related accident and was in intensive care at a hospital near his home in Virginia. As we heard details from Jeff's wife, Emily, I rushed to a plane and headed east, where Jane was to meet me.

It was June 2009. In a few days, I was to address a special session of the general assembly, with the budget and new economic development tools on the table. A lot was riding on that session, but for the moment, I was a father first.

Our son was hurt.

Apparently, Jeff had been knocked down by a stallion and had banged his head against the pavement. Initially he insisted he was fine, but as Emily was driving him to the hospital to be checked out, he began showing signs of a severe concussion.

By the time I got to University Hospital in Charlottesville, Jeff was in a drug-induced coma to help the healing process. Despite a doctor's assurance that Jeff would eventually be fine, we kept an anxious vigil. I had watched a number of friends lose a child, but you never think it will happen to you. You can imagine the fear that had gripped me when Emily had called and I had heard the concern (and shakiness) in her voice. That told me how serious this could be, and I couldn't get to Virginia fast enough. Once I was there, I couldn't stop the thoughts that rushed through my head.

You never stop being a father, whether your child is two or 42. It's a lifelong honor and a lifelong responsibility. You worry, you hope, you dream, and when things go wrong, you just want to help—every minute of the day.

That 24/7/365 mentality is kind of like being governor. You hurt when your people hurt, you grieve when they grieve, and you just want things *to be better*. Simply put, you *care*.

During our wait, I received a call on my cell phone from Tim Kaine, then governor of Virginia (and later the Democrats' nominee for vice president of the United States). I'm sure the Virginia state troopers had alerted his office that I was in Charlottesville and had told him what was going on. Tim inquired about Jeff and asked whether there was anything I needed or anything he could do. It was very kind of him and reflected the type of person he is: a caring, sincere individual.

When Jeff finally woke, I talked to him for a little bit although he really wasn't all there at that time. But the next day, the real Jeff had come back, and Jane and I felt like a huge weight had been lifted from our shoulders.

Fortunately, Jeff fully recovered with no side effects or lingering problems.

But the scare had forced us to step back and remember what was important in life. It had reminded me why I was in public service. A few days later, I conveyed that message in my televised speech to the general assembly, one of the very few times I ever talked about my family and personal life in such a public setting.

"In politics, it's easy to get caught up in the policy of the moment, as if this were some abstract, nebulous exercise," I said. "It's not."

I continued:

Our decisions—to act or not to act—directly impact people's lives.

We're here today because Kentuckians—our family members, our friends—need us.

This isn't about politics, it's about people.

We're in the throes of a severe economic crisis.

But even as our families are struggling to cope, life goes on.

I was reminded of that several times over the last week, in vivid and emotional ways.

About a week ago, my son Jeff—who is an equine veterinarian—was critically injured at work in a horse-related accident.

Jeff is on his way to a full recovery, but for a while, that outcome was uncertain.

Jane and I spent many anxious moments in an intensive care unit, sick with worry, fear, and helplessness.

Every parent understands what I'm talking about; it doesn't matter how old your children are, their vulnerability is unnerving.

Life is indeed fragile.

Then today, I experienced emotion at the other end of the spectrum.

My other son, Andy, and his wife, Britainy, gave birth today to their first child, William Bradley.

He is Jane's and my second grandson.

And as you might expect, I'm here tonight feeling pride that's indescribable.

Every grandparent, I'm certain, can relate.

My fellow Kentuckians, there are moments in life that bring into focus what really is meaningful.

Whether it's praying for your child's recovery or touching your new grandson's tiny fingers.

Tonight, let us remember for whom we're working.

TELEPROMPTER MAGIC

The Kentucky General Assembly has 138 members. Thanks to the quirks of demographics and vagaries of the electorate, in any given legislature, you get a diverse assortment of characters and backgrounds.

This story speaks for itself.

Every year the governor appears before a joint session of the House and Senate to give a speech called the State of the Commonwealth.

It's a big occasion, televised live by Kentucky Educational Television, and it generates lots of media coverage, with reporters, lobbyists, legislators, and local officials parsing every word. Governors talk about the year that just ended and set the tone and agenda for the year ahead.

Now I didn't use a teleprompter in my day-to-day speeches, but for that very important annual speech, I did. The stakes were high, the speech was typically 45 minutes or more, and I had very specific things to say. I didn't want to ramble or repeat myself, and I didn't want to be seen flipping pages of my speech.

The teleprompter device itself consists of two tall "towers" standing in front of the podium, one on each side, as anybody can see. They hold glass screens on which an electronic image of text scrolls as I deliver the speech. The towers are designed to be as unobtrusive as possible, but ... well ... they're still there.

During the 2010 State of the Commonwealth, one of the things I talked about was the success of a new business incentives program I'd worked with the legislature to pass the previous year. To show how it was helping us to recruit businesses, I cited a representative list of projects announced in the previous year and the number of jobs each created.

For example: "Eighty-nine new jobs at Sazerac North America distilleries in Owensboro and Frankfort, 150 new jobs at Safetran Systems in Crittenden County, 100 new jobs at EQT in Pikeville" and so on.

It was a long list, with 11 different businesses, locations, and job numbers. And it was only one part of the speech, which was almost 4,000 words long and contained a whole lot more numbers and names and facts and such.

After the SOTC, we had a reception at the Governor's Mansion, as is traditional, during which officials offer congratulations, talk about the speech and the session ahead, and just mingle.

I was standing there saying hello to various folks when a long-time legislator came up to me. I won't name him. But his comment went something like this (and he was serious!):

"That was a great speech, Governor. Very inspirational. But I have to tell you, I'm really impressed. How in the world did you memorize all those company names and numbers? There must have been a ton of them, and you never looked at your speech even once. I could never do that."

Indeed.

SLEEPOVER AT THE GOVERNOR'S OFFICE

The protesters came expecting (and seemingly wanting) to be handcuffed and jailed. Instead, I offered them hospitality.

And with that, what was planned as a confrontation (and would have been a public relations nightmare) turned into a low-key discussion of differing opinions after which everybody emerged with dignity and respect—even if everybody wasn't satisfied.

It was Friday, February 11, 2011.

Late in the morning, a group of 20 protesters converged on the governor's office, saying they planned to stay until either I ordered a stop to a controversial mining practice in Kentucky or I had them dragged off to jail.

Inside my inner office just a few feet away, I had a quick discussion with my senior staff. We needed to be strategic and thoughtful, I said, because the situation was ripe for mishandling.

For one thing, among the group of activists were Wendell Berry, Silas House, and Erik Reece—three Kentucky authors of considerable renown who commanded a national audience. Berry, in particular, is widely considered one of Kentucky's all-time intellects and in 2005, was on the Smithsonian's short list of "35 Who Made a Difference." And for another thing, on at least two occasions in the previous few years, similar protests held in the governor's office of an adjoining state had ended in widely distributed images of uniformed officers carrying protesters away in handcuffs.

"We are *not* going to do that," I said emphatically.

Instead, we decided to "disarm" them.

So despite my busy day, I carved out precious time and surprised the protesters by coming out to talk to them in the outer reception area. It was a respectful if pointed discussion.

They opposed surface mining, in particular, a kind of surface mining called mountaintop removal, and said it permanently damaged the air, water, and land. They thought state government wasn't doing enough to protect communities and the land. Among other things, they wanted Kentucky to withdraw from a lawsuit we had joined against the US Environmental Protection Agency. And they invited me to Eastern Kentucky to see the situation in person.

I agreed to the visit, but I didn't share all of their beliefs about mining. While I respected their passion and concern, I thought they were demonizing the entire mining industry. Done right, mined land could be restored, I said. And they weren't considering the overall economic picture. Coal meant jobs, not just in the industry itself but even more so in a huge manufacturing sector supported by cheap electricity produced by coal. In a down economy, I couldn't jeopardize jobs.

We talked for a half hour or so, and while they appreciated that I had come out to talk, in the end, there was little agreement and they weren't happy with me or my words. Berry later called it an "unsatisfactory conversation" and a "standoff" but acknowledged that I "listened evidently with care."

When I returned to my office, I told my staff what we were going to do about the sit-in: nothing. We were going to lock the doors of the capitol building at its usual closing time and tell the protesters that they were welcome to stay in the outer reception area (and there was a bathroom down the hall). But otherwise, the building's usual rules would apply: A Kentucky State Police security guard would be on campus and the doors to the building would be locked. If they left the building, they couldn't return, and no one could join them.

The way I figured, there was no need to escalate the situation or to give them the public arrests they wanted. Besides, they weren't being disruptive; they were passionate advocates trying to make a point, and in fact, they were respectful of my staff and its workday. (As my communications director, Kerri Richardson, told the *Lexington Herald-Leader*, "As far as we can tell, they aren't doing anything wrong." What Kerri didn't add is that she and others on staff were big fans of Berry, Reece, and House, and actually had some of those authors' autographed books in their government offices. My speechwriter even had a framed Berry poem on his wall.)

Once they realized they weren't going to be arrested and instead were going to be allowed to stay, the protesters sent out for sleeping bags, blankets, pillows, books, and refreshments. Sometime Friday evening, we left for the weekend, but not before my chief of staff, the late Mike Haydon, bought the protesters a vegetable tray and snacks, and we offered drinks, napkins, and the like.

Fourteen of the protesters, including Berry, had decided to stay, and with supporters following on social media, they amended the protest's narrative. What was initially billed as a "historic sit-in" was now touted as a "slumber party" and a "sleepover at the governor's." As evening turned into night, they took photos, gave interviews, and posted periodic updates via blogs and Twitter. They continued to do so throughout the weekend, and on Sunday, they were seen waving to other protesters gathered outside.

Come Monday, three days later, they emerged—ending what one media outlet had elevated to a "four-day occupation"—for the previously planned "I Love Mountains" rally on the Capitol steps, held annually to promote environmental bills during the legislative session. Speakers criticized me and mocked my words, but I didn't take it personally. Besides, even Wendell Berry acknowledged publicly that he had been treated "with hospitality and perfect kindness"—even if, as I later heard, the protesters said that they had been outfoxed by the governor.

However, just as I promised, seven weeks later, I visited Floyd County to take a tour of communities near mining sites, courtesy of guides from the group Kentuckians for the Commonwealth. I also met with residents and officials in Harlan County to talk about economic development.

The moral to the story? Treating people with respect goes a long way, and we proved it the day the protesters came to get arrested and left with their freedoms intact and voices heard.

THE WHITE HOUSE:
HUMAN AFTER ALL

The aura of the presidency is overwhelming for most people, and they tend to think of the president and the White House in almost super-human terms.

However, an incident early in my governorship illustrated that the residents of 1600 Pennsylvania Avenue NW—no matter which party is in office—are just as human as you and me.

In 2009, a little over a year into my first term, a horrific winter storm hit Kentucky, placing 110 of our 120 counties in a state of emergency. Heavy ice that began January 26 brought down trees, power lines, cell phone towers, and almost anything else standing. The ice storm was followed by a week of snow that complicated repair and rescue efforts. Power was knocked out to almost 800,000 families, businesses, and hospitals; drinking water was cut to more than 200,000 families; and by the time it all ended, 36 people had died.

Just two days into the storm, I realized that we needed a major disaster declaration immediately so that we could access help from FEMA, Homeland Security, and other federal agencies. So on January 28, my office called the White House, gave them details, and asked for a declaration as soon as possible.

That evening, a call came to the Governor's Mansion where Jane and I were waiting. I picked up the phone and the operator said, "Governor Beshear, this is the White House calling. Can you hold for the president?"

"Yes, ma'am," I said and waited for about 30 seconds.

The operator came on the line again. "Governor Beshear, can you hold for the president?"

"Certainly," I said and proceeded to wait for another 30 seconds.

For a third time, the operator came on the phone and said, "Governor Beshear, can you ..."

But before she could finish her sentence, an exasperated voice in the background said, "Oh, just hand me the phone."

President Obama then came on the line to tell me that he had signed the disaster declaration. It was good news, and I was thrilled that additional resources were coming to Kentucky. Inside, however, I was chuckling. It seemed that the folks in the White House, who had been in office for only two weeks at that time, had not yet figured out how to transfer calls.

So you see, they are human after all.

FRIENDS IN HIGH PLACES

This essay could also be called "Governors stick together."

As I described in several other essays, the damage caused by the ice storm that hit Kentucky in the last week of January 2009 was of a magnitude never before seen, and thus the response was unprecedented in scope as well. On a state and local level, I called on every resource at my disposal, from road crews to public health workers to volunteer firefighters to the entire Kentucky Army National Guard, plus Air National Guard units.

Thanks to a presidential disaster declaration, we also had federal resources—including the Federal Emergency Management Agency, Homeland Security, and the Army Corps of Engineers—activated and working with our teams in Kentucky. The federal response was in most ways powerful and effective, but—not surprisingly—several of the federal agencies seemed to be at cross-purposes, making it difficult to obtain accurate information.

That became painfully evident as we desperately tried to find massive generators that could temporarily supply electrical power to places like hospitals and nursing homes. Due to fallen wires, poles, and transmission towers, electrical power was out to almost 800,000 families and businesses, including those like hospitals with vulnerable populations and no backup power.

We kept getting conflicting reports of the arrival and location of the generators we had requested. But whether it was too much red tape or poor interaction among agencies, nothing seemed to be actually happening—and unless it did, and quickly, more people were going to die.

I was out with the National Guard and Kentucky State Police reviewing damage when—in desperation—I called my friend Janet Napolitano, who had just recently been appointed secretary of Homeland Security. I had met Janet in 2007 when I was running for governor and she was governor of Arizona, and our friendship had strengthened during meetings of various governors associations.

Janet got on the line immediately, and I explained our situation related to the generators and expressed my frustration with FEMA and the Corps of Engineers.

"I want to help," Janet said. "What do you want me to do?"

I said, "Janet, I want you to set up a conference call with the heads of these agencies within the hour, and I want you to tell them in the strongest possible terms that their heads will roll if we don't get our generators immediately, because there are lives on the line."

"I'll do it," she replied, and in the next hour, we had that telephone call. I won't repeat the words Secretary Napolitano uttered during that call to a bunch of high-ranking officials, but suffice it to say, the heat generated during that call could have melted a lot of the ice across Kentucky! More importantly, our generators showed up immediately.

Thank God, I had met Janet Napolitano and developed that relationship when we were fellow governors. There's no telling how many lives it saved.

THE NEWEST GENERATION

When I was elected to my first term in 2007 and began assembling my staff, I was able to grab a number of people with experience in Frankfort, such as Joe Prather, Larry Hayes, Eddie Jacobs, Tom Preston, Sally Flynn, and Mary Lassiter. (Although in Mary's case, experience didn't mean "old.")

Naturally, a few reporters and bloggers took some potshots at me for bringing back the "geriatric" crowd, those whose hair was as gray as mine, or who had lost their hair altogether (again, Mary was the exception). The criticism, I assume, was meant to imply that the Beshear administration was tired, decrepit, and stuck in the past.

But the fact is, a good number of the important members of my staff were young, new to state government, and full of energy, ideas, and optimism for the future—and I have proof.

My evidence? Weddings and new babies.

I can't tell you how many members of my relatively small staff got married during my eight years, but six members of my communications staff alone tied the knot.

And births?

We celebrated at least 23 new babies during my term, in the Office of the Governor alone. Sally, my amazing executive assistant and the person who made the office run, taped pictures of almost all of them on the wall next to her desk. And that doesn't count the staff members who came to Frankfort with toddlers.

Along with my three grandchildren—Nicholas, Will, and Lila—I watched a whole lot of kids grow up during my eight years in the Governor's Office.

Seeing Sally's pictures and hearing the cries of the babies when they came to visit reminded us all that the work we were doing would affect not just us but also the generations that followed.

And let me tell you, answering "Will this make Kentucky stronger 50 years from now?" was a pretty good litmus test for just about any decision I was called on to make in the Governor's Office.

RELATIONSHIPS MAKE THE WORLD GO 'ROUND

I learned about the importance of relationships and the ability to communicate and deal with people early on. My father and his brother were partners in Beshear Funeral Home in Dawson Springs, and my mother was a funeral director. They drew business from a four- or five-county area around Dawson Springs because they treated families with respect. They listened, they sympathized, they consoled.

Consequently, families came from miles away because they wanted Brother Russell or Brother Eddie (courtesy titles because they were also lay Baptist ministers) to take care of mom or dad. We grew up in a home right next to the funeral home, and we saw our parents in action every day.

But an experience unrelated to the funeral home business taught me up close and personal the value of relationships.

All of the Beshear children worked to earn money during the summers. As a young teenager, I mowed lawns. When I turned 16, I applied for the most coveted summer position around Dawson Springs—employment at Pennyrile Forest State Park, just nine miles out of town.

These jobs were political; i.e., you needed to be on the right side of the state administration in the capital, Frankfort, in order to get one.

Back then, political fights in Kentucky on a state level were between factions of the Democratic Party, and my family had apparently been on the wrong side in the last governor's race.

After hearing nothing from the local Democratic contact about my application, I called, only to be told that my application had "not yet come back from Frankfort." This was apparently code for "you are not going to get a job."

I told my mom where things stood, and she told me to call Clint Meadows about the Pennyrile job. At that time, Mr. Meadows was possibly the wealthiest person in Dawson Springs, and his home was located on, appropriately, "Meadows Hill." More importantly, he was a Democrat and a prominent contributor to campaigns, and my mom had worked for him years before.

"Mother," I said. "I don't even know Clint Meadows."

But she insisted. "It doesn't matter. He knows me and our family."

So I reluctantly picked up the phone and called him. He answered, and I said, "Mr. Meadows, this is Steve Beshear. I am the son of Russell and Mary Elizabeth Beshear."

He said, "I know who you are. What can I do for you?"

I told him that I had applied for a job at Pennyrile for the summer and would like to talk to him about it. He invited me to come to his house to see him, so I jumped in the car, drove up Meadows Hill to his residence, and knocked tentatively on his door. Mrs. Meadows opened the door and invited me in to this beautiful, well-kept, well-furnished living room. Mr. Meadows came in, shook my hand, and asked me to sit down.

"How can I help you, Steve?" Mr. Meadows asked.

I explained that I needed to work that summer to earn money for college, and that I had applied at Pennyrile but had been told that my application had not yet been approved in Frankfort. After a few more formalities, Mr. Meadows thanked me for coming to see him and said simply, "Let me see what I can do." Without another word, I thanked him and left.

Two days later, our phone rang. It was the local Democratic contact. "Steve, your application just came back from Frankfort," he said. "You will start work in two days at Pennyrile."

And just like that, Mom had taught me that age-old lesson: It's not always what you know that counts; it's sometimes who you know that matters. The good relationship that she had established years ago with Mr. Meadows paid off for me.

The value of relationships was a lesson I never forgot, and one that served me well both in life and through eight years as governor.

WENDELL FORD:
A KENTUCKY LEGEND

I have a framed photograph that moved with me from the governor's office to my office at home. It depicts leadership and service, and more importantly, a Kentucky legend who epitomized those traits.

The image was captured at the University of Kentucky in Lexington, the day before the 1996 presidential election. President Clinton was on his way to being re-elected, and I was running for the US Senate. He and I are standing at the edge of a stage, smiling and waving to the crowd.

If you look closely at the photograph, which is in the photo section of this book, you see the impish smile of a third person standing behind the president and me, way off in the background. These days, some might call it a photobomb.

That person is the late US Senator Wendell Ford.

His being in the background was an appropriate place, because that's where he liked to maneuver. The senator from the Bluegrass State wasn't the flashiest politician—you didn't often see him out front grabbing headlines, at least not intentionally. He was too busy getting things done. As majority whip and later minority whip of the Senate, his job was to round up votes—by persuasion or other means—for the party's priorities, in this case, the president's.

Senator Ford was good at it.

I heard President Clinton tell the story about how his tax reform bill was passed in 1993. According to the former president, after counting the potential votes, it appeared that the measure would pass by a single vote. But one senator was wavering, so Wendell babysat the senator for 24 hours until he walked onto the floor and voted for the bill. "I got all the credit for tax reform, but Wendell Ford made it happen," Clinton said.

That was Wendell Ford's strength—figuring out what it took to put the votes together and then *making it happen*. Usually from the background.

That's why the senator liked to describe himself as a workhorse, not a show horse.

Nevertheless, he was one of the most interesting and effective leaders to cross Kentucky's political stage in the 20th century, ranking with Alben Barkley and John Sherman Cooper as Kentuckians who've made their mark as statesmen in this great nation.

A native of Western Kentucky, Wendell didn't go to college after high school, opting instead to enter his father's insurance agency business. He married the love of his life, Jean (they were married 71 years), and together they raised two children.

When he got into politics, he became the only Kentuckian ever to win election to consecutive terms as lieutenant governor, governor, and senator. In every office in which he served, his methods were simple: Wendell Ford listened, he cared, and he got the job done.

I met Wendell when I was elected to the state legislature in 1973 and he was governor, and over the years, he became both a mentor and a friend. I watched him closely. I listened and I learned. And when I came to Governor's Mansion in 2007, I told myself that if I was half as good a governor as he had been, then I'd consider my term a success.

When Wendell passed away on January 22, 2015, I was asked to say a prayer at the service in the Capitol rotunda in Frankfort. I chose Proverbs 31:8–9, a verse that honored Ford's penchant for sticking up for vulnerable Kentuckians: "Speak up for those who cannot speak for themselves, for the rights of all who are destitute. Speak up and judge fairly; defend the rights of the poor and needy."

Both former President Clinton and Vice President Joe Biden also honored Ford by speaking at the later Owensboro service.

A few weeks later, while I was sitting in Vice President Biden's office in Washington, he gave me one of the highest compliments I have ever received.

"Steve," Biden said, "you know who you remind me of? My friend Wendell Ford. You go about the job very quietly and just get it done."

I was stunned … but pleased as well. I don't deserve my name being mentioned in the same breath with Senator Ford's, but it sure made me proud when Joe Biden did it.

MY KINGDOM FOR A TIE

Kentucky governors get to do a lot of fun things, not the least of which is crowning the Mountain Laurel Festival queen.

It's a wonderful atmosphere: a beautiful cove deep in the mountains at Pine Mountain State Park in the southeastern part of the state. Dozens of beautiful young ladies representing universities and colleges across Kentucky decked out in formal gowns and displaying the ultimate in grace, dignity, intelligence, and poise. Colorful flowers, formal attire, a parade, and music. And usually a blazing hot sun beating down on the crowd.

This festival has been going on since 1931 and has become a homecoming for hundreds of folks who grew up in the area and annually come back to visit. Governors have been crowning the queen at the festival for years, and I joked many times that the real reason I ran for governor was to be a part of this tradition every year.

The governor traditionally wears a summer tuxedo—black pants with a white jacket and black bow tie. I would annually fly down to Pineville that morning, tux in hand, speak at the governor's luncheon, change into the tux, and proceed to the cove for the crowning of the queen.

But one year, things did not go as planned.

That year, after lunch, I proceeded to the room reserved for me to change clothes, and then realized that I had forgotten to bring my black bow tie. It was just 20 minutes before the beginning of the crowning ceremony and I was tieless.

That would not do.

I quickly alerted Eddie Jacobs, an assistant who traveled with me in his role as "body man." Eddie jumped in the car, drove over to the cove, and found Edith Asher, one of the longtime organizers of the event who happened to be a big supporter of mine. After hearing of the problem, she marched over to one of the young teenage escorts, who was dressed in a tux, and told him to take off his bow tie.

"The governor needs your tie," she said.

Who knows what the young man thought, but, tie in hand, Eddie beat a path back to the lodge, where I hurriedly finished dressing, got over to the cove, and performed the Kentucky governor's annual duty.

As I walked in, I will never forget the mischievous smile on Edith's face. She knew she had saved the day. And, needless to say, I never forgot my tie after that!

BURYING THE HABIT

Smoking is a powerful addiction, one that grips some people harder than others, and even some people who desperately want to quit find themselves unable to do so, at least for very long.

But some people *are* able to quit, and the stories of how they succeeded run the gamut, from long, repeated, and painful strategies to short and quite dramatic declarations.

The story of how my father, Russell Beshear, quit smoking definitely falls in the latter category.

Dad was born in 1909, and he started smoking as a teenager. After he and Mom married and started having children, Mother's mom, Nettie Joiner (we kids called her "Ninnie"), came to live with us and helped raise my siblings and myself. Ninnie was on my Dad for years to give up cigarettes, but she had yet to succeed when she passed away in 1960, at the age of 80.

At the cemetery, as the workers began to fill in the grave, my father took the cigarette he was smoking out of his mouth and, with tears in his eyes, threw it into her grave, saying, "Nettie, you always wanted me to quit smoking, and so that will be my *last* cigarette."

And it was.

With that act, my dad had literally buried his smoking habit. Years later, shortly after we were married, Jane and I also succeeded in quitting smoking cold turkey—but not in such a dramatic fashion!

VICTORY

No, this is not about me winning some election.

It's about one of Kentucky's best ambassadors who couldn't speak English and ran around on four legs—the First Dog of the commonwealth, Victory.

Known by everyone far and wide as "Tory," this rough-coated Jack Russell puppy landed in our arms just before Christmas 2007, right as I entered the governorship, and for eight years, she brought joy to everyone who came in contact with her.

Tory was immediately adopted by the staff and security detail at the Governor's Mansion, as well my staff in the Governor's Office. Everyone knew that while you could disagree with the governor or First Lady, you had better not disagree with Tory!

Tory played a number of roles over my eight years. First and foremost, she became the First Lady's best friend and constant companion, and during stressful and difficult times, Tory would be up in Jane's lap bringing a smile to her face.

Under the watchful eye of Ann Evans, the executive director of the Governor's Mansion, Tory entertained schoolchildren and adults who toured the historic home, as well as our grandchildren when they visited. Tory helped us recruit businesses to Kentucky (see the story on Champion Petfoods), she received her share of fan mail from her young fans, and she even inspired a children's book, "Sam Saves the Mansion." Constantly marking her territory around the capitol campus on every walk, she wanted everyone to know that the capitol grounds were her domain.

When we lost Tory in 2016, it broke our hearts, but she will forever be known far and wide as the First Dog of the commonwealth.

GOLFING WITH TIGER

I started playing golf relatively late in life (at age 55) but quickly fell in love with the sport. I became a student of the game, taking lessons, going to golf schools in Florida, and reading golf books and magazines, all in an attempt to get better. It worked. In about six years, I had my handicap down to 13, but then I did a fool thing called running for governor. Needless to say, my game suffered from lack of playing time, and my handicap during the next eight years shot up to 22.

Being governor, however, helped me enjoy some extraordinary experiences that even lifelong golfers would envy.

I have had a hole-in-one (the par 3 13th at Lexington Country Club), and played Augusta National (including the nine-hole par 3 course). In 2008, at the Ryder Cup held at Valhalla Golf Club in Louisville, Kentucky, I was allowed inside the ropes to follow my favorite Kentucky golfer, Kenny Perry, as he helped the USA bring home the cup. (For non-golfers, "inside the ropes" means being actually out on the course with the professionals— always keeping a respectful distance, of course.) I had the same experience two other times at Valhalla—in 2011, when I watched Tom Watson win the PGA Senior Championship, and in 2014, when I followed Rory McIlroy as he won the PGA Championship. I've met Jack Nicklaus, Arnold Palmer, Gary Player, Lee Trevino, and several other big names in the golf world.

I also had the honor of playing a round with Kenny Perry at his public course in Franklin, Kentucky, and I played in pro-ams with Phil Mickelson and Bubba Watson.

But one of the most extraordinary experiences was the time I played with Tiger Woods.

Jim Justice, the owner of the Greenbrier Resort and now governor of West Virginia, invited me to play in the pro-am before the PGA tournament at the National Historic Landmark in July 2015. "By the way," he said, "you'll be in a foursome with Tiger Woods."

How could I say no to that?

I flew into the local airport on a Tuesday about 4 p.m. I was met by a West Virginia State Trooper who was assigned to me while I was at the Greenbrier. When we arrived at the resort, he suggested that I leave my clubs, hat, and shoes in his car. "Your foursome tees off at 7 a.m.," he said, "so I will be here at 6 to pick you up and take you down to the pro shop where you can warm up."

That made perfect sense, and so I took his advice.

But when I walked out of the Greenbrier at 6 the next morning, there was no West Virginia State Trooper. We started calling his cell phone, but it kept going to voice mail. Panic began setting in about 6:30 a.m., and so I caught a ride down to the pro shop. I explained what had happened, and the staff there had a solution: "We'll put together a set of rental clubs, and you can put on those shoes that the tournament gave all of the participants as a gift."

I rushed over, sat down, put on the shoes, and grabbed the set of rental clubs. It was five minutes until 7 a.m., and I had to be on the first tee right then. So out I went with a pair of shoes that weren't yet broken in and a set of rental clubs with which I'd never even taken a practice swing, much less played a round, and I didn't even have a hat. Talk about panic city!

And there was Tiger Woods, one of the best golfers if not *the* best golfer in the history of the game, waiting for me on the first tee. As I introduced myself to him and the others in our foursome, I looked around and saw that some 200 people were standing there watching us—or rather, watching Tiger Woods.

The announcer stated, "First on the tee, Tiger Woods," to loud applause from the gallery. Tiger proceeded to lace one straight down the fairway some 300 yards.

Then the announcer said, "Now on the tee, Governor Steve Beshear of Kentucky."

Every golfer will sympathize with the full-blown anxiety coursing through my head. Here I was, about to play a round with Tiger Woods himself, something that every amateur in the world would love to do, and I had to step up and tee off in front of 200 people with a rented driver that I had not swung at all.

Well, I felt like throwing up. I walked to the tee like a man being forced to walk the plank, stepped up, and somehow hit a drive straight down the fairway some 210 yards. I looked to the heavens and thought, "Thank you, Lord. It's okay if I don't hit another good shot all day long."

Incidentally, Tiger was a very nice guy to play with and conversed with the rest of the foursome all through the morning. The West Virginia State Trooper—who will remain nameless— finally showed up with my clubs, hat, and shoes on the 7th hole, having set his digital alarm for 5 *p.m.* He was more panicked than I had been on the first tee and apologized profusely. I laughed and told him everything was okay, but I joked that "had I missed teeing off with Tiger this morning, you would be in big trouble!"

Still, when I flew into West Virginia a few weeks later, I presented the sheepish state trooper with a gift—an autographed alarm clock.

Section VIII

CONCLUSION

WHAT KENTUCKY NEEDS

Whether you're identifying which car to buy or considering whether your business should add a second shift, the process for making a decision is pretty standard: You gather facts, seek advice, weigh options, and then make the best choice you can.

In politics, however, the process of decision making has a large wild card that needs to be added to the equation.

It's called getting re-elected.

And for some politicians, it trumps everything else.

In politics, you can gather all the facts and listen to all the experts you want. However, as politicians have been discovering with much surprise and humiliation since the dawn of democracy, if your constituents don't agree with the decision you wind up making, they may well vote you out of office in the next election— no matter how researched and "right" that decision was.

Therein lies the practical consequences of a fundamental philosophical question that politicians have debated for centuries: Just what is the role of an elected representative in a representative democracy?

Through centuries of English political history, there existed one school of thought that suggested the role of elected officials was simply to carry out the will of the people. *"Vox populi, vox Dei"* went the saying, or in English: "The voice of the people is the voice of God." Among many applications, "vox populi, vox Dei" was used to support the belief that it was the responsibility of each member of Parliament to reflect his constituents' thinking, no matter what. If a majority of constituents supported position A on an issue, then that's what the member's vote should be. To look at it another way, the elected official was simply a microphone for the people he represented.

But the philosopher and political theorist Sir Edmund Burke thought the role of an elected representative was a little more complex. Burke, himself a member of the British Parliament in the late 18th century, believed that officials were obligated to make the decision that was best for the common good or the national interest, even if at times that decision ran contrary to popular opinion. In the end, according to Burke, the member must not pander to constituents' whims, but—as he famously wrote in his Speech to the Electors at Bristol—instead use his "unbiased opinion, his mature judgment, [and] his enlightened conscience" to make a decision. Representatives had the time, ability, and wherewithal to learn about and understand issues better than voters did, and the people put their trust in that role.

So why is this esoteric discussion germane to this book and this era?

Because Kentucky's future—and I'm talking both about the quality of life for our people and the competitiveness of our statewide economy—rests on the willingness of its elected officials to tackle difficult issues by moving beyond "vox populi, vox Dei" to embrace Burke, regardless of the political consequences for them or their party.

To put it in less lofty and more blunt language, Kentucky needs its leaders to worry less about winning elections and more about improving the state long term.

What sorts of specific issues am I talking about?

On issue is tax reform. Kentucky needs it. Our antiquated system of taxation is ineffective, unfair, and based on an economy that no longer exists. Like governors before me, I commissioned a task force and attempted to modernize our system, but, also like governors before me, I was told by legislators that they wouldn't look seriously at those ideas during election season. So I compromised and proposed a less aggressive set of changes. Unfortunately, for state legislators, it's *always* election season, so they never want to address tax reform, at least not the kind of tax reform Kentucky needs.

If the general assembly tackles tax reform again, as some leaders are discussing, one of the primary goals of that effort *has* to be to raise additional revenue—not by raising taxes, but by making sure everyone pays their fair share. That means a progressive income tax should remain part of the mix. That means things like closing loopholes, ending unnecessary tax credits, and expanding the base of the sales tax.

A word of caution: Apparently, the current administration is getting its tax advice from the same supply-side economists who advised President Reagan and Governor Brownback of Kansas. They put forward a very politically appealing idea— just cut everybody's taxes, particularly those of the wealthy and the business community. As the theory goes, two things would then happen: One, the wealthy and the business community would take most of the money they save from not paying taxes and invest it in creating more jobs, the benefit of which would "trickle down" to all the rest of us. Two, because of extremely low taxes, Kentucky would become such an attractive place to do business that companies from far and wide would flock to the state and create thousands of new jobs, resulting in new tax revenues flooding into the state's coffers.

Sounds great, right?

The only problem is it doesn't work.

After President Reagan did it, the country went through a recession and he ended his term with a historic budget deficit.

After Governor Brownback did it, no flurry of jobs resulted, just deficits that caused schools in Kansas to close early and roads to begin falling apart for lack of maintenance money. The only thing that trickled down for Kansans was a loss of educational opportunities for their children and a rapidly deteriorating physical infrastructure. So cutting taxes and praying for economic expansion as a way to invest in your people isn't a solution—it didn't work for Reagan, it isn't working for Kansas, and it won't work for Kentucky.

Another issue is substance abuse. Kentucky has some of the worst rates in the nation. The commonwealth needs to put significantly more money into expanding treatment options and increasing capacity at in-patient rehab centers. With help from the legislature and many others, including the First Lady's Recovery Kentucky program (started by Governor Ernie Fletcher), we did a lot to combat substance abuse during my eight years. But there's more to do, especially with the latest spike in heroin use in Kentucky, which mirrors a national trend.

Unfortunately, in the current national political climate, "law and order" is the new mantra and helping people who are addicted translates to "soft on crime." A lock-'em-all-up approach might be popular politically, but it's also counterproductive and shortsighted. Yes, we need to arrest and incarcerate hard-core dealers, but the long-term, effective solution to handling users is treatment, not prison. Many leaders in Kentucky privately understand this, given that the heroin epidemic has touched so many of their friends and relatives. However, understanding isn't enough. They need to be more vocal on this issue, and they need to put their concern in the form of policy and budget allocations.

Coal is another issue that needs a more pragmatic approach. It is a finite resource that faces increasing pressures from market forces that favor other energy sources and from federal regulations designed to make our water and air cleaner. As a result, mining jobs and coal production have decreased significantly, and this trend shows no signs of changing, no matter who is governor or president. This will continue to carry huge consequences for Kentucky for two reasons: One, coal-fired plants have historically produced 90 percent or more of our electricity, and our manufacturing-based economy depends upon the resulting low electricity rates. And two, many counties in Kentucky's Appalachian region and Western Kentucky coalfields have depended heavily on the coal industry for jobs and income for generations. To protect manufacturing jobs and many of our families, long term, Kentucky has to both continue to push clean-coal technologies, and diversify both its energy production and its coalfields economy in a big way with efforts like SOAR.

Another huge issue for Kentucky's future is smoking and tobacco use. When it comes to preventable illnesses and deaths, every study concludes that *nothing* else is as devastating to Kentucky. Unfortunately, our smoking and tobacco use rates are among the highest in the nation. Again, we made progress in this area. But much more can and should be done, starting with stronger statewide protections from tobacco smoke in public areas and for employees. The majority of states have smoke-free laws, as do many Kentucky cities and counties, and surveys show Kentuckians support such laws. Yet legislators continue to worry that smokers will punish them for infringing on their freedom to smoke anywhere they please even when it harms bystanders.

A fifth issue has to do with infrastructure. Kentucky needs to work with Ohio to replace the functionally obsolete Brent Spence Bridge that carries Interstates 75 and 71 over the Ohio River at Cincinnati. The Brent Spence annually ranks among the most congested and most unsafe interstate corridors in the nation, and it is an impediment to economic growth. Shortly before I left office, the two states were prepared to move forward on a $2.6 billion plan to renovate the bridge and build a new one next to it. Unfortunately, despite decades of discussion, Northern Kentucky legislators effectively killed the project by shepherding through a provision that prohibited tolls on the bridge. Although many of them admit privately that tolls will indeed be needed to finance the bridge, they say they can't afford politically to publicly support what they know must be done.

I could go on and on.

For a better future, Kentucky needs more cooperation between rural and urban areas. It needs political leaders who move away from the shackles of 24/7 partisanship and from sound-bite governing. It needs more emphasis on career and technical education (college isn't the best route for everyone) as a way to build a stronger workforce. And it needs to continue making health coverage accessible for all citizens and kids, not more expensive and harder to get—even if that means supporting an initiative that has President Obama's name on it.

But all of these issues are a tough sell politically in some quarters.

That's why we need elected officials who have courage, vision, and persistence—and who understand that sometimes they have to look past what's popular and choose what's best for their people.

I think in the United States today, most politicians privately feel as Burke did: The people of their district elect them and then expect them to use their best judgment. But then along comes a controversial issue, and the line gets blurred quickly. Many politicians might know that raising a particular tax or strengthening a particular regulation is the right thing to do, but they fear the wrath of voters and hide behind the rationale that "the majority of my people are against this; therefore, I have no choice but to vote against it."

In other words, they run for cover, and they justify it with polls and surveys.

In our own state legislature, it was amazing how 10 phone calls would come in on an issue and suddenly those 10 opinions became the ironclad and rock-solid "My constituents say . . ." in the words of a legislator. Or how an organized letter-writing campaign by a special interest group was seen as evidence of some groundswell of grassroots support or opposition.

It's also interesting to see politicians use polls and surveys to govern with a finger to the wind. Look, I polled a lot through the years, both as a candidate and as a governor. But there's a huge difference between using survey results to tell you exactly how to vote and using them to find out more about the public's concerns and to research messages and themes. When I needed to cut the budget but wanted to preserve education funding, I used polling to test messages (as in actual words and phrases) as a way of figuring out how to best "sell" that decision. I didn't need a poll to tell me that investing in our children would strengthen Kentucky.

In my political life, I tried to approach decision making as a two-step process. First, determine the right thing to do. (In some cases, this is obvious; in others, I needed a lot of research and debate.) And then second, determine how to do it and, at the same time, survive politically.

Too few elected officials go through this process, opting instead to hide behind the opinions of the most vocal constituents or cater to special interests. What this means is that not enough gets accomplished. Not enough officials are willing to take the risk of losing the next election to move the country or their state in the proper direction.

During my eight years as governor and as lieutenant governor, attorney general, and a state legislator before that, I certainly wasn't perfect on this decision-making process either. There were times when I "wimped out" and took the easy way out. But most of the time, I made myself do the right thing because I wanted to be able to get up each morning, look at myself in the mirror, and not be ashamed.

I admit that became easier during my second term, when I realized I never had to run for re-election again. It gave me freedom to be more outspoken and to take riskier stands, the most visible of which was to become the national torchbearer for implementing the ACA. While embracing a president who was unpopular in Kentucky was still a big risk politically, by doing so, we transformed the future of the commonwealth by making affordable health care available to every Kentuckian for the first time in history.

Back in 2011, during my re-election campaign, I was given a heads-up on the refreshing nature of that second-term freedom by none other than Governor Mitch Daniels of Indiana, a Republican who had won re-election just a year before. We were working together on building new bridges across the Ohio River between our two states, and we were discussing some controversial issue, probably the tolls that were required to pay for the needed spans.

I must have lamented in some way how, with my re-election campaign underway and having to balance being governor with being a candidate, I always felt like I had to weigh every word and decision 100 times as much as usual.

It was a stressful time.

But Governor Daniels just smiled. "Steve," he said, "come November, you're going to feel differently. And you're going to like how you feel."

He was right. I *did* feel differently, and I *did* like how it felt. And it was amazing how much we were able to move Kentucky forward because of it.

THANKS FOR THE RIDE

Wow, what a ride! Serving as governor of Kentucky was such an amazing experience. It became an all-consuming passion for both Jane and me, and we gave it our all 24 hours a day, seven days a week, for eight years.

The sheer number of meetings and events was overwhelming, but we thrived on it. It took two sets of security folks on eight-hour shifts per day to keep up with us, and we were much older than all of them.

But our commitment to this state didn't start with the Governor's Office. Our political life started back in 1973 when I was elected a state representative at age 29, when Jane and I walked door to door asking for votes. We never stopped after that. As we raised our two sons, Jeff and Andy, we instilled in them both the love of family and the commitment to help others that they both evidence to this day.

In becoming an equine veterinarian, our son Jeff found a calling that gets him out of bed every morning with a smile on his face. He has built a highly successful equine veterinary practice in Virginia, where he lives with his wife, Emily, and their son, Nicholas. Emily is a top-level event rider and trainer, and she manages their farm operation. And Nicholas, one of our three favorite grandchildren, is at the top of his class in school and is growing into a fine young man who loves horses, too.

Our younger son, Andy, lives in Louisville with his wife, Britainy, and our other two favorite grandchildren, Will and Lila. After law school and private practice, Andy is now Kentucky's attorney general, and by all accounts, is acquitting himself well as the people's lawyer. Britainy is the perfect partner in that political world, and in addition, is one of the best mothers on earth. Will and Lila are a precocious handful, in the best possible way.

Jane and I were not surprised that Andy chose public service as a calling. During both of my terms as governor and during both of my election campaigns, he served as a valuable adviser to me on political, legal, and policy issues, and he served as a sounding board. He reassured me when I was right and wasn't afraid to tell me when I was wrong.

So yes, Jane and I are very proud of our family, just as other doting parents and grandparents are. And all of this has given us some of the best memories anyone could ever have.

I will never forget watching Jane appear on *NBC Nightly News* to explain her Horses and Hope program that is saving the lives of our backside workers at our horse tracks. And on a lighter note, I will always fondly remember kicking a soccer ball with Will and Lila in the rotunda of the Capitol in the evening when the building was closed and most of my staff had gone home. And no one in the Winner's Circle at the Kentucky Derby was ever more elegantly dressed than grandson Nicholas.

But many friends over the past few years have asked, "Why do you two do this? Why do you subject yourselves to all of the scrutiny and criticism?"

Some people in our position might answer by pointing out that as governor and First Lady, we got to hang out with some important people, like the president of the United States, US senators, and famous actors, athletes, and military heroes. As Kentucky's governor, I also got to hand out the trophy to the winner of the Kentucky Derby every year—and that's not half bad!

But to Jane and me, the answer to the question of "why?" is simple, and it is embodied in an event that happened to me as I was finishing up this book in fall 2016, almost a year after leaving office.

I had left my law office in Lexington and entered an elevator on my way to the parking garage. Two young men were in the elevator with me, and we passed some quick pleasantries during the short ride. I didn't think much of it as I drove home.

But the next day I received the following e-mail from a fellow named Kevin Havelda:

> I *thought I would take the opportunity to say "hello" in a more formal message since I didn't want to bother you on the way out of the office last evening. I was one of the two men on the elevator with you as you left the office. I had to smile as you got on just as I did, and I thought how funny life can be at times. I'm a big fan of yours, and judging from [law professor] Biff Campbell's introductory remarks before you were given your award at the University of Kentucky College of Law Alumni Awards at this year's Bar Convention, I'm in good company. I could tell you how I've been a fan of yours when you were running for governor and I was a senior at Centre [College] and met you prior to your gubernatorial debate there, but if your memory fails as much as mine, that story will be lost upon you. Suffice it to say your most lasting contribution to me came in the middle of my second year of law school. ...*
>
> *Forgive me for badgering you with such a tale, but I'd be remiss if I didn't take the opportunity to finally say "thank you," now that we have been re-acquainted. Albeit, on an elevator when we were both rushing home.*
>
> *During my second year of law school, I had the misfortune to undergo a minor medical emergency, necessitating a fairly major surgery. As someone who did not make much money from my teaching venture in a previous profession with Teach For*

America and in a charter school in Brooklyn, my medical options were limited upon being admitted into law school in my mid-20s. With the news of my medical condition, my world came crumbling down. I thought I'd have to drop out of school, and put my offer [from a law firm] on hold. In short, I was as low as I'd ever been.

But for kynect, and the compassion of professors like Biff and many more, I was able to have world-class medical care, remain enrolled in law school, and graduate near the top of my class. My doctors were top notch. I recovered better than expected. Because of kynect, I received the medical care that I should have received, but never could have hoped for.

And last night, I shared an elevator ride down from my office with the man whose courage and leadership made that possible. Funny how things turn out.

It's a strange feeling to feel so indebted to a total stranger. So in a way, this is my small way of saying "thank you." Thank you for your courage. Thank you for your vision. I know it wasn't easy. It probably still isn't. But what you did mattered. It still matters. It matters to a lot of people in this state, including people you've never met, and some you'll never know. I doubt most of them will be as lucky to share an elevator with the man who did so much for their lives, and for the lives of their loved ones. And it mattered to me. It always will.

So if you've read this far, just know that despite my good-natured banter last night, I was really thinking of all of this, and how incredibly fortunate I was to have you as my governor. In a way, the only reason I was riding on that elevator was because of your work. So thanks for the ride, Governor.

That is what being governor and First Lady is all about.

As Jane and I look back on our eight years in the Governor's Office (and frankly our entire political lives), there is nothing that gives us as much satisfaction as knowing that we made someone's life better.

When I was on my way out of the Governor's Office, a headline in the *Lexington Herald-Leader* said, "Steve Beshear Governed with Compassion."

No political victory can ever compete with that, because in the end, helping people is the only thing that really matters.

So thank you, Kentucky, for giving us such an opportunity. And yes, it was indeed a great ride!

ACKNOWLEDGMENTS

First, a huge "thank you" from both Jane and me to our office staff, cabinet secretaries, and the thousands of dedicated state employees who made the eight years of the Beshear Administration such a success.

These unsung heroes include the state troopers who patrolled lonely roads at night, sleep-deprived plow drivers who worked in dangerous conditions to keep highways passable, and social workers who made heartbreaking decisions to help children in distress. They also include the teachers, inspectors, and number-crunchers who often worked 15-hour days and weekends—regularly missing family dinners, soccer games, and sleep. Kentucky families are better off for your commitment, compassion, and professionalism.

Second, to the Beshear family.

Jane and I met at the University of Kentucky in 1967 on a blind date. From that moment on, we have been constant companions. She sacrificed a teaching career because she felt our sons needed a full-time mom. Largely because of that decision, Jeff and Andy grew into wonderful adults. Jane has also served as a positive anchor for me, keeping my feet on the ground and my head in the real world, at least most of the time. Her love and support of all of us has been constant and unconditional.

Our sons, Jeff and Andy, have been the joys of our lives. What we gave them in love, support, and guidance they have returned a hundredfold by becoming intelligent, responsible adults dedicated to their families and to making the world a better place, each in his own way. They each found great life partners. Jeff and Emily gave us our grandson Nicholas, and Andy and Britainy provided us with Will and Lila. Jane and I have been truly blessed!

My dad, Russell Beshear, was a successful local businessman and an eloquent preacher who worked hard around the clock to provide for us. Mary Elizabeth Beshear, my mom, was the outgoing and more flexible parent. She made laughter a part of our daily lives and raised five active, rambunctious kids. Together, Dad and Mom made us their life's work and gave us a moral compass that has served us all well to this day.

My brother Bob became a successful pediatrician, leading the charge for more neonatal beds for Kentucky children and later fighting to bring health care access to hundreds of thousands of Alabama's children. My sister Nancy came of age when opportunities for women were limited, but she fought through that glass ceiling to earn a master's degree and become a librarian, raising two kids in the process. My sister Mary Ann earned a master's degree and has enjoyed a career with the Kentucky Department of Education. She has been one of the driving forces behind the great strides made in Kentucky in K-12 education, and she currently serves as chief of staff to the commonwealth's education commissioner.

All of us owe a special debt of gratitude to our brother David. He has led an interesting life—everything from working on a shrimp boat to running his own successful landscaping business. But when my parents reached that time in life when their health began to fail, David moved in with them and cared for them around the clock for years, allowing them to finish out their lives in the comfort of their own home. Thank you, David, from all your brothers and sisters.

A STRONGER KENTUCKY, INC.

A Stronger Kentucky, Inc. is a corporation organized exclusively for charitable, religious, literary, educational, and scientific purposes under section 501(c)(3) of the Internal Revenue Code of 1986, as amended.

The organization supports efforts to promote the health and well-being of the citizens of the Commonwealth of Kentucky. Funds were donated to A Stronger Kentucky, Inc. to produce and publish this book, and proceeds from the sale of the book will be donated to charitable and educational causes.

I want to thank the following friends whose generous financial support of the organization helped make this book possible. They include:

Jerry and Madeline Abramson
Ann Bakhaus
Robert M. Beck Jr. and Kathryn M. Beck
Bob Benson
Skip and Joyce Berry, Wehr Constructors, Inc., Louisville/ Lexington, Kentucky
Larry Bond
Kaitlyn and Sherman Brown
Mark Bryant

Rebecca B. Byers
Deno and Jo Curris
Mike and Margaret Denham
Adam H. Edelen, Chief of Staff to Governor Beshear 2008–2010
Colmon and Victoria Elridge
Carol and Tracy Farmer
Lori Hudson Flanery
Dr. and Mrs. Oliver Keith Gannon, Mount Sterling, Kentucky
Cammie and Will Grant
Mrs. Mike Haydon
Larry M. Hayes
Hollie Hopkins
Holly McCoy-Johnson
Alston and John Kerr
Frank and Mary Lassiter
Jamie Link
Honorable Crit Luallen
Jonathan Miller
Thomas B. Miller
Len and Georgiana Peters
Joe and Jennie Prather
Terry Sebastian and Ryan Readnower
Robert Stewart
J. Roger Thomas
Winn and Sally Turney
Bob and Judy Vance
Ambrose Wilson IV
Barbara Young
Thomas O. Zawacki

ABOUT THE AUTHORS

Steven L. Beshear was elected governor of the Commonwealth of Kentucky in 2007 and served until 2015. An attorney, Governor Beshear has a long background in public service. He served as a state representative in the Kentucky General Assembly, attorney general, and lieutenant governor before being elected governor.

Beshear is a native of Dawson Springs in Hopkins County, Kentucky. He earned a bachelor's degree and law degree from the University of Kentucky and served as an intelligence analyst in the US Army Reserve. He currently owns a consulting firm, Hourglass Consulting, LLC, and recently served as a Senior Leadership Fellow at the Harvard T. H. Chan School of Public Health.

He and his wife, Jane, have been married since 1969 and live on a small farm in Clark County. They have two sons—Jeff, an equine veterinarian, and Andy, currently Kentucky's attorney general—and three grandchildren.

Dan Hassert wrote Steve Beshear's speeches throughout Beshear's terms as Kentucky's governor. Hassert was a newspaper reporter and editor for 19 years.

A freelance writer, he lives in Covington, Kentucky, with his wife, attorney Monica Dias, and his two children, Abby and Jake.